"Borrowed Plumage"

APPROACHES TO TRANSLATION STUDIES
Founded by James S Holmes

Edited by Henri Bloemen
        Dirk Delabastita
        Ton Naaijkens

Volume 19

"Borrowed Plumage"
Polemical Essays on Translation

by

Eugene Chen Eoyang

Amsterdam – New York, NY 2003

The paper on which this book is printed meets the requirements of "ISO 9706:1994, Information and documentation - Paper for documents - Requirements for permanence".

ISBN: 90-420-0854-7
©Editions Rodopi B.V., Amsterdam - New York, NY 2003
Printed in The Netherlands

To Trish —

whose plumage
I have borrowed for years

Table of Contents

Divertissements

Introduction

This collection of essays relating to translation is, admittedly, eclectic as well as polemic. They address both the practice and the theory of translation. It's interesting that these two words almost always take on the *a priori* sequence of "theory" before "practice", whereas the actual situation in translation is that practice almost always occurs *before* theory. People are engaged happily (or agonizingly) in translation without any idea of the theory behind it. No field develops theories empirically more than translation. That is why the first three essays appear under the rubric of "Practice" and is followed by four chapters under the rubric of "Approaches". "Theories" — in the plural, to emphasize their speculativeness — occupy the next chapters. The book concludes with a section called "Divertissements" which includes essays not a little tongue in cheek.

Despite their motley nature, these essays are all polemical in one way or another, whether attacking the overemphasis on the text as a model of literature (Chapter 3), or the overliteral scholarship of some sinologists (Chapter 4), or the literary naiveté of a political sub-editor in China (Chapter 12) or the rhetoric of post-colonial theorists (Chapter 5), or the pieties about translations being always inferior to the original (Chapter 9). The chapters are not intended as a seamless exposition of a grand "string" theory of translation: they offer what might be occasional insights now and then. What I want to convey is the endless fascination of the subject, one which I hope the reader will share, at least in part. The chapter on humor (Chapter 2), is both about the jokes that can't be translated as well as the humor that can, but it also includes the considerable humor that mistranslations have themselves generated. This is a subject that can be, at the same time, intensely serious and intuitively amusing.

I subscribe neither to the translation-must-read-like-a translation school nor to the translation-must-read-like-an-original school. I am, complementarily, faithful to both schools. There is much to commend in each. But I can subscribe to both because I believe that each theory addresses different audiences: the translation as defamiliarized, often challenging, text assumes a committed scholarly audience, one that will accept no compromise with the original, an audience of exigent Vladimir Nabokovs. The translation that co-opts the original and makes it appear "naturally" native include all those who enjoy the King James Version of the Bible and Fitz-Gerald's Rubaiyat of Omar Khayyam, both of which are at some remove from the originals, yet both are considered treasures of English literature — whatever the originals. I've developed this taxonomy at some length in the middle chapters of my *Transparent Eye*, and have no need to revisit that analysis here.

The first section, on Practice, includes Chapter One, "Commerce and

Communication: Translation as International Trade" and Chapter Two, "Crossing the Borders of Humour: The Intersection of Different Logics" began as a paper titled, "Translation and Cross-Cultural Communication: Doing Business in the Global Village", which was first presented at the Beijing Language and Culture University, at an international symposium on "Translation and Cross-Cultural Communication," co-sponsored by Beijing University, Beijing Language and Culture University, the University of Copenhagen and the Copenhagen Business School, in Beijing, September 12-14, 1997. Chapter Three, "Translating the Secular and the Sacred" was first presented at the Panel, "Revising Methodology in a Multi-Cultural Context: Translation Studies and Literary /Cultural Histories," which was part of the Workshop on Translation and Modernization at the 13th Congress of the International Comparative Literature Association in Tokyo, 23-28 August 1991.

The next section emphasizes "Approaches". Chapter Four, "'Speaking in Tongues': Translating Chinese Literature in a Post-Babelian Age" was first presented at the International Conference on the Translation of Chinese Literature, convened in November 19-21, 1990 by the Council for Cultural Development and Planning, the Chiang Ching-kuo Foundation, and the National Taiwan University. It was subsequently included in the volume, *Translating Chinese Literature*, edited by Eugene Eoyang and Lin Yao-fu (Bloomington, Indiana: Indiana University Press, 1995), pp. 292-304. Chapter Five, "Translation as Co-optation: Getting Past Post-Colonialism", and Chapter Six, "Hegemonies of Translation and of Transliteration" were first presented before the "Diggante" Public Forum, Stockholm, Sweden, on April 11, 2000. Chapter Seven, "'Here and Now' vs 'There and Then' in Translating Chinese Literature," was first presented on April 28, 1995, at the Research Centre for Translation at the Chinese University of Hong Kong, to which I was kindly invited as a "Renditions" Honorary Fellow.   Chapter Eight, "Déjà lu: Recurrence, Allusion, and Plagiarism in Translation" opens the section on Theory, and was presented as part of the Nobel Symposium on the Translation of Poetry and Poetic Prose, August 24-28, 1998. An earlier version was offered on 20 August 1997 at the XVth Congress of the International Comparative Literature Association in Leiden, and was in press at the time of the symposium. That version was published in *Translation Quarterly* Nos. 7 & 8 (1998), pp. 33-67; it also appeared subsequently in the Proceedings of the Nobel Symposium, under the title, *Translation of Poetry and Poetic Prose*, edited by Sture Allén (Singapore: World Scientific, 1999), pp. 269-295. Chapter Nine, "'I lose something in the original': Translation as Enhancement," was first presented at the conference of the American Comparative Literature Association, March 26-28, 1998, in Austin, Texas. It was subsequently offered at the Nobel Symposium 110 on the Translation of Poetry and Poetic Prose, and appeared in *Translations of Poetry and Poetic Prose*, pp. 296-313. Chapter Ten, "Translating as a Mode of Thinking, Translation as a Model of Thought," was originally presented at the Second International Conference on the Translation of Chinese Literature, Taipei, Taiwan, December 19-21, 1992. It was subsequently published in *Perspectives: Studies in Translatology*, 1996, vol. 1 (Museum Tusculanum Press: University of Copenhagen), pp. 53-69.

The last section is titled "Divertissements" and includes three essays that might be call *jeux d'esprit*. Chapter Eleven, "Peacock, Parakeet, Partridge, 'Pidgin': An 'Ornithology' of Translators", was prepared for a visit to Lingnan College in February 1996, and was intended as a half serious, half entertaining survey of different species of translators. Chapter Twelve, "Primal Nights and Verbal Daze: Puns, Paronomasia, and the People's Daily," was first presented at the 8th Tamkang Comparative Literature Conference, Tamkang University, August 17, 1991, and was subsequently published in the *Tamkang Review*, 32,1-4 (Autumn 1991-Summer 1992), 253-262. The translation appeared on the OpEd page of the *New York Times* on March 31, 1991. Chapter Thirteen, "Hong Kong Place-Names: Colonial or Postcolonial?" originated as a talk presented at a meeting of the Institute of Linguistics (Hong Kong Branch), YMCA, Tsim Sha Tsui, May 20, 2000, and was subsequently published in *The Hong Kong Linguist*, 22 (2001), 1-6.

A word on the transliteration. Rather than mislead the reader into thinking that one system of transliteration prevails, or that one system is superior to the others, I employ both the Wade-Giles system and the pinyin systems. A conversion table is offered for those who wish to know which is which, but those who read Chinese directly will be able to dispense with either transliteration. There is another reason why I maintain two translation systems. Writing as I do from Hong Kong, I am imbued with the reality — far from contradictory — of seeing things from a "one country, two systems" perspective, in transliteration systems as well as in political ideology. Wade-Giles has been used in North America until about twenty years ago, and in Taiwan up to the present whereas the pinyin system prevails in China, and in North America since the seventies. Untidy as the situation is, there is no universally accepted transliteration system, although pinyin has gained wider currency in recent years. Students and scholars of Chinese should be familiar with both, even if the differences can sometimes be nettlesome. In this book, the system used reflects the provenance of the original presentation from which the chapter derives. When the paper was offered in China, I adopted pinyin; and when I presented in Taiwan, I used Wade-Giles. Chapters Four, Ten, and Twelve, for example, reflect the Wade-Giles system prevailing in Taiwan; Chapters 1 and 2 were originally prepared for an audience in China, and hence adopt pinyin. The remainder of the chapters were offered at different venues worldwide — Leiden; Stockholm; Tokyo; Austin, Texas; and Hong Kong — and may switch between transliteration systems, though the predominant system adopted is pinyin. (Hong Kong, anomalously, still uses a modified Wade-Giles, even though it has been — officially — part of China since 1997.) Adopting a mixture of transliteration systems will obviate two pitfalls: one, it will avoid a distracting politicization of transliteration systems, which may make one or the other system unwelcome in certain parts of the world; two, it will dispel the myth that standard putonghua is all absolutely standard. Transliterations are very approximate and very inadequate markers of sound transcription, even when they are conventional linguistically. For those who, mindless of the vagaries of reality, insist on consistency, I maintain that it is impossible, since many of the older books adopt the Wade-Giles system, and most of the newer publications use pinyin. A surrounding context using pinyin may cite a reference that uses Wade-Giles, which (in most cases) differ from pinyin orthography. I won't even mention even more archaic transliteration systems, vestiges of which can still be found: "Peking" as in "Peking [Beijing] University"; "Canton" [Guangzhou], Mukden [Shen-yang], as in the "Mukden Incident", Dairen [Dalian], etc. If one were to regularize all the references into one transliteration system, comprehensibility, not to say recognizability, would be compromised. Not many would recognize Hong Kong if transliterated as Xianggang. Residents of Shanghai are uniquely fortunate among urban dwellers in China: their city, when transliterated, is the same whether it's Wade-Giles or pinyin. The non-native student and scholar of Chinese, not unlike most of the speakers of Chinese in China who negotiate more than one dialect, must be fluent in more than one transliteration system.

There are many who have contributed directly or indirectly to these essays (though all the mistakes and misjudgments are mine): my friend and present colleague, Joseph Lau, has engaged me in many challenges in translation, most of which resulted in some insight into the subject, even if, or especially when, a solution was unavailing. My former mentor, Irving Lo, began my interest in translation as my teacher and the chief convenor of "The Sycamore Six" many years ago, which included William Nienhauser, Jr., now at the University of Wisconsin, Charles Hartman, now at the State University of New York at Albany, and Jerome Seaton, now at the University of North Carolina. Those after-hours "workshops", as demanding as they were congenial, resulted in a goodly number of translations (including mine) which were to appear in Irving Lo's *Sunflower Splendor: Three Thousand Years of Chinese Poetry* (Doubleday, 1975), which he edited with Wu-chi Liu. I am grateful to my former students, Jia Zhijie and Ge Liangyan (now at Notre Dame), for provoking me to translate the poem discussed in Chapter Twelve, and to Wann Ai-jen (now at Purdue University) for helping me refine my initial versions. To Eva Hung and David Pollard (both at Chinese University of Hong Kong), I owe much, not only for their hospitality in 1994 when I had the honor of visiting CUHK as a "*Renditions* Fellow" (it was for that occasion that I prepared the study that appears in Chapter Seven as "'Here and Now' vs. 'There and Then' in Translating Chinese Literature") but also for their continuing encouragement in succeeding years. At the Nobel Symposium on Translation in 1998, to which I was kindly invited by Sture Allen, I received very constructive feedback in the most cultivated setting, especially from Emanuela Tandello, Seamus Heaney, Eliot Weinberger, Tim Parks, Inga-Stina Ewbank, and Goeren Malmqvist.

Many of these ideas were first developed in a course in translation that I have taught at Indiana University, off and on, since 1976. To the students in that course, representing many cultures and languages throughout the world, I am grateful first for their attention as I developed my views on translation, then for their responsiveness to those notions they found convincing, and finally for their skepticism when they were dubious.

I am also indebted to the Office of Research and Staff Development at Lingnan University, which supported the research projects that culminated in several of these essays, as well as to the Office of Research and Graduate Development of Indiana University for supporting the costs of preparing the index, which Sean Conner very capably prepared.

I also must thank the Teaching and Learning Technical Laboratory at Indiana University, especially Erick Carballo, for helping me navigate the tricky shoals of desktop publishing, especially difficult in a text involving Chinese fonts and my insistence on using Macintosh Appleworks (in preference to the otherwise obligatory Microsoft Word, whose Chinese character generator is a nightmare to use).

Marieke Schilling of Rodopi Publishers has been wonderful to work with, and I wish to cite her for her unfailing patience, cooperation and support.

My debts to my wife, Patricia, are past enumerating, and my dedication tells only part of the story.

Eugene Chen Eoyang
Bloomington, Indiana
July 25, 2002

Practices

1. Commerce and Communication:
Translation as International Trade

Introduction

Trade among and between the peoples of the world is the stuff of history textbooks, which focus on interchanges between peoples that have taken the form, most notably, of commodities and services — commodities in terms of goods and produce shipped from one place to another; services in terms of skills and technology imported by craftsmen migrating from one country to another.[1] The spread of ideas — whether of Greek philosophy to Rome, or of Buddhism from India to China to Japan — has also been accounted for in surveys and monographs. But what has scarcely attracted notice is the trade in objects at once more abstract than goods and services and more concrete than ideas and systems of thought. I refer, of course, to translations. As indicators as well as embodiments of international trade, translations occupy a special role in the history of world civilization. They mark the crossing of linguistic borders, borders which often but do not always coincide with national borders, and they constitute a dialectic between the foreign and the native which may reveal a "balance of payments" in the intellectual realm, between nations and cultures.

What I should like to propose is that we study the historical fact of translation and the products of translation as if they were items imported or exported from a point of origin. Translations that are exported — i.e., translated out of one's native, source language into foreign, target languages — can be differentiated from translations that are imported — i.e., translated out of a foreign (target) language into one's own native (source) language. In developing an analysis of an intellectual "balance of payments", I should like to propose, at least in theory, a translation index, a "transindex" (TI), which will constitute the number of imported translations divided by the number of exported translations that any country produces. In other words, the number of translations into one's native language constitute the dividend; and the number of translations out of one's native language constitute the divisor. We may posit several values for this "transindex": where the number of imported translations equal or approximate the exported translations, the "transindex" of TI can be said to be at or near the value 1. Where the TI is greater than 1 (>1), we may say that the country is in a state of indebtedness, where it is <u>importing texts from for</u>eign cultures more than it is exporting its own

---

[1] One thinks immediately of the Silk Road in ancient times, of tea and china in pre-colonial times, and opium in the colonial era; the import of skills and crafts is less well known, but it would include the introduction of Italian architects in northern Europe in the Middle Ages and during the Renaissance, the importation of Persian carpetmakers and marble workers in India which resulted in the construction of the Taj Mahal, an essentially Persian building in Agra. The import of Hessian soldiers on the English side, and of Polish soldiers on the side of the rebel Americans, are further examples.

texts into foreign languages. Where the TI is less than 1 (<1), we may say that the country is in a state of hegemony, where it is exporting its own culture abroad more than it is bringing other texts home.

As a speculative exercise, more to provoke interest and to spur further study than to present a conclusive case, I wish to consider some salient examples of translations that reflect indebtedness and translations that reflect hegemony.

Examples of Indebtedness

Two factors will tend to favor cultural indebtedness: the natural curiosity of people concerning new and different phenomena, and the understandable happenstance that one is more likely to know one's native language better than a foreign language, resulting in the greater likelihood of translating into one's own language than translating out of it (TI: >1). However, a TI of 1 may mean two things. Isolated countries and cultures will tend to be at a stultifying equilibrium (TI: 1), with no translations either in or out of one's own language (0 divided by 0). Dynamic, interactive cultures will tend to approach a full-valued equilibrium (TI: 1), where the import activity is matched by the export activity. Such an index might be a prism through which one can examine the changing valences in civilizations, and enable us to see historical trends that would otherwise not be obvious.

Take, for example, Greece and Rome: clearly more was exported by Greece to Rome than the reverse. The indebtedness of Republican Rome to Greece is a story too well-known to rehearse here: its admiration of Greek culture, typified in literature by Virgil's devotion to Homer, is commonplace.[2] Clearly, in the Republican era, Rome saw itself as the eager apprentice to the Greek master: its heuristic was to imitate Greek civilization and to follow Greek precepts. The indebtedness to Greece was repeatedly acknowledged, even celebrated. Lancelot Patrick Wilkinson opens his entry on Latin Literature in the *Encyclopedia Brittanica* with the bald statement: "Latin literature began as translation from the Greek, a fact which largely conditioned its development." However, it is not always acknowledged that the greatest debt that Rome owed to Greece was the ironic introduction of Christianity, despite Roman persecution, through the medium of St. Jerome's translation of the New Testament, from the koine Greek of the *Septuagint* into Latin.[3]

Another irony is that, had there been more translation from the Arabic and Persian into the Latin, Aristotle might have been more available in

---

[2] The indebtedness of Greece to earlier cultures — Egyptian, Babylonian, Phoenician, Indian — is less recognized, and has been obscured by the myth, promulgated by Edith Hamilton and others, that depicts Greece as a totally originary culture, the fount of Western civilization. Charles Homer Haskins was among the few scholars to point to other sources of western civilization.

[3] The hoariness of history and the now classic state of Roman culture and the Latin language tends to make moderns forget that Jerome was translating the sacred text into the Roman vernacular of the time, signified by the word "Vulgate".

Europe during the so-called Dark Ages, and might have spurred the Renaissance to occur earlier than it did. A largely unwritten chapter in world history is the role of Arabic in the revival of classical learning in Western culture. The rediscovery of Aristotle, through the Persian commentaries of Avicenna (980-1037) and the Arabic commentaries of Averroës (1126-1198), was the spur to the systematic, humanistic, and scientific study that inspired the Renaissance.[4] Richard Rudolph Walzer reminds us: "The number of Greek philosophical texts known in Latin versions before the days of the schoolmen in the later middle ages, was only a very small fraction of those known to the Islamic world."[5]

A contrastive example to the Roman reception and absorption of Greek culture would be the introduction of Buddhism into China that began roughly around the first century, and that climaxed in the massive project of Xuanzang in the seventh century to translate — voluminously — the Buddhist canon from Pali and Sanskrit into Chinese. "It is said he carried back to China 657 items packed in 520 cases. Of these he translated only 73 items in 1,330 chüan", (Ch'en, 238). One may take issue with the qualifier "only" in terms of the achievement, which was monumental. What it does signify is that Xuanzang, despite almost twenty years of concentrated work, for which he organized collectives of apprentices and experts, was only able to render a portion of the vast store of the scriptures he brought back.

The Chinese did not consciously imitate Indian culture as Rome did, and the introduction of Buddhism into China, extending over many centuries, was a process of almost surreptitious, underground subversion. Not until the eighth century was Buddhism officially recognized and accepted as a state religion, although its promulgation by the Empress Wu Zetian, a woman, forever contaminated its claim to validity in the eyes of subsequent male historians — who were, for the most part, professedly Confucian. Surreptitious or blatant, the importation of foreign linguistic goods into China certainly exceeded the exportation by the Chinese of its own culture.[6]

One wishes there were data available on the import and export in translation toward the end of the Tang Dynasty. Might there have been a reverse thrust from the one we saw in Xuanzang? Instead of absorbing influences from the outside and digesting them, might the latter part of the Tang been more involved in exporting the glories of Du Fu, Li Bai, and

---

[4]   Nor should one assume that this indebtedness went in only one direction. The internecine conflict over the centuries between Christian and Muslim obscures the fact that the Koran sees itself as the continuation of the mythos begun in the Bible: in the Koran, Jesus is, after all, the prophet who preceded Mahomet.

[5]   *Encyclopedia Britannica* (Chicago, 1968), v. 2, p. 189.5.

[6]   I am making a distinction here, which may be unnecessary, between native exportation of native culture, and foreign importation of that culture. Certainly, during this period and throughout history, Korea and Japan, imported a good deal of Chinese culture into their own traditions, but this was not the result of Chinese scholars translating out of their own language, but of Korean and Japanese scholars learning Chinese in order to render Chinese classics into their own tongue.

Bai Juyi? We know from inferential evidence that the countries that became Korea and Japan were familiar with these poets, but was that a function of Chinese translating the corpus into the native vernaculars, or was it more probably the result of satellite cultures (as they saw themselves) developing scholars familiar with Chinese?

Similarly, Elizabethan England, perhaps the most dazzlingly productive period in English literature, was undoubtedly a "borrower" culture, one that relied heavily on what they regarded as superior continental traditions. Difficult as it may be for moderns to recall, the Elizabethans thought the language they inherited was a crude instrument, compared to the more sophisticated continental tongues, particularly French, Spanish, and Italian. "The nation had grown conscious of its cultural inferiority to the Continent," F. O. Matthiessen writes, " and suddenly burned with the desire to excel its rivals in letters, as well as in ships and gold." Translating into one's native tongue was, Matthiessen insists, "an act of patriotism"(3).

Patriotism did not hesitate to identify with the foreign. The translator borrowed from the French of Montaigne in John Florio's rendering; from the Italian of Castiglione and his *Courtier* presented in English garb of Sir Thomas Hoby; from the Greek of Plutarch, as distilled by Sir Thomas North through Jacques Amyot's French version; or from the Latin of Livy, Pliny, and Suetonius, as revivified by Philemon Holland. The notion of nationhood depended not on an autonomous existence, but on availing oneself of the wisdom from abroad, whether contemporary or ancient. Admissions of inferiority were spurs to action rather than defeatist self-denigrations. The result was a period in which literature flourished in England as never before.

Perhaps the most remarkable accommodation of translation was the invention in Japanese during the Meiji Restoration of a special language to render foreign words in a native tongue. Masao Miyoshi, among others, has described this medium of Japanese as crucial to the receptivity to Western ideas and Western concepts. Perhaps unique among the world's languages, Japanese devised a special sub-language to accommodate foreign works: "when the narrative requires expository clarity, it resorts to the stiff 'translation' style invented for handling the Western literatures" (Miyoshi, xiv). In a sense Japanese co-opted the foreign as part of the native, even as it distinguished one from the other, rendering both of them equally accessible and transparent. The net effect was a comfort level with the foreign in Japanese that did not exist, for example, in Chinese.

The introduction of foreign ideas into Japanese has, of course, a long tradition: and the invention of the special syllabary for foreign words had its precedent in the existence of *kanji* or Chinese characters, which were adopted from China, and which, while not a syllabary, retained a semantic character that was marked by its Chinese origins. A native syllabary, *hiragana*, was developed to accommodate indigenous expressions. Finally, another syllabary called *katakana*, evolved specifically to accommodate Western vocabulary. Doubtless this receptivity to the new, and the foreign, is a key factor in the speed with which Japan developed from a medieval culture, with little significant contact with the West until Admiral Dewey entered Tokyo harbor in 1855, to a world power in two generations, and a world leader in finance, technology, and manufacturing in five generations. The sense of "patriotism" which acknowledges one's own inferiority that one encountered in Elizabethan England, the impulse to catch up with other cultures and countries, may be found in Meiji Japan in the second half of the nineteenth century. In other words, love of country does not always take the form of a jingoism that vaunts one's homeland as supreme, nor does patriotism require that one deny the superiority of others in certain skills and technologies (a denial all too familiar in the history of China — despite repeated evidences, military and economic, to the contrary).

Though we do not have actual data to make a precise determination, we can speculate that the TI for early Republican Rome, early Tang China, Elizabethan England, and Meiji Japan, was significantly greater than 1 (TI: >1). In each case, this tendency to borrow from foreign cultures in no way reflected an absence of patriotism: indeed, each period can be characterized as one in which the native culture and the allegiance to one's country was in the ascendant. In anticipation of the analysis to follow, let us characterize this as the "patriotism of struggle," in which pride of place and of homeland take the form of a rapacious curiosity for, and a self-deprecating respect toward, other traditions.[7]

Examples of Hegemony

The situation with regard to imperial Rome from the viewpoint of translation is somewhat complex: the Roman Empire effectively dominated its subjugated territories culturally, with Latin as the medium of scholarly discourse for more than a millennium. Within that sphere, translation took the form of a conversion into a vernacular, which did not occur very often, given the fact that literacy was confined to the elite, and translations of the sacred texts of Christianity being restricted to those in ecclesiastical authority. As for the import and export of translation, the situation is not very clear (the single most important exception being, as we have seen, the translation of the Bible into Latin). Translations out of Latin into non-European vernaculars appear to be rare: Walzer, in the aforementioned *Encyclopedia Britannica* article, mentions that "the only Latin author ever translated into Arabic in the middle ages was the Christian historian Orosius" (EB, vol. 2, p. 188). With the decline and demise of the Roman Empire and the emergence of the nation-states in

---

[7]   One should note that in all instances but one — the borrowing was from a civilization at least as, if not more ancient, whether the Greek, as with the Romans, the Indian with the Chinese, or the European with the Elizabethans. Meiji Japan experienced the modernist trauma, so difficult for traditionalist cultures to comprehend, of learning not from a more, but rather from a less, ancient tradition.

Europe, translation of Latin texts into the vernacular became commonplace. Gilbert Highet makes the point that the English Romantics did not so much rebel against their Neo-Classic predecessors in their fondness for the classics as prefer the Greeks to the Romans. Charles Homer Haskins devoted an entire chapter to "The Translators" in his *The Renaissance in the Twelfth Century*, focussing on the circuitous route by which Greek science and philosophy was transmitted via Syriac, Hebrew, Arabic, and Spanish into Latin. Ernst Robert Curtius sees the hegemony of translating out of one's culture (though he used the word "empire"):

> The renewal of the Empire by Charlemagne could be regarded as a transferral of the Roman imperium to another people. This is implied in the formula translatio imperii, with which the translatio studii (transferal of learning from Athens to Rome to Paris) was later coordinated. The medieval Empire took over from Rome the idea of world empire; thus it had a universal, not a national, character. (28-29)

The politics of translation is, of course, a complex issue. The control in translation stems from the adamic precept that whoever determines the language of discourse exerts dominion over the objects (and subjects) discussed. The namer dominates the named. I agree with Eric Cheyfitz in his *Poetics of Imperialism* — subtitled: "Translation and Colonization from The Tempest to Tarzan" — when he says that translation is an act of "usurpation", but, unlike Cheyfitz, I see the *translatio imperii* more clearly in translations out of a language than translations into a language.[8]

Closer to our own time, we have the example of the enormous productivity of the Foreign Languages Press in Beijing, which has been publishing translations of Chinese literature into Arabic, French, and English for nearly fifty years. With the possible exception of the Gorky Institute for World Literature in Moscow, the Foreign Languages Press may be the world's leader in producing exported translation. Yang Hsien-yi and his wife, Gladys Yang, have headed an extremely productive team of translators who have produced translations of virtually every significant work of literature originally written in Chinese. During the same period, and especially spanning the ten years of the Cultural Revolution (1966-76), one can safely assume that the translation "balance of payments" in China, its TI, was considerably under 1, as virtually no western works were being rendered into Chinese. It would be interesting to chart the changes in the TI in China since 1979, when China opened up to the West. My personal and anecdotal impression is that, not only are significant Western works being voluminously translated into Chinese,

---

[8] Cheyfitz sees two kinds of translation, one uncovering, the other eliding, the difficulties of intercultural communication. He focuses on the colonial treatment of an illiterate society, where an oral society is considered a culture, and a literary society a civilization. In these instances, translating has inevitable hegemonic effects. But, there are instances where near-equals, both literate, can learn from each other without evident hegemonic impositions.

there appears to be little lag time between original publication and the appearance of the Chinese translation. In other words, there has been a radical reversal of the TI that prevailed in China before 1979. Surely this reflects a less insular, less complacent attitude toward foreign cultures: there is as much appreciation for what one can learn from others as for teaching them about one's own culture. Although I can only speculate on what the TI index in China might be today, I feel sure that it is closer to equilibrium, and may very likely be greater than TI 1.

By contrast to the Elizabethan period, when England was in the ascendancy, it would be interesting to examine the Transindex of the Victorian era. One imported translation into English, of course, stands out: Edward Fitzgerald's Rubaiyat of Omar Khayyam. And towards the end of the period there were the translations of the wisdom books of the East which F. Max Mueller edited under the title, The Sacred Books of the East. Nevertheless, the Victorian period is likely to be one where one expects considerably more export translation than import translation, the imperialist tendencies of the British Empire being what they were, and taking into account the British attitude about their own culture, to say nothing of their attitude toward other cultures. The Transindex for the British in the 19th century would, I suspect, be low, less than 1 (TI <1). The most notable export in translation of this period, though it was not undertaken by Englishmen, would be the Schlegel-Tieck version of Shakespeare which Germans to this day consider superior to Shakespeare in accessibility and colloquial fluency. Dickens's influence in Europe was also enormous, and we know that Dostoyevsky, among others, very much admired Dickens for his humanity and his wit. Still, if we saw in the Elizabethan period an example of translation viewed as evolving out of the "patriotism of struggle," the translation activity in the Victorian period is more likely to have evolved out of a patriotism that was not so much struggling, as complacent. Such a vantage point as the one I'm recommending here, is that we can use the Transindex to distinguish between a physical and geographical insularity and a cultural and intellectual insularity. No one can claim that England, an empire on which the sun never set, was physically or geographically insular; but an examination of the translation "balance of payments" might reveal a cultural insularity that might explain her consequent decline. Would a Transindex provide a clue as to the ascendancy or the decline of a culture? Might it be a pulse that would indicate a country's vital signs?

For example, the fledgling Germany under Frederick the Great was an "importing" country, especially of French culture; so was early nineteenth-century Russia, borrowing from the French as well, progressing within a century and a half from a medieval nation to a modern monolith. Did France herself not undergo a period of "patriotic struggle" earlier on, absorbing the higher wisdom of older traditions, the Italian and the Roman? And did translation into French not play a crucial role? Was Spain not enriched by borrowings from Moorish culture before it reached its peak in the sixteenth century? These speculations are beyond my competence to analyze, but they may be worth pursuing.

Test Comparisons

One comparison that could be made would be to examine the translation activity in China during the late Qing, and in Japan during the Meiji. Might the receptivity to foreign ideas, specifically Western, not have been a factor in Japan's ability to adapt, and China's failure to modernize? The situation in China is, of course, complex, because in a sense half of its history over the past millennium has involved foreign occupation: the Yuan in 1279-1368, and the Qing in 1644-1911. It may be that China thought it had already adapted to the foreigner (i.e., the Manchus), and was loathe to adapt to another. And, of course, China's notion of the foreigner saw them distinctly as a military threat, one more incursion on the homeland, whereas Japan had had the proud tradition, reinforced since the time of their rebuff of the Mongols in the late 13th-century, and unique among the nations of the world prior to the establishment of the United States of America, of never having been invaded by a foreign power. (In that respect, in World War II, the United States and Japan were like two previously undefeated pugilists.)

In the absence of precise figures on books translated into one's native language, and out of one's native language, it may be difficult to establish accurately a Transindex (TI). However, figures for book imports and book exports are readily available, so that one can easily compile a Book Trade Index (BTI). These ratios would probably be proportional to the ratio of works translated into and out of a particular language. The BTI for the United States in 1991 would be, according to Publisher's Weekly (June 29, 1992), 402,622 units imported, compared with 776,454 units exported, which yields a BTI of 0.518. Since the Book Trade Index is less than 1 (BTI <1), that would suggest a Translation Index would also be less than 1 (TI <1).

By a rough order of approximation, in 1985, the total number of translations published in the United Kingdom and the United States (1,121 and 1,389) total 2,510 by contrast, some 26,690 titles were translated with English as the source language.[9] Assuming that these represent or approximate the total translations out of English and those into English, that would translate into a combined TI of 0.09 — a very low Translation Index indeed. If we compare this with Japan in the same year, 1985, the figures are as follows: 2,892 translations into Japanese published; only 254 translations published out of Japanese, yielding a TI of 11.38 — a very high Translation Index.

---

[9]   This figure is inevitably inflated, since the UNESCO data charts translations with English as a source language: this would also include original works first published in Anglophone countries other than the United Kingdom and the United States, such as Canada, Australia, and South Africa. To my knowledge, no data exists that chart the translations imported in the same language subdivided by country.

If we look at the former U. S. S. R, in 1985, some 8,039 titles were translated into Russian, whereas some 6,337 titles were translated out of Russian, yielding a TI of 1.27, or near equilibrium. France, for the same year, has a TI of 0.7 (4,679 into, 6,327 out of French). The first observation one makes about these figures is how wide the gamut is, from Japan with a TI of 11.385, and the U. K. / U. S. with a TI of 0.094. France, Germany, and the U. S. S. R. (the former Soviet Republics) are nearer equilibrium.

There are a number of methodological difficulties with the calculation of the TI: some of the data, while helpful as corroboration, may not always give reliable evidence of import/export activity in translation. For example, UNESCO's Statistical Abstracts provides book exports, measured in terms of millions of dollars: while this is useful in calculating the economic "balance of payments" in the book trade, it may not be a reliable measure of the trade in translations.

	Translations Imported	Translations Exported	Translation Index (TI)
France	4,679	6,327	0.74
Germany	6,305	4,847	2.18
Japan	2,892	254	11.39
US / UK	2,510	26,690	0.09
USSR	8,039	6,337	1.27
Source: *Publisher's Weekly*, June 22, 1992, p. 24.			

Second, not all countries are equally monolingual: translations imported into the United States can be safely assumed to be translated into English, but translations imported into Canada may be just as likely to be translated into French as English. Third, where the source language is found principally in one country, it is relative easy to assess the number of translations into and out of that country, but where a language is spread out over many countries — as with English, Spanish, and, to a certain extent, French — the Translation Index may reflect not a particular country's hospitableness to other cultures as the receptivity of the language culture, which may not be coterminous with a specific nation.

Still, these methodological difficulties aside, I believe even an approximate calculation of the Translation Index is worthwhile as a way of measuring what might be interpreted as a polarity between complacency and curiosity. The country that imports very few translations can be said to feel no curiosity about other languages, other countries: it is satisfied that it has all it needs within its native language, whereas a country that imports ideas from the outside reflects a curiosity about developments not accessible in the native tongue. The TI does not reflect economic dominance: note that Japan and the United States are at the opposite ends of the spectrum. Japan has a high TI, reflecting insatiable curiosity about the rest of the world, whereas the United States has a very low TI, reflecting persistent ignorance of, and indifference to, developments abroad. It should be noted that the persistent criticism that the United States levies against Japan about severely restricting imports from the West does not apply to books and ideas, where Japan virtually leads the world.

Perhaps there is a lesson in that anomaly.

2. Crossing the Borders of Humour:
The Intersection of Different Logics

This chapter will consider one of the litmus tests of translation — the rendering of a joke from one language to another. It is not true that humor cannot be translated: some jokes may, indeed, be untranslatable, but there are others that do survive translingual transport with the wit intact.

As I shall be much occupied with China, let me begin with a panda joke. A panda walks into a bar, orders a sandwich, eats it, takes out a gun, shoots at the ceiling, and leaves. This behavior puzzles a bystander, who asks someone to explain this bizarre behaviour: he is told that there's nothing unusual — since that's what pandas do. "What do you mean, that's what pandas do?" the bystander asks. "If you don't believe me," he is told, "look up the definition for panda in any reference work, and you'll see what I mean." The bystander looks up an encyclopedia, and reads the following: "Panda: large black-and-white mammal, resembling a bear, found mostly in the mountains of southwest China. Eats shoots and leaves."

I tell this joke by way of illustrating the difference between translation and cross-cultural communication. This joke cannot be translated, except into a language where counterparts can be found for: a word which can be a verb meaning "to discharge a bullet from a gun," as well as a noun referring to the tender young branches of trees, i. e., "shoots"; and a word which can be both a verb meaning "to depart" and a noun referring to what grows on trees, i e., "leaves". No other language, to my knowledge, has exact counterparts to these ambivalent meanings.

Translation can transmit information between two cultures, but it cannot convey these subtleties of language and meaning inherent in any culture. For the sake of convenience, let me refer to the first as "definitive sense," and the second as "indefinite nuance." Jokes are a way of playing with definitive sense to create indefinite nuance. What is "lost in translation" is precisely cross-cultural insight: translation offers the illusion that meaning is universal and that all languages are semantically equivalent to each other, whereas cross-cultural communication focuses on the individual and regional — the particular rather than the general — and shows that each language and culture is clear and distinct, and that each has its unique character.

It's only fair that I share with you as well a story which can only be appreciated in Chinese:

在美国，有一些学生不仅汉语学的好，而且对于中国人的礼貌及客气话，都学的不错。有一个学生，他老师请他吃饭，烧了几个菜，客气的对他说：［请坐，请坐。没有甚吗菜，就是便

饭] 那位学生为了要表示他的汉语
水平，很得意的回答，说 [啊,老师太客气，这简直不是 "便反
"。假如是便饭，也不是小便饭，是大便饭！]

The crux of the humor in this anecdote, which I'm told is a true story, lies in two intersecting semantic propositions: one, that, in Chinese, to refer to something as big (大) rather than small (小) is a form of compliment, raising its importance and value rather than denigrating it; two, that the idiom in Chinese for urinating is (小便) and for defecating is (大便). What the student wanted to say was something like: "What you have cooked me is hardly a small thing, it's a big thing." But the net result of the student's attempt at elegance and politeness was to say to the teacher, "You haven't cooked me a urinating dinner; you've cooked me a defecating dinner."

Let me venture another so-called "joke", which is both unfunny and funny — depending on who the audience is. This joke was especially popular in Eastern Europe before the fall of the Iron Curtain. Americans find this "joke" totally impenetrable, whereas the Rumanians, Czechs, Bulgarians, and Hungarians I have tried it out on find it hilarious. Here is the joke. A man goes to a hotel: the clerk at the reception desk asks: "A double bed or twin beds?" The man is indignant, and shouts: "Comrade, not even if I were alone would I want a double bed!"[2]

East Europeans, with memories still fresh from the rigid moral codes of the former Soviet bloc, are reminded of the sycophants and the lackeys who tried to ingratiate themselves with authorities by insisting on their anti-decadent (read: "anti-capitalist") convictions.   In this case, the absurdity is based on the presumption that celibacy under the Soviets was as admired as ideological purity. Hence, the outlandish protest that one would not want a double bed "even if one were alone". The joke doesn't work with American audiences, because in most American jokes, it is the presumption of preternatural lust that provides the thrust of the humor, whereas in the former Soviet Socialist republics, it was politically correct to proclaim, even to insist on, one's sexual innocence.

Having told two jokes that don't translate from one language to another, or from one culture to another, let me relate a third that does lend itself to translation.

When I visited China in 1979, a driver once asked me if I had ever tasted dogmeat. I said no. "It's very tasty," he told me. "Why don't you invite me to America," he asked, "I'll run a dog over for you, we'll cook it, and you'll see how delicious dogmeat can be." "No, thank you," I replied, "You don't know how much Americans love their dogs. They hate people who kill dogs more than they hate people who kill people."

---

[1]   A story I owe to Professor GE Liangyan, a former student, who teaches at the University of Notre Dame.

[2]   I heard this joke from the folklorist, Andrew Vazsonyi, in the 1980's, prior to the fall of the Iron Curtain, when we spent a memorable evening discussing the reasons why this joke was both funny and unfunny.

Years later, I related this incident to a friend. "Why, yes," she said, "Did you know that Koreans are also fond of dogmeat?" Then she added: "I once invited a Korean to visit the U. S. and he wanted to try everything typically American. At a restaurant, we looked at the menu, and he noticed an item called 'Hot Dog'. 'Is that typically American?' he asked. 'There isn't anything more typically American than a Hot Dog,' I told him. 'Well, in that case, I'll order a Hot Dog.' When the food was brought to the table, my Korean friend was aghast: his face turned ashen. 'What's the matter?' I asked. He said: 'That's the only part of the dog we don't eat!'"

Now, this incident, unlike the first two "jokes", can be rendered quite easily into virtually any language.[3] But, aside from its translatability, the story illustrates one of the important lessons of cross-cultural studies: that one is so inured by the conventions in one's native language to the "dead metaphors" that one forgets their literal meanings. Foreigners make mistakes that sometimes remind us of what we've overlooked in our own tongue.

The frustrations caused by cross-cultural misunderstanding can also be the source of cross-cultural insight. A woman once told me that, living in Switzerland and knowing very little French, she had to improvise in order to identify without words what she wanted. Mimicry is one way of trying to describe things, but gestures alone are not always sufficient. Sometimes a combination of word and gesture is needed. Going to the butcher in search of chicken breasts, this woman from the United States did not have enough French to say "blanc de poulet" or "filet de poulet" — which is what the French say when they want to specify the white meat part of the chicken. So, adding a bit of ingenuity to what little French she had, she made a gesture with both hands cupped towards her chest and added the words ". . . de poulet." She was rewarded for her ingenuity, to say nothing of her earthiness: the butcher understood immediately. (Doubtless he looked forward to selling her "blanc de poulet" again.)

Another challenge to cross-cultural understanding can be found in the buses in Hong Kong. When I arrived at the end of the summer, just before the beginning of classes, there were two schedules for the shuttle I took to Lingnan College.[4]

I went in one morning according to one schedule, concluding thereby that it — let us call it Schedule A — was accurate. Then, when I went home that day, I consulted the times in Schedule A, only to find out that the other schedule — let's call it Schedule B — was accurate for the afternoon. I remonstrated with the college authorities and told them that

---

[3] "The translation of jokes," writes Anne-Marie Laurian, "is a path to a greater understanding among people and a sounder communication in the world" (126): she concentrates on translation of humor from English to French; Qaiser Zoha Alam deals with intralingual translation, from Indian English to British English; Katsuo Tamaoka and Toshiaki Takahashi focus on humor in English as understood by the Japanese university student; Mark Herman writes a regular column on "Humor and Translation" for the *ATA Chronicle*.

[4] As it was known then: Lingnan became a university in 1999.

the bus company issued Schedule A which gave times correctly in the morning, and Schedule B which gave times correctly in the afternoon. "Why don't they provide a reliable schedule?" I asked, which I thought was eminently reasonable. "We've tried to get the bus company to print a reliable schedule," I was told, but they refused. "Why?" I asked. "Because," came the response, "If they printed an accurate schedule, they were afraid that they would always be late." (It should surprise no one that the shuttle service was soon discontinued because not enough people used it.)

Minibuses are a unique Hong Kong institution: they seat sixteen people, can pick up and drop passengers where they want and if they want, and sometimes they do not have a standard fare: they charge according to the weather conditions (the fare is higher when it rains) and on the volume of the passengers (the more crowded, the more expensive). As a result, one is never sure what the fare is upon entering the bus.[5]

Still, there is a logic to this seeming madness which may make even more sense than a uniform standard fare: in economics, it's called the law of supply and demand.

Human communication is incredibly intuitive in its ability to disambiguate between variables: we recognize people not by knowing their exact weight or height or by their coloring at any given point, but by the circumstances in which we encounter them, which is why we are befuddled when we encounter someone outside the customary context: we may know we know the person, but out of context, it's difficult to identify them. What makes our intuitions powerful are the presuppositions we make in any circumstances: the person we see in uniform behind the cashier's counter in a shop is suddenly a vaguely familiar stranger whom we can't quite identify if we encounter them, say, as a juror in a courtroom. Our perceptions leap to a recognition on the basis of assumptions that are correct in the preponderant percentage of the cases. However, to show that presuppositions are at work, even when we are scarcely conscious of them, I offer a photograph of a woman buying fruit. No one can fail to make the mistake of seeing more than meets the eye: our presuppositions make us see something which really isn't there. Our minds immediately form a context of meaning which is far less innocent than a clean-cut woman picking out and weighing, one in each hand, two canteloupes.

Cross-cultural communication requires that we recognize the lenses through which each culture sees the world; it demands that we acknowledge that no perception proceeds from a neutral, totally objective base; and it encourages our minds to think out of our specific cultural boxes, to appreciate a different, even opposing perspective. Effective cross-cultural communication involves the recognition of "pseudo-universals": the fact that cultural paradigms are not, in fact, universal, even if their familiarity may give them an air of universality in any culture. It also means that one must "translate" semiotically, as well as verbally, not

---

[5]   These practices are found more often in the New Territories, not so much in Kowloon or Hong Kong Island, where the procedures tend to be standardized.

only meaning, but situation and circumstance. I offer two examples, one to illustrate different cultural semiotics, the other to illustrate semiotic translation.

At a dinner with Chinese friends at a Chinese restaurant in Singapore, I was developing a stock semiotic analysis, half in jest, half seriously, about the paradigms of dining in a Chinese and a Western milieu. In Western culture, the tastiness of one's meal depends not at all on how many others one dines with: ordering from a Western menu is an individual enterprise. Aside from curiosity, one's dining experience does not depend on what other people order or how many other people one is dining with. One's food is unaffected whether one eats alone or with half a dozen other diners. Not so at a Chinese meal, as anyone knows who has eaten Chinese food alone. It is much less satisfying to eat Chinese food alone than in the company of a number of people (ideally as many as eight). Eating a Chinese meal involves ordering for the table; it's not an individual experience where it's every person for him- or herself. This is a reflection of a deeper paradigm: the emphasis on the collective in Chinese culture and on the individual in Western culture. When I was developing this theme, my Chinese interlocutors broke into a smile. "Do you find my analysis absurd?" I asked. "No," they replied, "We're laughing because we are recalling the sight of eight Englishmen at the same table in this very restaurant last week: they each ordered exactly the same thing — sweet and sour pork." What is perfectly natural for eight Brits in this instance would seem absolutely bizarre to most if not all Chinese.

Chinese preconceptions of a meal differ from the Western: in the one, the meal is what an individual orders; in the other, the meal is a communal feast in which the individual partakes, and each one participates in ordering for the whole.[6]

My second anecdote involves a Hawaiian-American woman who decided that the American fondness for pizza could be transplanted to Japan, where she began a frozen pizza business. What she didn't account for were several cultural disparities involved in the making of pizza: what we might call "pizza presumptions." First, cheese is a defining ingredient in pizza, but most Japanese do not care for cheese; second, pizzas must be baked, and most Japanese do not have ovens.[7] Ingeniously, to solve the first problem, she substituted tofu for mozzarella, and addressing the second problem, she designed pizzas that could be panfried on the stovetop.

---

[6] People from Beijing are sometimes known to eat a meal of nothing but *jiaozi* (dumplings), but that is another matter; when a meal consists of more than one dish, no Chinese would order exactly the same item as everyone else. The decision is collective and not individual (when there is no designated host), and the meal is the construction, semiotically conceived, of all those present as one, and not of eight separate individuals.

[7] This was more true in the 1980's than now, of course, and many more Japanese do have ovens in their homes.

(Marc Rivière)

Nevertheless, when her business began to pick up, she ran into some unexpected difficulties. The Japanese complained about her pizzas: they weren't perfectly round, they said. Now, in all the millions of oven-baked pizzas prepared daily in the United States, I can state with confidence that few if any have been perfectly round. Indeed the irregularity of shape is the identifying trait of an oven-baked pizza. But before one attributes this insistence on perfect roundness to an excessive Japanese penchant for precision, one needs to ask about the configuration of the pans used if frozen pizzas are to be cooked on the stovetop: predominantly, they are perfectly round. So, what seems bizarre to an American accustomed to irregularly shaped oven-baked pizzas makes good sense to Japanese who cook their pizzas in a pan.

Some cross-cultural disparities may be caught in certain classic mistranslations. A series of "found" quotes in various countries have been circulating every so often for years, discovered by different editors as if for the first time, although by now they have been published, with exactly the same wording, over and over again, under different headlines and in different journals and newspapers.

Here is a sample:

> In a Copenhagen airline ticket office: "We take your bags and send them in all directions."

> On the door of a Moscow hotel room: "If this is your first visit to the USSR, you are welcome to it."
> In a Japanese hotel: "You are invited to take advantage of the chambermaid."

> In an advertisement by a Hong Kong dentist: Teeth extracted by the latest Methodists.

> In a Bangkok dry cleaner's: "Drop your trousers here for best results."

> In a Rome laundry: "Ladies, leave your clothes here and spend the afternoon having a good time."

> In a Tokyo bar: "Special cocktails for the ladies with nuts."

> On the menu of a Swiss restaurant: "Our wines leave you nothing to hope for."

(These samples appeared in Richard Lederer's *Anguished English* (in the chapter "Lost in Translation"); they also appeared in *The Far Eastern Economic Review*, September 28, 1989, under "Traveller's Tales". Paul Ames of the Associated Press, with a byline from Brussels, Belgium, reports that much of the same material is displayed on a bulletin board in the European Community's Centre Borschette office complex; this reference was sent to me by a friend who copied it down from a bulletin board at the University of South Carolina in Columbia, South Carolina in July or August 1997: it appeared under the title, "Broken English: EC showcases best of the world's worst grammar." Further research revealed that Ames's piece also appeared in the November 22, 1992 City Edition of the Chicago Tribune, under the title, "Linguistic Lulus Draw Global Laughs." Mr. LIU Jian, of the reference department of the Indiana University Library, informs me that he saw the same listing on the Internet "a long time ago.")

How many of these gaffes, in fact, tell the truth? Might that Swiss restaurant be telling us something crucial about the wines they serve? Might the Roman laundry be thinking of something else besides cleaning clothes? How can grammar disambiguate between "special cocktails with nuts" and "ladies with nuts"? How many weary air travellers would agree with the Copenhagen airline ticket office: airlines do take our bags and send them in all directions! And though I've not been to Moscow, I'm told that many visitors would voice the same sentiments as those found in the hotel room: many people would say about Russia: "You're welcome to it."

Ignorance of language or the semiotics of symbols in other languages has produced famous howlers which are not only embarrassing, but fatal to market prospects. Among the most famous, of course, is the name for a model of Chevrolet, Nova, distributed in South America without any awareness that "no-va" in Spanish means, "no-go". "Robo car washes" indicate the height of technology in the United States, but in Spanish, "robo" means "I steal". Colgate toothpaste in Argentina has an ominous ring: it's understood as "go hang yourself"; and the suggestion of Braniff Airlines vaunting its leather seats, "viajar en cuero", actually means "to travel naked" (not "travel on leather"). Not to be outdone, Continental Airlines, who put their initials "CA" repeatedly on their silverware, was not aware that "CACA" is "baby talk for excrement."[9]

Perhaps the most interesting instance I know of fruitful cross-cultural misunderstanding occurred in 1963, when President John F. Kennedy went to the Berlin Wall and made his famous "Ich bin ein Berliner" speech. As a metaphor for the universality of the Berliner experience, living on the border between Communist and Capitalist worlds, Kennedy's declaration resonated throughout the world. However, in another sense, Kennedy's use of "ein Berliner" might lend itself to a possible misunderstanding, since to those who live in Berlin, the phrase "ein Berliner" means a kind of jelly donut. Some commentators have mistakenly characterized this as a mistake, and claim that "He should have said 'Ich bin Berliner' — eine Berliner is a jam doughnut, short for Berliner Pfannkuche, a 'Berlin pancake'" (Read and Fisher, 285). But there are no reports that Kennedy was met with any guffaws in the Berlin audience, and certainly no one mistook his meaning. On the contrary, if Kennedy had said "Ich bin aus Berlin" or "Ich bin Berliner" (according to Read and Fisher), the rhetoric of the situation would have betrayed him. For had a Berliner heard Kennedy say, "Ich bin Berliner" or "Ich bin aus Berlin", he would have thought Kennedy a liar, uttering a falsehood: Kennedy didn't, after all, come from Berlin.

Saying "Ich bin ein Berliner" was absolutely appropriate for a foreigner, who was only "borrowing" the German language to make a

---

[9] I owe some of these examples to Jack Child (23).

point.[10]   It may have marked the speaker as foreign; far from distracting the audience, the phrase underscored what he was saying as metaphor, not as literal truth.   Conversely, to hear a Berliner state "Ich bin ein Berliner" would be a statement of fact, not a metaphor.[11]

What translation cannot address, and what cross-cultural communication uncovers, are the premises and presuppositions that every language is subject to, with the natives often being the last to be aware of it.   Elsewhere I have attacked the assumption by Western linguists that every language has a grammar, and that grammar is, traditionally, conceived in Western terms (Eoyang, 1997).

There are presuppositions in even the scientific method, in such "neutral" subjects as social science research — which are not as unbiased as one might initially assume. Here are two examples. The first is the use of questionnaires by Western researchers in canvassing the opinions of select populations to explore differential or homologous attitudes in different cultures.   (I have in mind questionnaires that examine comparatively the attitude of Japanese and U. S. employees.) The more scrupulous social scientists take great pains to ensure the "objectivity" of the questionnaire instrument by translating the questions into the native language; the meticulous even go so far as to translate the translation back into the original language to see that no distortion has occurred. There is, in this precaution, two basic cross-cultural fallacies: the first is that equivalence can ever be achieved in translation, and the second is that the answer to questions will always have the same degree of earnestness and reliability across cultures.

Questions and answers on matters of judgment and opinion are rarely, if ever, semantically neutral. The rhetorical situation must be considered. Take, as one example, the intrusiveness felt by an American when asked about his or her age, a sense of being intruded upon that a Chinese would find puzzling. Or, asking about one's salary: in the U. S. this inquiry would be offensive, and even close friends are reluctant to ask about salaries, whereas in China, this is virtually public information, and one has no qualms about asking. How could answers to questions of this sort be equally valid in every culture?

Questionnaires also assume, erroneously, that respondents in different cultures will answer with the same forthrightness.   Cross-cultural experience shows, however, that answers from respondents from different cultures may represent different values, and may well be motivated by different concerns. In Japan, respondents will be prompted by what they

[10]   Surely it is willfully disingenuous to suggest, as Read and Fisher do, that Kennedy should have avoided the "eine Berliner" construction. For a Berliner to take Kennedy for a jelly donut is as improbable as it would be for a New Yorker to take someone who says, "I am a New Yorker" for a magazine. Besides, no Berliner would expect a foreigner to know the "jelly donut" meaning of "eine Berliner". I first cited this anecdote in a paper presented in 1990, before the publication of Read and Fisher's book.

[11]   In this regard, as *metaphor*, "Ich bin ein Berliner" is better than "Ich bin aus Berlin" or "Ich bin Berliner" — which in Kennedy's case would have been contrary to fact. I make no speculation as to whether Kennedy's speechwriter was aware of these nuances.

think the researcher wants to hear or what they imagine their employers might prefer; in the United States, respondents are more likely to offer independent opinions — regardless of their effect. Americans are also more likely to answer forthrightly questions about their personal lives: the Japanese, perhaps like Asians in general, are more likely to be more discreet and evasive. I suspect that Chinese respondents to questionnaires would differ in their motivation from both the Japanese and the American.

A second example of mistaken paradigm assumptions would involve the statistical notion of a "bell curve," where it is assumed that in any population, the configuration of a graph will resemble the shape of a bell, where the norms and the average will occur somewhere around the mean of any distribution. The configuration of the "bell curve" too often becomes *de rigueur* in the assessment of grade distributions at schools and colleges. If an instructor gives grades that do not fit the "bell" curve, it is assumed that his evaluations are unfair and contrary to a fair-minded assessment of realities. But the concept of a "bell curve" assumes independent instances, individualistic, differentiated, and randomly plotted: given these conditions, it is probable that any distribution will tend to be sparse at either extreme and more plentiful at the middle, and the norm will approach the mean, with a gradual incline up and down at either end. But in more conformist, less erratically individual populations, the curve would resemble more nearly a plateau rather than a bell. What I am saying is that the expectation that a bell curve describes a "normal" sampling is a cultural prejudice that assumes certain characteristics of the population being surveyed. Shapes other than those resembling a "bell" may be more normal for different populations and different distributions.

Too often, what is presented as objective is not as neutral culturally as it pretends to be; what is presumed to be self-evident is self-evident only to some people and not to others, and what is vaunted as universal is merely a local or regional conviction falsely extrapolated beyond its provincial context. Aristotle's universal is a function of his experience; Confucius's universal is another matter, reflecting a different experience. The true universal is what we find in both Aristotle and Confucius.

We must embark on a campaign of what James Hamill calls "Ethno-logic", which he defines as follows:

> Ethno-logic is a part of the social sciences, and its goal differs from that of formal philosophical logic. Whereas formal textbook logic seeks to identify how abstract logical systems work, ethno-logic attempts to learn how people think . . . Ethno-logicians must collect data using methods that can reveal the knowledge system standing behind their consultants' thought patterns (cf. Hamill, 59).

An ignorance of "ethno-logic" leads to the pious insistence by Western politicians and diplomats on "the rule of law" as if there were only one species of law, and that law is universal rather than merely Western. The Universal Declaration of Human Rights promulgated by the United

Nations in 1948 includes, among its thirty articles, certain claims that are not shared by all cultures. "All human beings are born free and equal in dignity and rights" is a belief that Western culture — particularly its Anglo-American component — adheres to, but the faith in its validity is not universally shared.

Nor is the codicil that maintains that an accused is innocent until proven guilty[12]: the exact opposite is part of the tradition of many Asian cultures. In traditional China, for example, the magistrate was at the same time the prosecutor, and those indicted were often tortured to extract a confession, on the not unreasonable assumption that the guilty were prone to lie.[13] In modern Japan, there is the case of Shoko Asahara (alias: Chizuo Matsumoto), the leader of the Aum Shin Ri kyo sect, accused of masterminding the attack which released deadly gas in the Tokyo subways on March 20, 1995. The Japanese courts found it difficult to maintain the presumption of prior innocence when no lawyer wished to be associated with him, and no one volunteered to represent him in a court of law. (The court eventually appointed legal counsel to represent him, but one can hardly rely on the earnestness and the enthusiasm of such legal representation.)

Even the definition of a human being as an individual, implicit in Western notions of the human, may not be accepted in all cultures. There is considerable scholarship establishing the fact that a shift in attitudes toward the self occurred in Europe during the twelfth century (cf. Morris). And John Benson reminds us, for example, that "though there was a perfectly good Latin word for 'self' [in the twelfth century]. . . there is no medieval word which has anything like the meaning of 'personality'" (Benson and Constable, 284). A modern notion of the self that does not involve "personality" would be, for us, incomprehensible. Contrast this with the Japanese perspective: "the Japanese attitude toward personality (not any particular trait, but 'personality' itself) is basically profoundly negative" (Miyoshi, xi)

The insistence by Western ideologues on "human rights," by which they mean, implicitly, "individual rights", ignores the hegemonic imposition of a distinctly Western concept alleged to be universal. The Confucian concept of *ren* 仁 for example, stresses relatedness and connectedness as the essence of what it means to be human — more than the autonomy of the self or the separateness of the individual. If we proceed from this different premise, then entire presuppositions about privacy and personal property, not to mention copyright and patents, must be called into question.

---

[12] The actual wording: "Everyone charged with a penal offence has the right to be presumed innocent until proved guilty according to law in a public trial at which he has had all the guarantees necessary for his defence."

[13] Indeed, the adversarial character of Anglo-American law, which may be a vestige of the chivalric code of the medieval joust, See my "Western Agon / Eastern Ritual: Confrontations and Co-optations in World Views," in: *Thresholds of Western Culture: Identity, Postcoloniality, Transnationalism.* London: Continuum International Publishing 2002, which also appears (as Chapter Four) in *Two-Way Mirrors* (Lexington, 2004)

The whole discourse on "Asian Values", advocated by Lee Kuan Yew of Singapore and Mahathir Mohamed of Malaysia, sought a middle ground between the insistence on absolute individual freedom that some advocate in the West and absolute collective tyranny that prevails in some parts of the world. The "piety" of American homilies on freedom reflects, typically, an American virtue and an American vice: admirably, with the best of intentions, Americans want the rest of the world to enjoy the freedoms they enjoy; not so admirably, however, this fervor for freedom sometimes tends to denigrate — unwittingly — those who might not share the same enthusiasm for freedom.

There is a hegemonic thrust in even a slogan as seemingly unexceptionable as the one we hear in the United States: "To make the world safe for democracy." Despite the American distaste for monarchy, there are countries in which monarchies are popular: Thailand, Spain, the Netherlands, Denmark. Isn't it a cultural bias to assume that only the benefits of a democratic world are worth having? One of the ironies of ultra-liberal positions is that they insist that everyone choose democracy — or else. Nothing could be, of course, more undemocratic and illiberal. There is a fascism not only of the right, but of the left as well. No wonder, some Asians see no difference between "To make the world safe for democracy" and "To make the world safe for Coca-Cola"!

None of these questions can be adequately addressed without recourse to both translation and cross-cultural communication, the one to establish a common ground of understanding, the second to explore areas in which basic paradigms differ. For discourse in the global village, translation and cross-cultural communication are complementary, not interchangeable. Both are necessary for a full understanding between people of different cultures. Translation highlights what we have in common; cross-cultural communication emphasizes what we have that is different.

The progress of civilization throughout the world would not have been possible without translation, but studies of translations by themselves can hardly uncover the underlying differences which make each culture unique. We must avoid the natural but misguided assumption that understanding proceeds only from understanding identities. It is wrong to posit a heuristic that seeks self-affirming equivalences, analogous to the tendency, among the insecure and the provincial, to "like" only those people who are "like" us. True understanding must proceed to an acknowledgement of differences between cultures and individuals, so that we might begin to "like" people who, indeed, are not "like" us. Only in that way can the idiocies of the conflicts in Northern Ireland, in the Middle East, East Europe, and in Afghanistan be resolved.

What we must strive to discover is not merely the common ground between us, but also what is uncommon in each of us.

3. Translating the Sacred and the Secular: Hermeneutics and Interpretation

This chapter explores the following dialectic relationships: between the sacred and the secular, between the oral and the textual; and between hermeneutics and interpretation. The premise of this discussion is that an enhanced understanding of these relationships will provide a context for a more accurate analysis of the problematics of translation. We may posit at the outset the contingent and parallel significance of translation to our concerns, recognizing that in traditional humanist hermeneutics the theory of translation is subsumed under the category of interpretation (Mueller-Vollmer, 3).

What is translated in canonical sacred and secular texts — despite their common status as "classics" — is clearly different with respect to their status as truth, in the one case soteriological and spiritual, in the other case logical or empirical. While there is little distinction made in translation theory between sacred and secular source texts, the process that renders the first is crucially different from the process that transmits the second. As for oral and textual sources, the meaning derived from each takes the form of translation, but the translation of oral forms involves on-the-spot interpretation; there is an imminence and an immediacy that is vital to the discourse. In the case of texts, translation borders on exegesis of a fixed artifact, or "explication de texte," a form of literary archaeology that "figures out what the text is saying."

Traditionally, scholars of scripture have been rigorously exegetical. However, the ontological status of scripture is complicated, because the reader's response is different for different readers: for the worshipper, the proper "reader's response" is to see oneself in the presence of "received truths" which one must neither question nor deny; to the ecclesiast and preacher, it is a source of inspiration; and to the scholar, it is a text, like any other text, to which basic philological principles apply.[1] The translation of scripture involves both fidelity to the work and fidelity to the faith. Luther's "protest" against Catholicism emerged out of both his insistence on the meaning of Scripture, "in their simple and ordinary sense" and his belief that anyone with "a right disposition" could feel the words of Scripture in one's heart" (Coward, 60).

We must, perhaps, first define our terms. By "sacred" we mean any concern with a transcendent being that involves devotional faith in the reality of that being; by "secular" we mean any concern with "worldly" mundane activities that does not presuppose the existence of a transcendent deity.

---

[1]   See my "Maladjusted Messenger: Rezeptionsasthetik in Translation" , Chapter 10 in *The Transparent Eye*.

Let us begin by differentiating sacred from secular "truths."

The truths in scripture are those vouchsafed to the reader either by intermediaries to divinity, or directly by God. The translation of these truths cannot be entrusted to anyone: traditionally, they have been assigned only to the faithful. Indeed, ecclesiastical doctrine demands of an exegete fidelity to the faith along with fidelity to the text. Faur's distinction of "semiotic" and "semantic" levels of understanding Scripture is informative. The first reads the signs in the text, grasps its literal meaning, and is associated with *peshat*, the purpose of which "is to expound the mind of the author as expressed in the text" (12). The second or semantic level, "corresponds to *derasha*, the rabbinic methodology of Scriptural exegesis," which "interprets the text independently of the intention of the author." As Faur reminds us, "at the semantic level, there is no objective meaning. *Derasha* is a creative composition of the reader functioning as an ecrivain" (13). But the license to provide exegeses is not entrusted to just anyone of sufficient scholarly or literary credentials: "this methodology is the exclusive prerogative of the Jewish people" (13). Maimonides, we are told, dismissed the criticisms of sectarians and non-Jews," because "since they do not belong to the Jewish people," their exposition is illegitimate. We have here the beginning of an institutional warrant of authority, that implies that true knowledge of scripture involves not merely knowing, but believing.

Faur draws an interesting contrast between Greek and Hebrew attitudes toward truth. Particularly after Plato, the Greek aletheia is "truth" in itself, it is context-free, and therefore universally valid; it "un-veils" and "discovers" the evident. This truth is static and absolute: like Euclidean geometry it transcends all contexts. (28) Hebrew attitudes, on the other hand, are "context-bound": its demands are that only the "world-within" provides the proper perspective, that truths cannot exist outside a context, independent of situations and circumstances: there can be no truth that "transcends all contexts." Truth has meaning only when the context of the message, in time and place, has been established. It is contingent on time and circumstance: as one commentator put it, "Revelation continues in time, so new torah becomes part of the Torah, as God speaks to generations without end" (Neusner, xix; quoted by Henderson, 57). Faur recalls Maimonides who "compared the deciphering of the significance of physical phenomena to a person in pitch darkness trying to glimpse his surroundings during a flash of lightning. Like a flash of lightning, truth is necessarily temporal. It cannot appear as a continuum, but only successively" (36).

Christianity combines the Greek notion of absolute truth with the Hebrew notion of a privileged access to truth. At the same time, it denies the Greek concept that absolute truth is accessible to anyone with a capacity to reason, and it denies the Hebrew belief that truth is contingent on time and place. But Christianity restricted access to absolute truth not merely to the faithful, but to those faithful who were literate. We may take as representative Paul's notion of the mysteries, as enunciated in 1

Corinthians. Paul maintained that those who were uninitiated, "poorly educated, or ignorant of religious teachings" — whom he referred to as "idiotae" — could not understand the word of God. Brian Stock's summary is helpful:

> The man who speaks in mysteries, he reasoned, talks to God, not to other men. . . . For 'if you pray with the spirit, how can one who takes his place among the uninstructed (locus idiotae) say Amen' (29)

As Stock puts it, "Paul does not tell us precisely who the idiotae are. In all probability they are not yet full Christians; that is, although they take part in the gatherings, they do not yet belong" (30). And Stock reminds us that "during the Middle Ages, the sense of idiota as someone partially excluded from participation in worship was extended to monastic lay brethren and even occasionally to heretics" (30). Christianity combined the Hebrew sense of the exclusivity of access to truth with the Greek concept of an absolute truth that was independent of context. It posited limited access to transcendent truth. Contrast these perspectives with the Confucian classics, which make no claim on transcendental truth, indeed, specifically disclaims any authority on such metaphysical questions. Here are the oft-quoted passages from the *Lun-yu* (Wing-tsit Chan translation):

> Tzu-kung said, "We can hear our Master's [views] on culture and its manifestation, but we cannot hear his views on human nature and the Way of Heaven [because these subjects are beyond the comprehension of most people]." (5:12)
>
> Confucius never discussed strange phenomena, physical exploits, disorder, or spiritual beings. (7:20)
>
> Chi-lu (Tzu-lu) asked about serving the spiritual beings. Confucius said, "If we are not yet able to serve man, how can we serve spiritual beings?" "I venture to ask about death." Confucius said, "If we do not yet know about life, how can we know about death?" (11:11)

Not only did Confucius declare his limitations, but subsequent commentators admitted shortcomings in his teachings as well. Henderson tells us, " . . . the main value of the Confucian classics was in their function as teachers of morality rather than in their literary excellence, intellectual profundity, or divine inspiration" (211). Nor was the perfection of canonical works a given for the Confucian commentators. After relating the attitude of such scholars as Han Yü of the Tang dynasty who suggested the deletion of a particular repetition from the Analects, Henderson writes: "Confucian commentators were perhaps not so insistent as their counterparts in other traditions on the nonsuperfluous nature of each detail in canonical works" (189).

The ontological status of the classic — whether the truth conveyed is transcendental or merely sublunary — will affect the status of the commentary that develop in connection with the classic text. In the case of sacred scripture, hermeneutics will take the form of exegesis on a perfect text: its purpose will be to excavate the one true interpretation of the Word of God. Thus translation, which inevitably involves and affects interpretation, is viewed as perilous, and likely to lead to a diminution of original meaning. Sir Thomas More saw the wholeness of the sentence and the sense of the original and the sacred integrity of Scripture in the same terms:

> . . . it is dangerous to translate the text of scripture from one tong into another, as Holy Saint Ierome testifieth, for as much as in translation it is hard alway to kepe the same sentence [i.e. sense] whole. (Kelly, 74)

Islam until very recently forbade the translation of the Koran, not merely to avoid the dilution of the cultural identity of its adherents, but also to avoid violating the sanctity — i.e., the perfection — of scripture. "According to Islam," Faur writes, "the Koran is untranslatable; it must be read and transmitted in the original alone" (16). "Muslims," one scholar has written, "are a 'people of the Book'. . ." (Coward, 81).

Despite a generally scrupulous attitude to script, the Jews had a more ironic approach to the sanctity of the sacred word. Henderson relates a well-known Talmudic tale, in which "God himself is an exegete who studies and interprets his own Torah" (87). Indeed, what might be inconceivable for a Christian God, an omniscient God "was not above learning from rabbinic interpretations of the Torah and, in one famous encounter with a rabbinic commentator, even admitted that 'my children have bested me. . . . " (Henderson, 87). One would seek in vain to find a similar ironic impiety in the Christian commentaries on the Bible. Indeed, what one does find, in Augustine, a St. Justin Martyr, or Origen, is a reverence for the original work, reflected in their conviction that there can be no imperfection, no inconsistency or contradiction in the Bible (Henderson, 118).

In a useful distinction, Henderson contrasts the hermeneutics of the sacred into two categories, between the classic text and the commentary, by quoting Wang Ch'ung's (27-97?) claim that "classics were composed by the 'sages' (*sheng-jen*)," whereas "commentaries were written by mere 'worthies' (*hsien-jen*)" but he goes awry in suggesting that this "hierarchical distinction between classic and commentary is reminiscent of the division in the Hindu tradition between 'revelation' and 'recollection,' or 'Sruti' (scriptural teaching actually revealed by God to man) and 'Smriti' (teaching of divine incarnations, saints or prophets, who further explain and elaborate the God-given truths of the scriptures)"(71). The distinctions, the Chinese and the Hindu, are each helpful in their context, but their conflation confuses an essential point. The classics of the Chinese canon are not prophetic books, nor are they the organ of the divine. The Lun-yu is not the word of God, but merely the wisdom of a sage:

Confucius, for all his influence in the Chinese tradition, is but a man, not an exalted being, nor part and parcel of divinity, as Jesus Christ is. (If Confucius has been worshipped in China it has been as a progenitor and as an ancestor, but not as a god with supernatural powers; Jesus on the other hand, had no offspring, but supplicants continue to pray to him as a god.)

What Confucius had to say was not, and is not, mystical or mysterious. Nor are the other Chinese classics. Ouyang Hsiu, the great Sung literatus, "remarked that the classics were, for the most part, simple and clear enough to be read and understood without the aid of a gloss" (Henderson, 71). Confucius expressly avoided metaphysical exploration, and concentrated on what he knew — a moderateness and a discretion which James Legge disparaged.

The arcaneness of such secular classics as the *Lun-yu* and the *Ta-hsüeh* must not be equated with the obscurity of sacred scripture. For in sacred scripture one is dealing with gnomic expression which masks, at the same time that it points the way to, deeper mysteries; in secular classics, one is dealing with allusiveness, which is a function of the fragmentariness of our understanding of the context for the original discourse. Gnosis involves a knowledge of spiritual things; it is what the Hindus called jñana. In this regard, obscurities are an aid, rather than a hindrance to enlightenment, for they "promoted interpretive zeal and ingenuity" (Henderson, 197). Augustine's remark, as quoted by Henderson, is apposite:" [The authors of the Holy Books] have spoken with a useful and healthful obscurity for the purpose of exercising and sharpening, as it were, the minds of the readers and of destroying fastidiousness and stimulating the desire to learn" (197).[2]

It is interesting that *jñana* in Buddhism expresses a different kind of gnosis: it is far from intellectual or discursive:

> Direct knowledge (jnana) is the refuge and not discursive consciousness (vijnana). This . . . principle . . . shows that sound hermeneutics are based not on a literal though theoretical understanding of the noble truths, but on direct knowledge (Lopez, 23).

"Direct knowledge" seems to refer to pre- or post-discursive thinking that might be construed as equivalent to intuition on the one hand, or to epiphany on the other. There is a sense in Buddhism that scripture is a means toward an end, and not an end in itself. Clearly the Buddhist concept of *upaya*, generally translated "skill in means," but which might be more easily understood as kerygmatic adaptability, suggests that "the Buddha's teaching was bound by context" (Lopez, 5). In this respect, Buddhist scriptures resemble more the secular Chinese classics than the Bible.

In the discussion of "sacred" and "secular" the factor of

---

[2]   It may be that Gnosticism had a direct influence on the compilation of the Bible as a sacred fount of wisdom, for Marcion, the second century proponent for collecting the materials that eventually became the Bible, was himself a Gnostic (Coward, 52)

comprehensibility figures prominently. Implicit in the character of "sacredness" is its integrity as mystery, not to say its mysticism or its mystique. No mystery can long sustain what is dispelled by clarity, and in this context, obscurity can sometimes be mistaken for profundity. Transcendental thinking by habit of thought, if not by definition, must needs be far-reaching, deep, infinitely subtle, capacious, and complex. There is a belief that that which is profound can't be simple and that which is simple cannot be profound. Paul's quote (I Corinthians, verses 9-10) may stand as the *locus classicus* for the equation of mystery and profundity, on the one hand, and divine revelation and truth, on the other:

> "What no eye has seen, nor ear heard, or the heart of man conceived, what God has prepared for those who love him" God has revealed to us through the Spirit. For the Spirit searches everything, even the depths of God.

Earlier, Paul told the Corinthians: "But we impart a secret and hidden wisdom of God . . . . . . (v. 7). Even the apparent lack of order in the Torah can be explained as evidence of divine mysteries: "Had the chapters of the Torah been given in their correct order, anyone who read them would have been enabled to raise the dead and work miracles; therefore the Torah's order has been hidden and is known [only] to God" (Henderson, 155).

In *Critical Assumptions*, K. K. Ruthven posits "word-worlds" and distinguishes between language-as-lens" and "language as body" (14). If we apply this to our consideration of sacred and secular texts, we will see that the obscurity of ancient secular texts arises not from the opaqueness of the lens, but from the fragmentariness of the object under review. In the case of sacred texts, language must protect the mysteries even as it transmits the meaning. Discursive analysis must be transcended, whether in Buddhist jnana or in Christian kerygma or in Jewish derasha. Language becomes a sign, perhaps even a signal, that points to, more than it expresses, meaning. Yet this highly functional status is belied by the power of that sign, so that what started out as a means becomes an end. We read in the Gospel According to John: "In the beginning was the Word, and the Word was with God, and the Word was God." This elevation of language to divinity, to the status of transcendental truth, is decisive for our consideration of the sacred and the secular. The Greek text has the word "logos," which involves what might be called the "textualization" of the word of God. For the "logos" suggests "reason" and "logic," a truth beyond specific contexts, a discursiveness that is analytical and fixed, retraceable and reproducible, like a template, or the type set for multiple copies of a book. The mentality this model of divine truth generates develops concurrently with oral traditions even before the advent of print, but certainly with the advent of Gutenberg, it is the text that reigns supreme — its hegemony challenged only in the present century by such researchers as Parry and Lord, and by such theorists as Ong and

Havelock. The shift from the oral tradition that led to the Bible, to the textual tradition, for which the Bible constitutes the divine authority, entails major consequences. Harold Coward writes:

> The consequences of the formation of this canon on the Christian experience of its scripture have been far-reaching. These writings were originally seen to be authoritative because of their connection with the apostles, who were regarded as eyewitnesses and thus in a position to attest to the revelation given in Jesus. But once these writings were canonized, it was an easy step to begin to view them not as testimonies to the revelation given in Jesus, but as being revelatory in and of themselves . . . . The written form of the New Testament now claims the "inspired" status that in the early church was reserved for the oral experience of the word. It is in this shift of the ontological basis of the New Testament revelation from the oral to the written that the roots of Protestant literalism may be found. This shift was further aided by the impact of printing, which made it possible for each person to possess his or her own Bible and to study it privately and silently. (54)

The irony in all this is that the Greek word "logos" did not originally mean "reason"; it did not even mean "word": what it denoted was anything "that was said" (Thomson, 17), with no particular emphasis on the structure of oral discourse. One could say about the Greek conception of Logos, as one cannot say about the Christian conception, "This Logos is not true" (Thomson, 18). In post-biblical uses of logos, and particularly in the context of the passage quoted from John, it would be preposterous to say that logos, or the word, — especially the word that "was with God, the Word that was God"— could be characterized as untrue. The authoritative character of Scripture — the word "authoritative" already embeds a textual bias — stems from a reverence for God that is reinforced by a reverence for the written word. We may define the notion of "sacred" - - at least in the West — as that which is transcendental and at the same time textual.

How far from that perspective is the ancient tradition of the Chinese classics, where the orality of the Lun-yü — the Chinese emphasizes the oral component in a way that the English translation "Analects" suppresses — is unquestioned. "A venerable tradition," Henderson writes, "traces the sources of the three primary commentaries (San-chuan on the Spring and Autumn Annals, particularly the Tso Commentary, to the secret teachings of Confucius himself, who conveyed the meaning of the classic orally to a few select disciples" (68). Henderson points out what is too often forgotten, that during the Former Han period (206BC-AD 8), "explanations of the Confucian classics were transmitted orally," as much because of the paucity of writing materials and the unavailability of paper as because of "the domination of classical studies by acknowledged masters who transmitted their teachings primarily by word of mouth" (68). The oral bases of the Chinese classics always require their contextualization more than their textualization. The validity of these classics for us is their applicability to the lives we lead. We comprehend these works only when we create in our minds a context of meaning in which the words are true. This accords with Gadamer's notion of understanding as projection: A person who is trying to understand a text is always performing an act of projecting. He projects for himself a meaning for the text as a whole as soon as some initial meaning emerges from the text. Again, the latter emerges only because he is reading the text with particular expectations in regard to a certain meaning.

> The working out of this fore-project, which is constantly revised in terms of what emerges as he penetrates into the meaning, is understanding what is there. (236; quoted by Lopez, 65).

This dialectic process, a variant on Heidegger's "hermeneutic circle," is precisely the process activated in oral discourse, in what might be called the dialectics of dialogue. In this process, there is no "prior" text, no "higher" truth, indeed, no divine authority. Lopez informs us that "a belief common to the major schools of Buddhist thought in Asia is that the Buddha did not teach the same thing to all, but rather expediently adapted his message to meet the specific needs of his audience" (5) "He adjured his followers," Lopez says, "to adopt only what they found to be apodictic:

> Like gold that is melted, cut, and polished,
> So should monks and scholars
> Analyze my words [before accepting them];
> They should not do so out of respect."

In fact, this notion of truth as malleable, of meaning as negotiable, forged out of the dialectic discourse between teacher and student, recalls the context of the oral tradition where the narrator and the audience, whether few or many, play dynamic roles in establishing the context of meaning. The written remnants of that discourse freezes a constantly shifting, immanently allusive process, and codifies the message. The very perniciousness of wrongly sanctifying the text is what rabbinic Judaism tried to fend off when it adamantly insisted on the primacy of the Oral Law over the Written Law: as Faur points out, "the oral Law is the interpreter system and the written Law is the interpreted system" (xvii).

With Western languages it is too often assumed that writing is the recording of speech: they embody what might be called a phonological bias. Their conception of texts as totally self-sufficient (pace New Criticism) is made possible by the assumption that the phonetic alphabet essentially puts on paper the speech transmitted by word of mouth. The belief in the completeness and the perfection of the text forces most exegetes to overlook the salient fact that the Old Testament, in Hebrew, records only the consonants, and the New Testament, in Greek, has no markings of the tones which were a phonemic feature of ancient Greek.

Recent scholarship, however, demonstrates the prior status of the oral tradition in transmitting the word of God. Faur makes this clear: The well known rabbinic rule, "Oral words may not be said in writing and written words are not to be recited orally," refers to the way in which these texts are to be transmitted, not to the way in which they should be recorded. The entire chain of transmission must be oral. One cannot refer to a written document as the source of a tradition or as a link in the chain of transmission. (100-101) Indeed, the "word of God" was conceived by Judah the Prince, a leading rabbinic authority (160- 220 C.E.) as God's presence in human discourse. In discussing the Shema, in which God addresses man, Judah claims that "the reader is the linguistic representative of God to himself" (49).

The oral elements of the New Testament, long overlooked, have been recently rediscovered. Nor are the assumptions about causal, sequential textual transmission, emanating in a single source, and radiating outward in time and space — a Biblical version of the Big Bang theory — as convincing as they once were. There is no original when it comes to oral teaching, no one instance of the kerygma superior to any other. "The concepts of original form and variants have no validity in oral life," Kelber insists, "nor does the one of ipsissima vox, if by that one means the authentic version over against secondary ones" (30). And if there is no priority in any version, neither can one credit the model of a prime message transmitted over time and space. For the distinctions between original composition and secondary transmission become blurred in oral discourse, where one composes even as one transmits: "if each utterance constitutes an authentic speech act, then the question of transmission can never be kept wholly separate from composition." One saying of Jesus cannot be preferred over another saying of Jesus; unlike manuscript versions, priority in time does not indicate priority of meaning. Even systematic theologians like Edward Schillebeeckx subscribe to this view:

> We can no longer in fact start, as people used to do at one time, from the single kerygma of a Jerusalem mother church, as it was called, which only later on branched out in various directions. The facts contradict that. (84; quoted by Kelber, 31) [3]

Kelber's model for the "concretion" of the New Testament is very nearly opposite to the Big Bang model, where a single powerful source disseminates its force outward. His vision of the formation of the New Testament is to see the manuscript tradition as a coalescence of the various

---

[3] There are overtones of "enigma" in "kerygma" (especially in English) just as there is puzzlement at the Qabbalah. Henderson quotes Maimonides: "The Talmud expounds the Mishna in a way that no one can ever arrive at through common logic" and then comments, "From the point of view of Qabbala the ultimate sense of a text is only semiotically connected with the script. The letters are only 'metaphors' pointing to a significance transcending the realm of words" (125). Rudolph Bultmann agreed with Enrico Castelli's formulation: " . . . that the 'Kerygma, comprises the essence of the event (in so far as it is mystery); and the possible historical analysis of the event does not do injury to revelation, because it [the analysis] is the revelation of the message and of the event (i.e., of history) at the same time" (Mueller-Vollmer, 255)

contemporary oral traditions. Kelber's formulation is memorable: "It is . . . a function of the written gospel to 'implode' this oral heterogeneity and to linearize oral randomness" (31).

The restitution of the oral dimension to the early evolution of the Bible uncovers a subtle but significant shift from the priority of the oral to the authority of the written; from transcript, the written vestige of oral discourse, to scripture, the hallowed text; from the oral witness of events to the sanctified written document; from testimony, in short, to testament. In the Old Testament, this shift replaces the Oral Law with the Written Law; and with the New Testament, the words of Jesus become the Word of God.

Two contrastive premises have emerged from our analysis. "From the one, writing represents literacy; oral transactions in themselves have no legitimate status. From the other, writing is used chiefly to record, it is ancillary to a reality conceived in physical, personal, and verbal terms" (Stock, 59). These polarizations recall Faur's distinction of truths that are context-free and truths that are context-bound. How one interprets a classic, whether sacred or secular, will depend crucially on one's view of the priority of the oral or the textual, and whether truth is contingent or absolute. Since the Middle Ages, the West has tended to assume "the bias of preserved records": "the most injurious consequence of medieval literacy," Stock maintains, " . . . was the notion that literacy is identical with rationality" (31). (We retain remnants of this prejudice in our word "idiot" which derives from the Latin word for "unlettered.") To seek the fount of wisdom, the bias tells us, seek out the canonical text. Faur reminds us that this Christian innovation runs counter to the Jewish belief that "the book that God wrote is everything that exists" (xxii). For Christians, the book that God wrote is the Bible, or with more evident redundancy, the book that God wrote is the Book. For Jews, that book is not any particular tome or volume, it is the phenomenal world, "everything that exists."

In a remarkable parable for translation, highlighting the allegiance in the act of translating for the audience as well as from the original, Henderson outlines the rabbinic institution for the public reading of the Torah. Two public readings were delivered: one was in Hebrew and dealt with "the accepted sense of the text (*peshat*); the other public reading was accompanied by the Targum or the Aramaic version, which was in the language of the Jews in rabbinic times.[4] The Targumim was not restricted to the text, but included explanations on biblical lore, exegeses of difficult passages, and legal perspectives on the events narrated. (The process was decidedly not New Critical.) As a result it took three times longer to get through the translation than the original. Faur tells us, "The recitation of the Targum . . . functions as a reader-response on the part of the audience. The meturgeman 'translator' stands by the reader. . . and recites the Aramaic version after every verse read from the Hebrew text" (xxi).

---

[4]   *Shema* is the Hebrew word with which the first verse . . . begins . . . "Hear, oh Israel, the Lord our God, the Lord is One . . . "(Faur, 49)

The first five books of the Old Testament, in other words, are regarded differently by Jews and Christians. "*Derasha* is grounded on the special 'Book/people' relationship; it is not simply the effect of a 'sacred' text, writing in a 'divine language' (Faur, xxi). The rabbinic view of scripture was dynamic, not static, and its view of the Torah was that it was a book, not a Bible.

How far from the view of a book as sacrosanct is the Chinese attitude toward *ching*, which is usually translated, without modification, as "classic," and which is often assumed to be Chinese scripture. Inadequacies in the *Lun-yü* were routinely recognized (Henderson, 184-186); some Sung and Ming scholars argued that the neo-Confucians . . . had even improved on the ideas of Mencius" (Henderson, 83). Nor were these *ching* considered whole and coherent, from which not a word should be deleted, nor any word added: they were, indeed, collections of ancient materials, mostly oral, almost miscellaneously and even indiscriminately collected: "in the Han era," Henderson reports, "there was a tendency to designate all pre-Han literature as 'ching' . . . few of the other works designated as classics carried nearly as much weight" as those which later commentators deemed essential. Prior to Chu Hsi, even the Four Books — the *Analects*, the *Mencius*, the *Doctrine of the Mean*, and the *Great Learning* — "were not recognized as classics or even, in the case of the latter two, as independent texts" (Henderson, 50); in fact, the *Analects* were sometimes regarded as mere commentary (Henderson, 51). Indeed, the word *ching*, which refers to writing on silk and bamboo, is wrongly translated as "scripture" or even as "classic" for it is a generic label with no evaluative force. There were, in other words, *ching* which we would not regard as classics as well as *ching* which are indisputable classics.

In this connection, it is hard to speak meaningfully of a Chinese "canon" in the same sense as the Western canon. As I have said elsewhere, "canon" is not a Chinese word. In the West, "canon" is variously defined as "rule, law, decree of the Church"; "a general rule of any subject"; the definition most apposite for our present purposes is: "A list of books of the Bible accepted by the Christian Church as genuine and inspired." What is canonical is what the Christian Church says is canonical, or, to put it more precisely, what a particular sect of the Christian Church determines as "genuine and inspired." The Old Testament in the Douay (or Catholic) version of the Bible is comprised of 46 books, as opposed to 39 in the Revised Standard (or Protestant) Version: both versions contain the same number of books in the New Testament (27).

If we read canon in this ecclesiastical, institutional sense, there are no "canons" in the Chinese tradition: Buddhism for example, does not label certain sutras inspired and others uninspired, some genuine or others not; nor are the texts of Taoism considered "canonical," for they are — in the primary resource — merely included in the *Tao Tsang*, the "Taoist Repository." Editors over the centuries have, of course, made the selection as to what to include, but their authority is bibliographic, not ecclesiastical. Hence, the Buddhist and Taoist texts are almost indiscriminately voluminous. One edition of the Taoist Repository, for example, the one from the Wan-li reign of the Ming Dynasty (dated 1607), comprises 520 volumes which contain a total of 5,486 separate titles. The Buddhist Classics are preserved in various compilations: one, the *Ta Cheng Tsang,* is divided into 1,460 sections, with 4,225 books! Surely a "canon" with thousands of titles is more like a repository than an anthology of recommended works (Eoyang, 1985).

The mythology of the book, and of the Bible as canonical, has persuaded translators to believe that what they are translating is a text rather than a tradition: too many translators have concentrated on creating a text when rendering an original even as they neglect the equally important task of creating an audience. For hermeneutics teaches us that meaning cannot exist without the context of a dialectical, "interactive" commentarial tradition. To merely translate the text is to do what the Talmud expressly prohibited: "Words that are in writing — you may not say them vocally, and vocal words — you may not say them in writing" (Faur, 135). (The need for these injunctions might be clearer for the Hebrew in the Torah, where only the consonants are recorded.) For the text is an inadequate rendering of what is said, it does not convey the logos in its original sense: it does not preserve "what is said," but only the traces and the dim recollection of what was said.[5]   In the impulse to preserve the original in translation, the view of the original as text binds us to a distorted view of meaning as fixed and inflexible. What it neglects is the chimerical nature of meaning, as well as its inherent ambivalence. "How many meanings may a given passage have?" Biblical exegetes has asked for millennia, and it is clear, even as early as Origen, that more than one meaning was involved (Coward 57). Even Luther, who inveighed against "the idea that scripture has several levels of meaning," saw messianic overtones in the Old Testament as well as its "simple and ordinary sense" (Coward, 60).

It may be helpful to recall that, as Kurt Mueller-Vollmer reminds us, that "the etymology of the term "hermeneutics" carries an obvious relation to Hermes, the messenger god of the Greeks, and suggests a multiplicity of meanings" (1). "In order to deliver the messages of the god," Mueller-Vollmer writes, "Hermes had to be conversant in their idiom as well as in that of the mortals for whom the message was destined. He had to understand and interpret for himself what the gods wanted to convey before he could proceed to translate, articulate, and explicate their intention to mortals." The challenge to the translator is to convey not the meaning of script, but a multiplicity of meanings which can be seen in and through the text.

This process is, inevitably and frustratingly, one of precise imprecision. (The overemphasis on text as scripture elicits the fault of its converse: imprecise precision, the result is an over-literal and often meaningless translation). There is no more poignant or realistic depiction

---

[5]   In this connection, it might also he mentioned that ancient Greek was a tonal language, and that the New Testament text has no tonal markings. Hence, the Bible may be seen as the Word of God without vowels in the one case and without tones in the other — a less than complete transcript.

of the enterprise of translation as interpretation than Faur's description of the rabbinic view:

> The Hebrew term for interpretation, peter (*pitaron*) /*psher*, implies the notion of compromise. Interpretation involves the integration of various elements. In Hebrew, it also means "lukewarm." In a sense, "interpretation" may be conceived as blending different elements, as when mixing hot and cold water. Thus "to interpret" is to integrate two or more signs and make a "compromise" which contains them all but is identical with none of them, just as lukewarm water is neither hot nor cold. (28)

Translators may perhaps not appreciate this less than heroic depiction of their enterprise, and we may hope that readers of translation will not be lukewarm to what they read, but this Janus-faced characterization of the translator, of Hermes mediating between the gods and the mortals, will strike the practising translator as altogether familiar — and apt.

Approaches

4. "Speaking in Tongues":
Translating Chinese Literature in a Post-Babelian Age

Glossolalia is the technical term designating a phenomenon, usually associated with religious ecstasy, where a communicant, in a state of divine possession, speaks languages with which he or she is not normally familiar. This form of oracular insight is characterized by three factors: (1) its extreme impenetrability for the listener, who is, presumably, not acquainted with the language being spoken; (2) the ignorance, at least on a conscious level, on the part of the speaker of what he or she is saying; and (3) a sense of the miraculous and divine, as if the individual were the mouthpiece for arcane truths which he is merely mouthing, but which are beyond his comprehension. The relevance of this phenomenon to Chinese literature is that some Western studies of Chinese texts strike me as perfect examples of scholarly glossolalia, or an academic "speaking in tongues." It is my purpose in this chapter to describe this phenomenon, to examine specific examples, and to consider the reasons for the strange power scholarly glossolalia has over its adherents.

Before we proceed, we might examine what we mean by "Chinese literature." Traditionally, the phrase designates first of all the Four Books — the *Analects*, the *Great Learning*, the *Mencius*, and the *Doctrine of the Mean*. Then there are the so-called Five Classics: the *Book of Poetry*, the *Book of History*, the *Book of Changes*, the *Book of Rites*, and the *Spring and Autumn Annals*. Then there is the entire corpus of writings in the literary language in various genres, the *fu*, the *lüshih*, the *yüeh-fu*. In modern times, all writings in the vernacular — from the *zhiguai* tales to the *yenyi* popularizations of history — are included. Indeed, the richness in both variety and scope of Chinese literature is scarcely matched. But despite the variety of levels of readership — from the semiliterate to the highly literate — there is one claim we can make about Chinese literature, indeed about any literature, without fear of contradiction. These works were intended to be understood by the targeted audience or readership.

It is a basic premise in translation theory that the reader of a work in translation should have the same access to the meaning in the translated text as the reader of the original text in the source language. The difficulties in finding exact counterparts from different languages, particularly languages which are not cognate, languages which represent cultures not historically related, are what make effective translation such a challenge. To test this theory from a commonsensical point of view, let us posit a nursery rhyme. However arcane that rhyme may be underneath the surface, its surface meaning should be readily understood. A translation of a nursery rhyme should not sound like a scholarly disquisition, nor should it appear erudite and forbidding. The difficulty in the process of translation is not inherent in an original text. Something simple and inevitable in one language may be difficult to capture in another language with the same simplicity, yet there is no reason for that difficulty in the process of translation to be reflected in the text of the translation. Art in translation — as with any art — is that which hides art.

This point, obvious though it is, cannot be passed over, because there are many who, speaking in tongues, present works of Chinese literature as if they were elaborate puzzles to confound the ordinary reader, yielding their secrets only to the scholarly initiates. If readers cannot understand what the scholarly translator of Chinese literature is trying to convey, it must be because they, the unintended readers, are dense: they don't, after all, know Chinese. But what casts strong, dramatic shadows in the glare of only one light source is far less imposing in the balanced light emanating from different directions: what may be impressive in a monolingual culture is rather commonplace in a multilingual context. I should like to examine this phenomenon in a multilingual audience and in the light, if not of a thousand suns, then of more than one sun.

In an interesting article titled "Polylingualism as Reality and Translation as Mimesis," Meir Sternberg posits a term, "translational mimesis," by which he means the reenactment of the original literary work in another language. Sternberg is speaking specifically about rendering the occurrence of a foreign language in the source text when it is being translated into another language. But his discussion raises interesting issues about what is preserved in translation. Sternberg, in considering the challenge of reproducing in one language an instance of polylinguality in another, suggests that "the interlingual tension between language as represented object (within the original or reported speech-event) and language as representational means (within the reporting speech-event) is primarily mimetic rather than communicative" (222). He posits three categories of "translational mimesis": "referential restriction," in which the objects described are normalized (or, as James J. Y. Liu would say, "naturalized") so that nothing is marked as foreign (Sternberg cites the works of Jane Austen); "vehicular matching," in which the very differences of language have a characterizational force, are, indeed, part of the mythos of the story (Sternberg cites Shaw's *Pygmalion* and Jean Renoir's movie *La Grande Illusion*): these works would be incomprehensible if the polylingual or polydialectical speech were normalized; and finally, "homogenized convention," in which foreign, even fantastic, creatures are assumed to speak the same language (no one finds it implausible, Sternberg points out, to see the White Rabbit speak English in *Alice in Wonderland*). This scheme is very fecund, because it provides a means by which rhetorical strategies can be more clearly examined.

The only — very slight — issue I would take with these categories is with their order. I would reverse "vehicular matching" and "homogenized convention" —- arriving at a sequence of increasing degrees of sophistication and cosmopolitanism. Referential restriction is provincial in that it limits the object in view to the monolingual; homogenized convention breaks that provinciality by considering so-called foreign objects, but renders those objects comprehensible in the provincial tongue; vehicular matching stretches the monolingual resources to include polylingual phenomena, in their polylingual character.

Let us examine each of these categories for the deconstructed perspective they offer. In the first case, there is an implicit cultural coercion. In order to appreciate Jane Austen, one must become, or imagine oneself as, English; to resist that ambivalently self-flatteringly and self-inflating experience would be to resist the charms of Jane Austen's wit and style. There is no reading Jane Austen without becoming English. Her genius was precisely to see the richness and the self-sufficiency of the provincial experience. For her, the life in her precincts was endlessly fascinating, and the earth-shaking events outside those precincts were matters of little or no import. (Which is why critics have remarked, with both admiration and dismay, that no one who reads Jane Austen's novels would not have any inkling of the Napoleonic Wars, which were occurring at about the same time as the action in her novels.)

Homogenized convention extends imaginative empathy to include the feelings of other beings, other species. It posits the pathetically fallacious premise that all creation speaks the same language we do. Thus animals speak a language we can understand without effort. On American TV, in *Hogan's Heroes*, even Nazis speak English routinely among themselves, and German appears a foreign language even to the Germans: what differentiates foreigner and native is an "accent." With homogenized convention, we encounter what might he called linguistic coercion: readers — even if they are native in the "foreign" language homogenized and conventionalized —- must accept the privileged subjective voice of the prevailing linguistic discourse. However, this technique posits a false universalism and overlooks the "prison-house" that each language represents. This notion homogenizes experience and erases all objective and subjective differences. It allows for no subjective stance from the perspective of the other.

A common symptom of this mind-set is the impatience one feels with someone who doesn't speak one's native language — an attitude more prevalent in dominant world cultures than among the dominated. An example of this are the questionnaires that were circulated in Florida and California some years ago about making English the official language: all the forms were in English, and advocates of the English Only Movement never thought about the inherent bias in such a poll. This conventionalizing of differences erases the multi-ethnic character of a civilization. A German reading an unflattering portrait of Germans in a French novel, or an American reading Akio Morita and Shintaro Ishihara's caustic critique of American society, *The Japan That Can Say NO*, which was not intended for an English-reading audience, or a Chinese-American being told in English that he speaks good English, know something of the intense feeling of humiliation and exclusion homogenized convention represents. Feminists objecting to thoughtless sexist language know something of the pitfalls and provincialities of homogenized convention.

Vehicular matching appears to be the most satisfactory exercise in translational mimesis: it extends the sensibility of the reader and reflects the true contrasts in the original between what is foreign and what is native. Yet, even here, there are pitfalls. Let us consider an instance in which, say, English is used in a Chinese fiction; let us further consider a translation of this fiction into English. The excerpt in English does not need translation, but unless it is editorially marked as foreign in a footnote, the reader will have no idea of the particular "framing" of this context in the original. The modishness of English when it is quoted in a non-English language, for example, the sense of modernity that the use of English evokes — all this is lost if the reader in translation fails to realize that the English in these expressions involves embedded exoticisms, not translated versions of native locutions. Such an instance could be mistaken for "homogenized convention" where everyone — even non-English-speaking characters — speaks English. But this example would actually be the obverse of "homogenized convention," because what is being presented is a "heterogenous unconventionality," someone who, exceptionally, uses a nonnative expression in the original. Lu Hsun's use of the Roman letter "Q" in "The True Story of Ah Q" is a case in point. Originally the phrase was a literary invention intended to pique the reader"'s curiosity. It is now, of course, so familiar, at least on the mainland, that it is no longer a novelty — either in Chinese or in English. Furthermore, this kind of locution may appear strange to some readers of Chinese unfamiliar with English. Indeed, Lu Hsun may have intended this to alienate the character from the reader. If one leaves the English untranslated, this novelistic effect is lost, even if the exact locution in the original is preserved. And, if one "translates" the already transparent English to another language "foreign" to the Chinese, then the particular characterization of an English-monger is erased.

Let us examine this gradient in provinciality: in the first case, there is an implicit assumption that only one language exists and that everyone speaks that language; in the second case, there is a recognition of difference, but that difference is erased by the assumption that despite those differences, everyone understands each other using the same language; in the third case, the differences are recognized for what they are and are preserved as such, either as extensions of the host language or as composites of more than one language. This last point reveals a flaw in Sternberg's categorical division between monolinguality and polylinguality. Individuals may be both monolingual and polylingual. When someone says "laissez-faire," is that speaker automatically French? Hardly. American economists routinely say "laissez-faire," and — what is more remarkable — even pronounce the phrase correctly, but the language they speak cannot — on that account alone — be characterized as French. The emergence of Franglais, indeed of Americanisms in all the languages of the world, indicates that there is an incipient, developing polylingualism in every language. Philologists could easily demonstrate a degree of polylingualism in every language, since each language develops out of other languages or blends in admixtures of other languages. English is one of the richest polylingual languages, consisting of Anglo-Saxon (itself a composite), Norman, Celtic, and Romance elements. The Elizabethan was a partially polyglot speaker of Latinisms, Italianisms, Anglo-Saxon, French, and Celt.

It is this polylinguality within monolingualism, as well as the multilinguality and bilinguality of a significant portion of the world's population, that is invoked by the phrase "post-Babelian" in the subtitle of this chapter. I define pre-Babelian as a world where everyone speaks one language; a Babelian world is one in which there are different languages mutually incomprehensible; and a post-Babelian world is a world where there are different languages but there are people who speak more than one language. Put simply, the pre-Babelian world is one with a universal language; a Babelian world is a world of many languages, with everyone monolingual; a post-Babelian world consists of many languages, but it also includes polylingual speakers. An ultimate post-Babelian world would be one where everyone speaks everyone else's language.

There is a hegemonic monolingual myth that has prevailed, which suggests that knowing only one language is the preponderant norm in human civilization and that knowing more than one language is the rare exception. Of course, this monolingual myth has been perpetrated through no arbitrary provinciality but through each language, which naturally tends to restrict or privilege the discourse in its own precincts. Also, it will not be surprising that discourse in a language will reinforce the perception of reality in that language and will downgrade if not neglect altogether the existence of other languages: by considering itself the language of the self and all other languages as "foreign," the language of the other, each language conveys the myth of universal monolingualism. But recent studies have indicated that the monolingual speaker of language may not have dominated human civilization as much as we may have imagined.

Nor has the bilingual and multilingual speaker been quite as exceptional as we might think. In Old Egypt, Milan Dimic reminds us, "the people of that country were divided into seven classes, one of which consisted of interpreters" (15). "The Mesopotamian civilization gave rise," Dimic writes (citing Kovganjuk [53f], M. Lambert [17-20], and H. Pohling [1261], "to the Assyrian and Babylonian multinational states. In the third millennium B.C. Sargon of Assyria proclaimed his victories in the many languages of his realm. Ancient Greek evolved from other languages in Asia Minor; even when its culture dominated, it fostered bilingualism . . . Wherever they settled, the Greeks and the Romans instituted private elementary schools and educated a bilingual or trilingual elite which held the new commonwealth together. The conqueror and the conquered had to know each other"'s language" (15).

Indeed, all conquest through the ages involved an encounter with bilingualism and multilingualism. All educated Romans were conversant with Greek as well. The spread of Christianity also promoted bilingualism, as did the spread of Islam. Bilingualism may be more the rule than the exception. "The famous Rosetta-stone from the second century B.C.," Dimic points out, "is in Greek as well as hieroglyphic and demotic Egyptian." Chinese, despite its apparent monolithic character in the West, is a polylingual and multicultural language, involving elements of Mongol, Turk, Tungusic, Thai, and Tibeto-Burman. There are manuscripts in Tun-huang, dating from the fifth to the tenth century, with texts that contain Chinese and Tibetan in interlinear configuration as well as texts in Sogdian, Uighur, and other Central Asian languages.

The myth of Babel described an era when all the world's people spoke the same language, an era which ended when God punished the world's peoples for overreaching and "confounded" their language so that the tongues they spoke were mutually incomprehensible. The Babelian era is one that divides the languages of the world into one that is "native" and the rest as "foreign." We have tacitly and implicitly assumed that we live in this Babelian era. But in fact, the realities are less simplistic. Leaving aside the question of relative degrees of mutual comprehensibilities — surely cognate languages are less opaque to each other than languages that are not historically related — the numbers of bilingual and multilingual speakers in history have already begun to establish a "post-Babelian" world.

W. Mackey estimates that 70 percent of the world's population is now bilingual. In Singapore, many of the inhabitants are descended from the Chinese and are brought up speaking Chinese, yet the "national" language is English, the language of instruction in school. For many Singaporeans, Chinese is "native" but English is their language of public discourse. The multilingual societies of Switzerland, Yugoslavia, India, Brazil, the Netherlands, and the nations of the former Soviet Union are but the most obvious examples of societies where knowing more than one language is not exceptional. One must add to these instances the worldwide emphasis on instruction in English: I once calculated the number of high school students in the Far East, where instruction in English is compulsory for all students, and arrived at a figure in excess of 50 million — which exceeds the total number of high school students in the United States, which was around 25 million. Hence, for every student in an American high school, there are two East Asians studying English. The world is not predominantly or uniformly monolingual, yet most of what is published — at least in the U. S. —reinforces a monolingual bias. As a result of the nationalism of the nineteenth century and the vestigial language chauvinism of the twentieth century (I refer to the attacks against Franglais in France and those in favor of "English only" in the United States), patriotism and monolinguality are viewed as inseparable. In only one language that I know of is the "foreign" incorporated generically and institutionally in the "native" language — and that language is Japanese. Can this feature of accommodating the foreign within the native linguistic medium be part of the reason for Japan's spectacular success in adapting not only to the modern world but also to a multilingual marketplace?

It is in this multilingual and polylingual context, this post-Babelian

reason" or "the right way"; or 說三道四
perspective, in which I would like to consider some pertinent questions of translation. Sternberg's analysis of the various modes of imitating polylingualism in translation offers a fascinating exercise in perspectivist criticism. By examining the different modes of portraying difference — by erasing it, by marking it, and by enacting it — he focuses our attention on the different strategies available to incorporate the strange into the familiar. His scheme can be seen as a paradigm of the process of understanding: how we progress from learning about the familiar by finding "equivalents" to the familiar; then, realizing that the new object had no real "equivalents" precisely because it is really new "to our ken," we mark its equivalence as "approximate"; until finally, realizing that the similarities between the new object and its approximate familiar equivalents are not as salient as their differences, we incorporate the new object in our native discourse and thereby extend our own language.

These fruitful discriminations are helpful in addressing one of the primary problems of translating from the Chinese. Let us take the word 道 translated variously as "the way", "the Way," and "the Tao," this word can be taken to represent succinctly Sternberg's three approaches to "translational mimesis": to translate 道 as "the way" is an attempt at "referential restriction": the word is treated as if it were exactly equivalent to an ordinary English word — no experience outside the semantic precincts of the host language being admitted; to translate it as "the Way" is an attempt at "homogenized convention": the sense is made accessible, but capitalizing the "w" marks the strangeness of the concept as special; and to translate it as "the Tao" is an attempt at "vehicular matching": the sense is opaque to the uninitiated: the reader is forced to grasp the concept with provisional recognition — true understanding comes only when the reader has encountered the original in its context or, more intuitively, has encountered the same vehicular matching in various contexts of meaning.

But Sternberg's scheme, while useful, fails to explain further anomalies which must be addressed with each of the three categories. In the first case, with the "referential restriction" of "the way" as translational mimesis, one captures the ordinariness of the expression, even if one misses the special philosophical significance of tao in Chinese. To the extent that the special meaning of tao is missed, referential restriction is clearly inadequate. Yet, in conveying the ordinariness of tao in Chinese, referential restriction in this case is more adequate than either of the other "more sophisticated" approaches. If anything, translating 道 as "the way" is not ordinary enough: it does not reflect the innumerable semantic and grammatical contexts in which 道 can he used, as in 知道 "to know"; 道地 "real, authentic"; 道理
"to make thoughtless comments".

Philologists, in their categorical way, point out these different uses of tao and imply that they are separate and unrelated senses of the word. Dictionaries have this propensity of offering different meanings, from which the language user is to select the most appropriate. Yet this digital and analytical approach is precisely what is wrong with dictionary translations: they embody a fundamental misconception about language. When a word has many different meanings and different uses, it can often suggest — and not only in the paranomasic compositions of poets — different meanings at the same time. Indeed, in the case of tao, the authority and profundity of the word inheres precisely in its seeming versatility in different contexts: in that sense tao does not define anything, it does not indicate anything, it is not the signifier to an elusive signified. It is, in fact, emblematic of what it means: the word can suggest speech, as in 說三道四, it can suggest a pattern or principle, as in 道理; it can suggest reality, as in 道地, or it can suggest the object of comprehension, as in 知道. The point is that each meaning is inherent in *tao*.

The word "way" in English does not occur in compounds involving speech, nor in phrases that involve principle, nor in a construction that suggests reality. It is not a word that resonates with all the other senses, the way tao does. One doesn't disambiguate the meaning of tao when one uses it the way that other words may be disambiguated — either phonetically or orthographically. For example, we disambiguate graphonyms like "c-o-n-s-u-m-m-a-t-e" phonetically: an accent on the second syllable denotes the adjective "consúmmate," whereas an accent on the first syllable denotes the verb "cónsummate"; we disambiguate homonyms like "stationary," meaning "to be at rest," from "stationery," meaning "writing paper," by writing one with an "a" and the other with an "e." "Bow," meaning "to bend forward," is differentiated phonetically from "bow" as in "bow and arrow" or "violin bow"; whereas "bow," meaning to bend forward, is differentiated from "bough," meaning "a branch of a tree," by its spelling.

Indo-European languages often enhance the process of semantic disambiguation — where the context of meaning determines which of two or more viable alternatives apply — by phonetic or orthographic means. Spoken Chinese, with its wealth of homonyms, relies heavily on context to disambiguate words of similar sounds. Written Chinese has words that require different phonemes to reflect different semantemes, as in 好 meaning "good" (3rd tone) and 好 meaning "to like" (4th tone) and 中 "center" (1st tone) and 中 "to hit the target." But the different uses of *tao* are differentiated neither orthographically nor phonetically.

Like the English word "run" — for which I count eighty entries in the Oxford Universal Dictionary — the semantic versatility of *tao* presents an interesting linguistic challenge. If a word has so many meanings, how can it be accurately or meaningfully used in each? One might also suggest that such words — which we might label as "maximally meaningful key words" — reflect the cultural emphasis of the language. The root etymon is so rich that the word becomes almost infinitely replicable in different semantic contexts without dysfunctional unclarity. Is there any significance to the fact that in traditional Chinese such a "maximally meaningful key word" is *tao* and that in American English the "maximally meaningful key word" is "run"?

Let us now consider the translation of some key terms in Chinese.

One of the most astute philologists, with considerable influence in sinological circles, was Peter Boodberg. His discriminations of meaning, flowing out of a vast erudition that included not only the major East Asian languages but most of the European tongues as well, are lasting contributions to learning. His exegesis of the term *jen* 仁 translated as "benevolence," "human- heartedness," "goodness," etc., is worth close attention. These renderings, however, are not the equivalent of jen but the fruits of a sense of *jen*. If one has *jen*, one will show benevolence, human-heartedness, goodness, etc. To translate the word in this way is virtually to equate cause with effect. Boodberg writes: "It is my belief that the primary etymology of *jen*, 'humanity,' cannot be successfully conveyed in English, short of creating a neologism, on the prototype of the German Menschlichkeit, such as 'manship,' 'manshipful,' and 'manshipfulness' (37). He also suggests a "Latin synonym of 'manship'," using a derivative of the plural *homines* rather than the singular homo, and comes up with "homininity."

Boodberg has also coined a few neologisms which have proliferated like viruses in certain translations of Chinese literature. Chief among them is the word "Thearch" for Chinese *ti* 帝, usually rendered "emperor." Less popular is his offering of "basilearch" for Chinese 王 *wang*, conventionally rendered as "king." In discussing these terms, Boodberg resorts to his knowledge of ancient languages, as in the following excerpt from his "Cedules from a Berkeley Workshop in Asiatic Philology" (217).

> WANG 王 "king," "prince," "emperor" (of the Chou dynasty) may best be metonymized as BASILEARCH. The etymology of WANG, like that of Greek *basileus*, is unknown; it seems', however, to be a Sinitic word but the native scholiasts can suggest nothing better than association with the homonym WANG, 'to go,' and the far-fetched school-etymology "king" = "one to whom the people go." Through a curious coincidence, this parallels the attempts of the Greek grammarians to decode *basileus* as some coadunation of *baino*, "to go," and *laos*, "people." HUANG 皇 "emperor," "august," is, on one hand, a cognate of WANG; on the other, an affine of KUANG 光, "bright glow," glory". The upper part of the graph, now written with the element "white" 白, the *Shuo Wen* 說文 interprets as being "original" 自, while the protograph is suggestive of the representation of a corona (of the sun), an aureole, perhaps an anthelion.
>
> Since HUANG was traditionally applied to the divine WANG of the highest antiquity, ARCHIBASILEARCH, ARCHIBASILIC (adj.) may prove to be hermeneutically acceptable, with ARGI- (<argos, "shining bright") as a paragram for the first element. For TI 帝"god", "emperor", the logical option is THEARCH or DIARCH (<dios, "divine"); for HUANG TI, ARCHIBASILIC DIARCH.

I have quoted this dense exegesis at some length, not only because of what it says but also because of how Boodberg says it. It represents a variation of the "vehicular matching" that we encountered in Sternberg's scheme. We may note in passing that aside from the Greek in the exegesis, there are a number of infrequently encountered English words whose meaning can be fairly well adduced from the context but are disconcerting nonetheless: "coadunation," "affines," "protograph," "anthelion," "paragram." "Anthelion" and "affines" are listed in some dictionaries, although in some cases only the adjectival sense of "affines," with reference to finite values in mathematics, is cited. The others are not to be found. One might not unreasonably ask why an exegesis of words requires its own exegesis.

As for the reliance on Greek, it is true that Boodberg came from a generation in which the educated were more likely to know Greek than not, but even so, why should it be reasonable to require of a reader who doesn't know Chinese that he know another foreign language — especially a language as hoary as ancient Greek — in order to understand the true meaning of Chinese?

There are other epistemological concerns. Given the democratic traditions of ancient Greek culture, is it reasonable to equate the autocrats of the Periclean Age to the specifically Oriental despots in ancient China? To render the huang-ti of ancient China as counterparts, if not equivalents, of the monarchs of ancient Greece is to convey certain overtones of reason and of the polis that may have existed in Greece but did not exist in China in the same way. And what about the principle of familiarity: should the reader of a translation not be as familiar with a term in translation as the reader of the original with its counterpart in the original?

Boodberg takes the notion of "vehicular matching" even further than Sternberg develops it. He is addressing an audience at least as polylingual as he is; but he is more polylingual than the normal speaker of the English language — if the locutions which he uses in his own prose are any indication. Indeed, in his era, Boodherg expected his students to be post-Babelian: only the most gifted attempted the study of the difficult non-Western languages — Arabic, Chinese, and Japanese — and only after mastering the most formidable Western languages — Latin and Greek. The study of Chinese was therefore the enterprise of *la crème de la crème*, which by definition would be a very small elite. The consequences of this approach, natural as it was for Boodherg and for sinologists of his generation, makes no sense today, when the study of Chinese is no longer restricted to the classical philologist.

The school of sinology to which I refer has produced considerable contributions to knowledge. I need only cite David Knechtges's work on the *Wen hsüan* and Edward Schafer's many volumes on T'ang poetic imagery. But in the school's idiosyncrasies and in its ideological impatience with translations that depart from their defense of "exact" renderings, there is a specious logic as well as a crucial misunderstanding of language. Philology is not an exact science, but even if it were, even if it were mathematics, the insistence on an absolute accuracy is chimerical. It is not irrational to "approximate" when translating, nor is approximation irrational; indeed, as the English mathematician G. H. Hardy reminds us in his *Mathematician's Apology*, "all approximation is rational" (102). He also provides some uncommonly valuable advice when he tells us that "sometimes one has to say difficult things, but one ought to say them as simply as one knows how" (47). Frankly, some exegeses of difficult points in Chinese literature are simply not said "as simply as one knows how."

Some schools of sinology remind me of the schools of divines which Thomas Hobbes took to task at the end of his *Leviathan*:

> the writings of School divines, are nothing else for the most part, but insignificant trains of strange and barbarous words, or words otherwise used, than in the common use of the Latin tongue, such as would pose Cicero, and Varro, And all the grammarians of ancient Rome. Which if any man would see proved, let him . . . see whether he can translate any School divine into any of the modern tongues, as French, English or any other copious language: for that which cannot in most of these be made intelligible, is not intelligible in the Latin. Which insignificancy of language, though I cannot note it for false philosophy; yet it hath a quality, not only to hide the truth, but also to make men think they have it, and desist from further search. (449)

A heuristic principle of epistemology is implicit in this attack. Hobbes is suggesting that one's ability to make clear a difficult or elusive point reflects the degree to which one understands the point. The test of "translatability" into "intelligible Latin" — we have already encountered snippets of unintelligible Greek —- is an x-ray that sees through the obfuscations of pseudo understanding. Yet there are those who have insisted that unless one subscribes to a certain school of sinology, one can't understand Chinese — and that includes those who are native Chinese! The perniciousness of this ideological stance is that it exalts academic politics at the expense of free intellectual inquiry. It substitutes method for matter and takes dogma for truth, and it substitutes one unknown for another unknown. Anyone who has experienced the difficulty of comprehending an exegesis intended to elucidate a difficult passage will recognize immediately what I am referring to. The trouble is that, faced with the impenetrability of the original passage, the naive student takes the impenetrability of factitious scholarship to be the warrant of insight. So, where one began being baffled by one text, now one is baffled by two texts. The problem is that many delude themselves into thinking that they now understand the original just because they have read what purports to be an exegesis. It is time to announce to the world that the emperor has no clothes, that if, on occasion, a reader doesn't understand something, the inadequacy of the exegete rather than the limitations of the reader may be at fault.

How many students of Chinese, encountering "Basilearch" for wang, will think that they have the truth and desist from further search? How many Western scholars of Chinese, too often failing to speak in Chinese, speak in tongues?

5. Translation as Co-optation:
Getting Past Post-Colonialism

Let me start with an excerpt about an English family in the Caribbean, Richard Hughes's minor classic, *A High Wind in Jamaica*. The children are fussing at bedtime on their schooner.

> LAURA. There's a cockroach in my bed! Get out!
> EMILY. Laura! Go back to bed!
> LAURA. I can't when there's a cockroach in it!
> JOHN. Get into bed again, you little fool! He's gone long ago!
> LAURA. But I expect he has left his wife.
> HARRY. They don't have wives, they're wives themselves. (56)

This bit of narrative frippery may seem far removed from concerns about translation and about post-colonialism, but I find it useful to begin my exploration with this narrative reminder of the difference between seeing others as alien, and seeing others as simulacra for ourselves. For these children, cockroaches are not something to step on, but beings that we might empathize with. There is, in this brief passage, a wise innocence, so at odds with what I will later call "imperialisms of the mind". These children have an imaginative sympathy for the vermin that others would despise; they are knowing in their intuitions, but not smug in their knowledge.

Subject Ironies

If the recognition of the evils of colonialism implied in the post-colonial mentality has taught us anything, it's that egocentricity, ethnocentricity, and monocentricities are all hegemonic, distorting, biased. But this identification has created a logical and predictable corollary. There is a deep anxiety among post-colonial thinkers that they are, indeed, the colonials of the present, the anti-hegemonic hegemonists of contemporary thought. "To wish class or nation away, to seek to live sheer irreducible difference now in the manner of some contemporary post-structuralist theory" Terry Eagleton writes, "is to play straight into the hands of the oppressor" (*Eagleton, Jameson, Said*, 1990, p. 23). The ironies are, to Eagleton as to others, inescapable: "All oppositional politics thus move under the sign of irony, knowing themselves ineluctably parasitic on their antagonists" (26). Even when the ideological distinctions are clear, reality has a way of confusing them. For example, First, Second and Third World categorizations are no longer stable, or as easily essentialized. As Jameson observes: "It would be easy to demonstrate a presence of other such voices in First World cultural situations outside the United States . . . in the United States itself, we have come to think and to speak of the emergence of an internal Third World and of internal Third World voices, as in black women's literature or Chicano literature for example" (49). It would appear, like the political chauvinists in the United States after the fall of the Iron Curtain, there is a certain nostalgia for the now vanquished enemy: the target, apparently, disappears once it is hit.

Even the premier demonizer of imperialism, Edward Said, admits a complicitous role for the victim, the object of the Western gaze: "Imperialism after all is a cooperative venture," he writes, "Both the master and the slave participate in it, and both grew up in it, albeit unequally" (*Nationalism, Colonialism, and Literature*, 74). The nativist instinct to oppose imperialism has its own ironic perils, Said warns us: " . . . it is the first principle of imperialism that there is a clear-cut and absolute hierarchical distinction between ruler and ruled. Nativism, alas, reinforces the distinction by reevaluating the weaker or subservient partner. . . ." The nativist impulse, to restore one's cultural essence, whether it's negritude, Irishness, Islam, or Catholicism, is, Said reminds us, "to abandon history. Most often this abandonment in the postimperial setting has often led to some sort of millennarianism . . . into an unthinking acceptance of stereotypes, myths, animosities, and traditions encouraged by imperialism" (82). The ironies in the post-colonial position are often bewildering. Sometimes, they take on such infinitely convoluted forms that one is confronted not with articulated assertions of meaning, but with verbal vortexes in which meaning flit in and out, as in the following incomprehensible passage, taken from Eagleton:

> The most effective critique of bourgeois society is accordingly one that like Marxism is "immanent," installing itself within the very logic of that order's own most cherished values in order to unmask the necessary disconnection of this ideal universal realm from the sordidly particularistic appetites it serves to mystify. (31).

But perhaps the greatest irony in post-colonial writing is that its decisive articulations were all written in the hegemonic languages of the imperialists: English and French. Raymond Schwab's *Oriental Renaissance* (*La Renaissance orientale*, 1950); Frantz Fanon's *The Wretched of the Earth* (*Les Damnés de la Terre*, 1961), Leopold Senghor's *Négritude, arabisme et francité; réflexions sur le problème de la culture*, 1967, and Aimé Césaire *Discourse on colonialism* (*Discours sur le colonialisme*, 1950) were all written in French. And how much impact would Edward Said's *Orientalism*, or Fredric Jameson's Marxist sympathies for the Third World, or Gayatri Chakravorty Spivak explorations of the subaltern have had if they had written in a subaltern language instead of English?

This irony might reflect the libertarian, self-critical, egalitarian ethos of the modern West, which not only brooks criticism better than authoritarian societies run by "Oriental despots", it sometimes positively revels in self-recriminations (at least in the U. S.). However, one should not be so quick to assume that the "orientalist" critique of imperialism has not already been made in subaltern languages. The point is that if they have been made, they've escaped the notice of hegemonic readers. What is significant is that the celebrated post-colonial texts were originally written in a hegemonic language, not translated from a non-hegemonic discourse. This neglect of theories composed in languages other than those in Western languages is well-nigh comprehensive — even, alas, in some nativist traditions.

Speaking not only for themselves, Ashcroft, Griffiths, and Tiffin (hereafter: Ashcroft et al) acknowledge "the persistence of European critical and theoretical domination of the study of post-colonial literatures long after the literatures themselves had begun exploring the fields now incorporated into, and legitimized by, the European theoretical hegemony" (139). Monolingual readers of "english"[1] may gain some inkling of this mainstream blitheness towards backwater theory from the experience, short-lived, of "commonwealth" literature. Ashcroft et al cite the Canadian critic Diana Brydon, in referring to the work of "the last two decades in contemporary critical theory": "We of course have been writing about these dangers for years, but in a discourse marginalised by its status as 'Commonwealth literature' and by its reliance, until recently, on the language of monologist or monocentrist criticism (Brydon 1984: 387; quoted by Ashcroft, 139). How many works of critical theory written in non-hegemonic languages would fit in the same category?[2]

The consequences of this insight involve not so much hegemonic languages, as the hegemony of language itself. No matter how liberal any language may be — and French and English are among the most libertarian in their outlook[3] — each language has its own mindset, its own hidden biases, its own way of looking at things. (I am not rehearsing the theories of Benjamin Lee Whorf, although his theories have, in my opinion, been more misunderstood than understood, but reflecting the work of the cognitive theorists like Lakoff and Johnson, in *Metaphors We Live By*.)

A compromise in post-colonial writing is that one has to use the language of the oppressor to overcome oppression or, as Raja Rao put it in 1938, "to convey in a language that is not one's own the spirit that is one's own." (Rao 1938,vii; quoted by Ashcroft, p. 39). In his preface to

---

[1]   I accept the conventional convenience, popularized by Ashcroft, Griffiths, and Tiffin, of distinguishing "english", as the world-wide medium of communication, from "English", referring to productions of the Anglo-American ambit.

[2]   Exceptions, of course, come to mind, most prominently, Mikhail Bakhtin from the Russian, Diontz Durisin from the Slovak, and Wolfgang Iser and Hans Robert Jauss, from the German. But none of these come from "Third World" countries.

[3]   By this I mean the accessibility in these languages to a wide spectrum of opinion, including those attacking the cultures these languages represent. I do not mean the receptivity of these languages toward "foreign" expressions — in that regard, English is much more accommodating than French.

Fanon's *The Wretched of the Earth,* Sartre said that "the Third World finds itself and speaks to itself through his [Fanon's] voice" (9). What he neglected to say was that Fanon's voice spoke in French, and that the message would not be transmitted to the Third World, unless they could read French, or the languages into which the original French text was translated.[4]

In characterizing the imperialist agenda polemically, Sartre imagines a scenario where "Everything will be done to wipe out their traditions, to substitute our language for theirs and to destroy their culture without giving them ours" (13) — which prospect has not been entirely avoided in the generation or more since. The terms of discourse are still "hegemonic" English or "hegemonic" French. Even the service of translation to post-colonialism is ironic: it gives voice to members of the Third World, as well as access to a First World audience, yet it requires that Third World concerns be expressed, not natively, but in a First World language. One of the consequences is that more and more First World scholars appropriate the voice of Third World advocacy. Depending on the adamancy of one's ideology and the vehemence of one's paranoia, these Western spokesmen and spokeswomen of post-colonial interests are either expropriators and distorters of what does not belong to them, or self-conscious apologists for the sins of the West in the past.

Part of the problem in most post-colonial critiques of the colonial and post-colonial is the adversarial cast of the logic and the rhetoric. Frantz Fanon's passionate recrimination of French colonial brutalities in Algeria in the 50's set the tone of combative demonization. "The colonial world is a world cut in two (29)," Fanon writes, "The colonial world is a Manichaean world" (31). The effect of this view of the struggle, as Ashcroft et al have pointed out, "is a radical division into paired oppositions such as good-evil; true-false; white-black, in which the primary sign is axiomatically privileged in the discourse of the colonial relationship" (125). These clear-cut oppositions, helpful as they may be in stirring up nationalistic passions, and effective as Fanon undoubtedly was in promoting the liberation of Algeria from its French oppressors, nevertheless traps Fanon and post-colonialists in an ontological circularity. For, once reality is thus bifurcated into binary, mutually exclusive categories, then there can be no admission of the complexity of multiple allegiances: to understand, much less sympathize with, the other is to betray the self. But absolute demonizations always fail: Fanon's hatred of the French did not extend to a distaste for the French language, or to the technologies that the imperialist languages, both English and French, gave access to. As Michel de Certeau, writing more than a decade after Fanon, observed:

> In Algeria, the imposition of Arabic in all areas would have led
> to a paralysis of scientific, technical, and cultural development;

---

[4] It would make an interesting study: the translation of anti-colonial classics in the languages of the Third World. But would it be published (and read) in the West?

thus it was resolved to teach the exact sciences in English or in French. Since its independence, Algeria has accepted. . . a "Frenchification" of the population as a whole. . . . (79)

The Manichaeanism posited by Fanon entails at least an inconsistency if not a contradiction, and renders the anti-colonial position hypocritical if not cynical. We encounter a phenomenon that might be called "ironic Manichaeanism".   Here is an example from Fredric Jameson.   In discussing the role of narrative fictions, Jameson writes: "in simultaneously articulating and deconstructing the 'Manichaean aesthetic' of post-colonial societies" (Aschroft et al, 174), and recognizes that the text "brings into being that very situation to which it is also, at one and the same time, a reaction" (Jameson 1981:81-82; quoted by Ashcroft et al, 172). To Jameson, this is a paradox, not a contradiction. The irony stems initially from the serial dialectic first adumbrated by Hegel, and elaborated by Marx: the paradigm is conflictual and combative. The old order must be destroyed to create a new order, but then the new order becomes the old order: it becomes the very establishment that it opposed in the first place.[5] There is, in this, something characteristically Western, and Freudian, because history is seen as a serial dialectic of constant and inevitable parricide, with one generation overthrowing the previous generation, in endless swings of the patriarchal pendulum. The futility of these dialectical swings was recognized by Michel Pécheux in his notion of "counter-determination" where one may inadvertently support that which one vehemently opposes, because one is locked in the paradigm of the system that one wishes to undermine (Pécheux, 169). Yet it is this ontological trap which still holds sway in the post-colonial mindset, even after the apparent demise of colonialism. Despite the adamancy of post-colonial critics, neo-colonialism remains a constant threat, and the "incorporating tendencies of European and American neo-universalism" (Ashcroft et al, 121) continue unabated. For example, according to Ashcroft et al, "it is perhaps an indication of the persisting hegemony of Europe that theories such as poststructuralism are adopted more readily than similar views derived from the conditions of the post-colonial experience" (164). We begin to recognize that "postmodernism, which has sought in recent times to reabsorb post-colonial writing into an international postmodern discourse, may themselves, in fact, be more indebted to the cultural effects of . . . colonialization and its aftermath than is usually acknowledged" (Ashcroft et al, 156) — one may well wonder if the post-colonial critique isn't, at bottom, self-defeating.

Perhaps the most outlandish, certainly the most ironic, anti-hegemonic exercise is Fredric Jameson's 1986 article, "Third World

[5] It is the dilemma of every revolutionary (pace Victor Serge), who succeeds when he most fails, and fails where he most succeeds. Among the revolutionaries who failed where they most succeeded, one can name both Mao Zidong and Fidel Castro; and among the revolutionaries who succeeded where they most failed we can list Zhou Enlai and Che Guevara.

Literature in the Era of Multinational Capitalism." Written after a sojourn in China, he argues that "All third-world texts are necessarily. . . allegorical, and in a very specific way: they are to be read as what I will call national allegories" (69). "Third-world texts . . . necessarily project a political dimension in the form of national allegory: the story of the private individual destiny is always an allegory of the embattled situation of the public third-world culture and society" (69). The breathtaking sweep of this claim, based on an analysis of a handful of stories and novels, most notably those of Lu Xun of China and Ousmene Sembene of Senegal, cannot be more imperious. Nor is the confidence of the analysis undermined one whit by the fact that Jameson read these works, presumably, in translation. This is a clear case of what mischief First-World defenses of Third-World literatures can lead to. For whatever virtues Lu Xun may have had, they are certainly not limited to the national allegorical reading that Jameson culls from "Diary of a Madman" and "The True Story of Ah Q." And to suggest that Ousmene Sembene's numinous and poetic novels represent a Senegalese national allegory undercuts precisely the uniquely uncategorizable nature of Sembene's writing.

But my point here is not to dispute Jameson's analysis. What strikes me in these passages is the arrogance of his attitude toward the Third World, the condescension toward backward peoples, the unchallenged assumption of Western superiority and the use of Western criteria in judging non-Western material. No colonial was ever as patronizing as this advocate of Third World interests. In addressing the effort to make an argument for the importance and interest of non-canonical forms of literature (note how Western literature has become canonical for the world!), Jameson writes, "Nothing is to be gained by passing over in silence the radical difference of non-canonical texts. The third-world novel will not yield the satisfactions of Proust or Joyce; what is more damaging than that, perhaps, is its tendency to remind us of outmoded stages of our own first-world cultural development and to cause us to conclude that they are still writing novels like Dreiser or Sherwood Anderson" (65). The assumption of Western development as paradigmatic, the characterization of other cultures as occupying a lower stage in an evolutionary ladder, the smug satisfaction in the perfection of modern Western culture — all these are more than a little reminiscent of the blithe and callous capitalist imperialists that Jameson inveighs against elsewhere.

Circularities of bias

More than overt ideology, more even than covert economic exploitation, the culture of colonialism persists in innumerable inadvertencies of presumption and logic, in premises assumed but not established in fact or reality, in realities that manifest colonialistic thinking which may be true, but not just. For example, definitions of literature on which Third World works are evaluated distinctly favor an aesthetic concept of unity and wholeness that derives from Aristotle: they privilege the text, whereas Third World traditions tend more toward the oral, and its episodic, improvisational, and fragmented aesthetic. There are generic presumptions as well: the tripartite division of narrative, lyric, and drama is widespread in the West, but they are hardly universal.

In Chinese, lyric and drama (in *The Romance of the Western Chamber* and, very differently, in *The Dream of the Red Chamber*)[6] are often conflated; in Japanese, lyric and narrative (in, say, Basho's "The Narrow Road to the North") are inseparable. And it is undeniably true that Third World productions must be translated into a First World language if they are to attract "world" attention, but — given the vagaries and pitfalls of translation — there is no justice in that truth. These are what I call "imperialisms" of the mind, which, despite considerable vigilance continue into the post-colonial age. There is, as Ashcroft et al point out, a hegemony of theory, where Western theory is applied to non-Western literature, but the world (read "the West") remains generally ignorant of, or uninterested in, non-Western theory.

There can be no question that translation is critical to worldwide recognition of non-western, non-hegemonic cultures: the preponderance of Nobel Prizes awarded to writers in English, French, Spanish, and German (to say nothing of languages cognate with these tongues) attest to the inevitable language bias of the Swedish Academy. Gregory Rabassa's translation of Gabriel García Márquez has been widely recognized by many (including García Márquez himself) as instrumental in his winning the Nobel Prize (cf. Chapter. And how likely would Kawabata's Prize have been, in 1970, if the Swedish Academy had been relied upon to have read him in Japanese before choosing him for the award? The eminent sinologist and member of the Swedish Academy, Professor Goeran Malmqvist has said, on more than one occasion, "that it is of paramount importance that works of Chinese literature be translated into the major Western languages." He has also suggested that had their works been faithfully translated soon after their publication, both Lu Xun [1881-1936] and Wen Yiduo [1899-1946] could well have won the Prize" (personal communication). Yet translation is, for post-colonial literatures, a two-edged sword: while it undoubtedly confers access, and attracts a substantially wider world audience, it also imports evaluative criteria that are not necessarily appropriate to the indigenous text. Even post-colonial critics as astute as Bill Ashcroft, Gareth Griffiths, and Helen Tiffin miss this point. In their influential *The Empire Writes Back*, they write of Indian literature, without apparent irony:

> It is frequently asserted that the work produced by contemporary writers in languages as diverse as Maratha, Bengali, Kannada, Telugu, Malayalam, etc., far outweighs in quantity and quality the work produced in english. This may well be the case, though until more extensive translations into english from these languages have been produced it is difficult for non-speakers of these languages to

---

[6]   The medieval Chinese form of the *bianwen* combined lyric and narrative structurally. Of course, the narrative-lyric-drama distinction is only a modern development in the West, since Shakespeare, most prominently, can be said to have combined all three.

judge. (122)

There are at least two problems with this otherwise unassailable assertion: (1) it entails the necessary privileging of works that can be effectively translated into english, and (2) it ignores the evaluative problematic of requiring works to satisfy the criteria and the tastes of an english-reading public. This is part of the implicit but chimerical "comprehensive" universalism of Western institutions of judgment. International prizes are awarded, presumably on a world-wide basis, but nowhere is the reality admitted: that one is judging only those items to which one has linguistic access, and that linguistic access is greater in some languages than others.

However, despite the alarms about globalization as the Coca-Cola-nization, the MacDonaldization of the planet — the West is not even close to eliminating the cultural diversity in the world. The problem is not whether the Western paradigms are to prevail globally or not: the challenge is to uncover the culturally specific bias of Western concepts. We have already mentioned the Western insistence on human rights, when what is clearly intended is individual rights, presumes a Western ontology of the human being. It assumes that one's humanity is defined in terms of selfhood, whereas many cultures define one's humanity in terms not of one's autonomy or independence, but in terms of one's relatedness to other human beings: this definition of the self, as I have argued elsewhere,[7] is by no means inevitable, or even inevitably persuasive. In many Third World sites, and especially in Hong Kong, there is frequent invocations of "the rule of law", as if that were an inviolable principle of civilization and civility. But what is being promulgated is not some culturally neutral principle, but the tradition not only of Western law, but specifically of the Anglo-American tradition of the law. To borrow an observation from Certeau which he used in another context, "In this way, a particular milieu imposes on everyone the name of the law, which in reality is only its law" (142). With these imperialisms of the mind, it would appear that Western colonialism, at least in the area of hegemonic thought, is alive and well, although some, like Samuel Huntington, have argued precisely the opposite.[8]

To illustrate a further hegemony we may contrast the causative dialectic of Hegel and Marx we adduced earlier with a simultaneous dialectic of traditional Taoism. The basis mode is oppositional; its basic strategy is confrontational; and its underlying worldview fundamentally

---

[7]   Cf. "When I find myself, what will I find, and who did the looking': Intercultural Challenges to the Self"; *The I of the Beholder: A Prolegomena to the Intercultural Study of Self,* edited by Steven P. Sondrup and J. Scott Miller; also *Two-way Mirrors* (Lexington Books, 2004), Chapter 13.

[8]   Samuel Huntington: "the powerful currents of indigenization at work in the world make a mockery of Western expectations that Western culture will become the world's culture." Huntington points out that "the proportion of the world's population speaking English is small and declining." Huntington concludes: "A language foreign to 92 percent of the world's population is not the world's language" (*Foreign Affairs,* November 21, 1996, p. 28).

Manichaean. Its preferred descriptor is neither the circle nor the square, not even, as in the famous Taoist symbol partial circles within a circle, but a straight line. Let us call this Manichaean Cartesianism. This preference for reifying the straight line as a mode of understanding, and of political control can be easily demonstrated.

Early colonializations by the Spanish and Portuguese, followed the irregularities of the topography. However, divisions established after Descartes, i.e. those territories colonized in the 18th century and after, such as the United States, Canada, Australia, Africa, we will find the presence, if not the predominance, of the straight line. It is, indeed, the hegemony of the Cartesian mindset that determines the political boundaries of French and English colonizations. Where these lines demark the internal divisions, as of states in the U. S., and of provinces in Canada and in Australia, the mischief caused has been minimal. But, the straight lines cast across the face of Africa has been the cause of more than a little disruption, cutting across as they do not only topographic features, but tribal homesteads and fluctuating boundaries, the consequences — witness the troubles in Uganda, Rwanda, Somalia, etc. — have been unhappy, if not disastrous. There can be nothing more arbitrary, less situational, more impersonal, less historical than to divide people according to the straight line calculations of a surveyor. The 48th parallel, separating North from South Korea, has been the scene of conflict for more than half a century; the nearly straight line along the 17th parallel, separating North from South Vietnam caused traumas, not only for the indigenous populations, but for France and the United States. This is not to say that natural borders have not been contested, but it is to say that straight line borders have little or no chance of success, because they are not reinforced by topographic, ethnographic, or historical realities.[9]

The model of Western dialectics is a continuing cause-and-effect model mirroring Newton's Third Law of Motion, which posits equal and opposite forces (cf. Eoyang 2002). Straight-line divisions are merely the cartographic manifestation of this way of "mapping" territories according to a Manichaean vision of the world.

---

[9]   The most remarkable, and peaceful, straight line border between nations is, of course, the one between Canada and the United States.

6. Hegemonies of Translation and of Transliteration

At the end of his book, *The Scandals of Translation*, Lawrence Venuti writes:

> because developing countries are notable sites of contest between cultural sameness and difference, they can teach their hegemonic others an important lesson about the functionality of translation. (189)

What I propose to do in what follows is to look at specific instances of decolonized translation, and to focus on the "linguistic and cultural differences that comprise the local scene". I have chosen two sets of examples, one from Hong Kong, and the other from the United States.

One way of seeing the colonial impact on a colony or a post-colonial reaction against the colonizer, would be to look at the translations of familiar Western children's songs. Here, too, there is a mixture of strategies involved so it is difficult to determine whether the superior culture has been abrogated or appropriated. In the renderings of these familiar lyrics, one can identify three different stategies: the first is semantic; the second, transliterative; and the third, transformative. I offer the Cantonese versions.

一閃一閃小星星，一顆一顆亮晶晶
yat shin yat shin siu sing sing, yat fo yat fo leung jing jing

仿似許多小寶石，掛在天空放光明
fong qi hui doh siu bo shek, gwa joi tin hung fong gwong ming

一閃一閃小星星，
yat shin yat shin siu sing sing, yat fo yat for leung jing jing[1]

Translated literally, this would read:

> A flash, a flash, little star, a drop, a drop of bright crystal,
> Just like many little jewels, suspended in the sky radiating brightness,
> A flash, a flash, little star, a drop, a drop of bright crystal.

If you have a wide semantic tolerance in your memory, you might find this faintly familiar, but if I were to sing it, you would recognize it

---

[1]   For these and the following texts and transliterations, I am indebted to Pauline Leung Po Lin and Joey Lee Suk-wan.

immediately:

> Twinkle, twinkle, little star, how I wonder what you are?
> Like a diamond in the sky, up above the world so high,
> Twinkle, twinkle, little star, how I wonder what you are?

Please note that most of the lines in the Chinese are very close semantically, but in order to preserve the rhyme, and to capture the childlikeness of the diction, there has been no attempt to capture "how I wonder what you are" — which comes out as "a drop, a drop, of bright crystal." The loss is, perhaps, not significant, because "drops of bright crystal" might be assumed to elicit wonder quite automatically. Because of the general semantic faithfulness (and the rhythmic accuracy: the same number of syllables having been retained), we characterize this strategy of translation as semantic.

For our second song, the crucial opening is not translated at all but transliterated:

> 瑪莉有隻小錦羊，小覡羊
> Malei yau jaet siu min yeung, siu min yeung, siu min yeung
> 瑪莉有隻小錦羊，羊毛白如雪，
> Malei yau jaet siu min yeung, yeung mo baak yue shuet

Because there is no requirement to rhyme, the Chinese can be quite semantically faithful to the original, and the lines can be rendered thus:

> Mary had a little sheep, a little sheep, a little sheep,
> Mary had a little sheep, her fleece was white as snow.

But for the word-for-word accuracy, the phrase I rendered "little sheep" could just as easily be translated, "lamb" (although, to be pedantic, if "a little sheep" is a "lamb", then a "little lamb" in this context should be rendered as a "little, little sheep"). But the first two words in the Chinese betray this as a foreign song, because 瑪莉 (Malei) is clearly a transliteration of an English name. We may characterize this effort as adopting a transliterative strategy to translation: what is preserved here is the distinct foreign provenance of the text.

For our third song, we offer something definitively and inescapably Western: yet it is unrecognizable in its Cantonese guise:

> 有隻雀仔跌落水，跌落水，
> yau jaet juek tsai dip lok shui, dip lok shui, dip lok shui
> 有隻雀仔跌落水，跌落水，
> yau jaet juek tsai dip lok shui, bei shui chung hui.

An accurate retro-translation of these lines might run as follows:

> There is a little sparrow who fell in the water, fell in the water,

> There is a little sparrow who fell in the water, which flushed him away.

There is the same childlike singsong simplicity to these lyrics, and they fit the melody quite well. The scarcely recognizable original is "London Bridge" (that ultimate symbol of Anglo-imperialism):

> London Bridge is falling down, falling down, falling down,
> London Bridge is falling down, my fair lady!

But where is London Bridge in the Cantonese version? Washed away, I suspect, not only by the waters but by the exigencies of translation. It has been transmogrified into a little sparrow. And there's no trace of "my fair lady"! Clearly, the strategy of translation here is transformative.

What are we to make of these different translation strategies, and how does our analysis affect our understanding of the relationship between translation and post-colonialism? First, we notice that, even at the extremely minute lexical level, where one would expect language to be most intractable, the most hermetic, we find accommodations to meaning in the first case, to nominalistic fidelity in the second case, and to rhythm irrespective of nominalization in the third case. Perhaps this dispels the myth, promulgated by theorists bent on abstractions or on rhetoricians eager to make a point, that cultures cannot be essentialized into entities that can be conjured up, abrogated, or appropriated.

And, finally, vernacular ethnic literature provides yet a third lexical prism through which to examine the way language reflects the colonial-postcolonial dynamic. Some fictions by bicultural, if not bilingual authors, illustrate the spectrum of possibilities in accommodations and co-optations of the foreign. John Okada's 1957 novel, *No-No Boy*, concerns two Japanese-American boys: one, Ichiro, who refuses to serve in the U. S. Army because he will be forced to fight against his parents' native country; the other, Kenji, who commits totally to being an American, enlists in the army, fights honorably, and returns home, with one leg amputated, crippled in body and spirit. Part of the dynamic depicted between generations is the willingness and reluctance of the parents to adapt to the United States. Ichiro's mother clings to her Japanese ways, whereas Kenji's parents are more Americanized. In depicting the conversation between Ichiro and his mother, Okada skillfully conveys a foreign tongue by careful use of stilted syntax:

> "Where have you been?" she repeated harshly.
> "With Kenji, Kanno-san's boy." He approached the counter and faced her. "You know him."
> "Ahh," she said shrilly and distastefully, "that one who lost a leg. How can you be friends with such a one? He is no good."

Lest we forget that we are overhearing a conversation in Japanese that's rendered in English, the context makes it perfectly clear: the "us" in the following paragraph is a translation of a "we" in Japanese:

> His discomfort seemed strangely to please her. She raised her chin perceptibly and answered: "He is not Japanese. He fought against us. He brought shame to his father and grief to himself. It is unfortunate he was not killed." (103)

By subtle strokes of defamiliarized but accessible English, Okada sensitizes the reader into "hearing" Japanese in English, a technique which Meir Sternberg calls "conventionalized homogenization," in which everyone, from foreigners to aliens to extraterrestrials speak the language of the narration – except that, in this case, by dint of subtle rhythmic variation and syntactical stiffness, the vestige of the foreign is preserved.

Writing some 35 years later, in his 1991 novel, Donald Duk, Frank Chin, the Chinese-American novelist, adopts several approaches, and posits a partially bilingual audience, one that understands a certain amount of Cantonese, as well as English. His first strategy is to offer transliteration alongside translation, to give a sense of the phonetic sounds involved:

> Mr. Doong calls to Uncle Donald Duk splashing and sizzling at a wok all his own. The words lob out of his mouth like military commands. "Ah-Sifu!" (Maestro in Cantonese to Donald's Dad.) "Ah-King sook ahhh! Aha! Ah-Sook!" (Familiar but very respectful.) "Ho see fot choy. What an honor it is for me to see you working at your art!" (64).

The use of the word "wok" unitalicized reflects the author's conviction that the reader is already familiar with this typically Chinese, all-purpose stir-fry pan. With the proper transliteration and uncanny parsing, Chin renders faithfully the cadence and rhythm of spoken Cantonese. He relies on the Cantonese we do know in English (at least in urban America), and translates what may not be familiar.

Elsewhere, he adopts a different strategy, of not merely pointing out that languages are different, but of spotlighting the extra-semantic differences between languages: he depicts the enunciated overtones of each language:

> "Like in my restaurants," Dad says, "I don't say sliced cross-section broccoli spear alternate with slices of Virginia ham and chicken breast. Sounds too laboratory science. Who wants to eat some kind of autopsy? Ugh! So, I say Jade Tree Golden Smoke Ham and Chicken. In Chinese, oh, it sounds even more beautiful. Yuke shur gum wah faw tur gai kow. Jade tree. Sounds so pretty you don't feel bad about paying too much money to eat broccoli ." (125).

The bilingual reader invoked is presumed to be proficient in either English or Cantonese and the reader, whatever his limitations, sees provisionally from a Cantonese-American perspective.[2] There may be some "exoticization" at work here, where English-only readers will experience the ineffable (not to say inscrutable) Orient, but Chin's project is precisely to undercut this kind of Orientalism with his asides and his contextual triangulations, so that by inference and from the glosses supplied, we are equipped with enough information to divine the meaning. The experience of reading is, in a sense, to become Cantonese-American, even if we are not.

Linguistic exoticism plays a larger role in Chin's portrayal of Cantonese-accented English, yet even here, the view of the character is intended to be interior rather than exterior:

> The old bald waiter at Uncle's pops out of the swinging door to the kitchen with plates of food in each hand and more plates stacked up his arms. He throws grabeyes onto people lined up to get in and breathlessly includes them in his constant patter as he lays out hot breakfasts and calls orders into the kitchen. "You hammaneck over ease, sticky potatoes. You by you'self! Sit right dere! Don't afraid! Sit! Yeah! Sit! Beckon anna scramboo, ricee no grave. Oh, Ah-King Sifu! Maestro! How many? Five! Wow! I kick somebody out for you, but bad for business to do things like that. But if you can't wait."
> "We can wait, Ah-Bok," Dad says, calling the baldhead Old Uncle. That's a lot of respect.
> "Pork chop, poachecks, Frenchie fries, you. Sausage patties, sunnyside ups. Okay. You a waffoo. I get the syrup, don't worry."
> (147)

Any reader who has encountered, at one time or another, a "Chinatown" proprietor in an English-speaking country, will be able to make out some of these accents. We recognize these phrases: "hammaneck over ease" is the Chinglish equivalent of "ham and eggs over easy"; "Beckon anna scramboo" is "bacon and scrambled [eggs]"; "poachecks" turns out to be "poached eggs"; and "waffoo" is "waffles". The brilliance of Chin's writing is that he manages to enact a Cantonese-accented english without demeaning the character who speaks it and with no narrative condescension. These locutions are not presented as solecisms, deviations from standard (correct) speech: they are a colorful segment of what Saussure distinguished as the *parole* rather than the *langue* part of language. They are as literary as the rural accents of Mark Twain's Huckleberry Finn, the adolescent slang of J. D. Salinger's Holden Caulfield, the Chicago street patois of Saul Bellow's Augie March, or the black vernacular of Mark Twain's Nigger Jim.

The examples from Okada and Chin are illustrations of how difficult and meaningless it is to maintain a purely post-colonial perspective.

---

[2] Even Mandarin speakers do not quite qualify, since they won't be able to guess at the original words from the transliterations of Cantonese: they may deduce the original approximately by translating the English verbatim, but that wouldn't control for synonyms.

Certainly, both Okada, as a Japanese-American, and Chin, as a Chinese-American, have an axe to grind against white, Anglo-Saxon, Protestant (WASP) imperialism and prejudices in the United States. But to characterize them as "post-colonial" undercuts their significance and denigrates their achievement. That would reduce their works to anthropological documents, to see them as ethnography rather than as literature, resulting in what would be, ironically, the cruelest hegemony — to take ethnic writers and to pigeonhole them as ethnic. *No-No Boy* and *Donald Duk* describe cultures as indigenous as Joyce's Dublin; as authentic as Hardy's Wessex; and as realistic as Flaubert's Paris.

Historical Precedents

The restriction to Marxist perspectives in post-colonial thought has had the unfortunate consequence of narrowing the consideration of cultural interaction to an analysis of modern capitalism and its spread. This strategy effectively precludes relevant pre-modern examples of "colonial" impositions of culture. Among the earliest would be the "colonialisation" of Roman civilization by Greek culture, with the (from the modern point of view) ironic reversal that the "colony" was the stronger military power. In Asia, an apposite phenomena can be cited in the relationship between Japan and China (one could include Korea as well), where the "dominant" culture exercised decisive influence on the local civilization, but — as in the case of Greece and Rome — without the advent of force. Is it merely a modern phenomenon that "cultural superiority" in our time is always assumed by force of arms? The Roman Empire, in its turn, certainly exercised its hegemony by the force of its culture as well as by military means: indeed, its sway over Europe in the predominance of Latin outlasted the Roman Conquest by centuries: indeed Latin dominated scholarly discourse in Europe until the twentieth century.[3]

A sense of cultural inferiority did not deter the Romans from developing their own civilization along the lines of their Greek model, nor did it inhibit the Japanese from evolving its own highly accomplished civilization, despite its indebtedness to the Chinese model. The imputation of inferiority in post-colonial discourse is always condemned, and there is little constructive analysis of an admitted inferiority — whether in culture or in technology — as a spur to positive development. One easily forgets that the most imperialistic country, England, grew out of very humble beginnings, and managed, in a short time, spectacular achievements. Moderns view the Elizabethan period as a Golden Age of English literature, yet few realize that its achievements were motivated by a deep sense of inferiority toward Continental (read European) literary traditions (see Chapter One). The introduction of F. O. Matthiessen's *Translation: An Elizabethan Art*, a neglected classic of scholarship, conveys this sense of buoyant inferiority, where one's shortcomings were not regarded as permanent disabilities, but rather as offering opportunities

---

[3]   Bertrand Russell and Alfred North Whitehead's *Principia Mathematica* and Ludwig Wittgenstein's *Tractatus Logico-Philosophicus* are vestiges of this Latin hegemony over

ripe for the taking:

> A study of Elizabethan translations is a study of the means by which the Renaissance came to England. The nation had grown conscious of its cultural inferiority to the Continent, and suddenly burned with the desire to excel its rivals in letters, as well as in ships and gold. The translator's work was an act of patriotism. He, too, as well as the voyager and merchant, could do some good for his country: he believed that foreign books were just as important for England's destiny as the discoveries of her seamen, and he brought them into his native speech with all the enthusiasm of conquest. (3).

Note the imperialistic diction used in this passage, with words like "voyager," "merchant," "conquest", all of which would become critical to the post-colonial critique. Yet, there is nothing combative or adversarial about these concerns, no recrimination of the Continent as hegemonic and oppressive. Of course, England was not occupied by what they recognized as superior cultural countries, and one can understand why they were free to contemplate their own inferiority as inspiration and impetus for developing a native literature that reflected the rich Continental tradition at the same time it established their own indelible identity. The trouble with the notion of "inferiority" as it is used in post-colonial discourse is that it is often presented as mere emotional rhetoric, a cruel debasement by insensitive hegemons of the local culture. The admission of inferiority by the natives then becomes a kind of "lackey" behavior, where the victim is perceived to embody the ideology of his own victimization.

To ignore the colonializations of the past is to perpetrate the myth that it is a recent phenomenon, and to miss the salient point that colonialisms are not all equal: it isn't that colonialism is bad, per se, or even avoidable — cultural diffusion cannot take place without some form of colonialism — but rather that the modern, particularly Marxist, notion of colonialism has some special characteristics. If we examine the pre-Marxist, more traditional instances of colonialism, we will be struck by the vigor with which "inferior" cultures prevail — in energy, in resources, in imagination, if not always in economic or military power — over previously "superior" cultures. The breakaway of the various literatures in english from the common root of English Literature — whether American, Canadian, Australian, Jamaican, South African, Irish, Scottish, Straits (Singaporean), Indian — can thus be appreciated not simply as "overthrowing the yoke" of the imperialist oppressor, but also as a form of nurturing and fecund co-optation, on the part of the receiver culture of the paternal literary stock. One can easily contrive similar scenarios of co-optation by Roman literature of Greek, by Latin American literature of Spanish, by Brazilian literature of Portuguese, by Japanese literature of Chinese, by Francophone and Quebecois literature of French.

In some respects, the self-contradictions inherent in the post-colonial stance and the dilemma of compromised subjectivity is inevitable in any monolingual discourse, even in any translation in a monolingual discourse. There is a linguistic hegemony in any language, which necessarily privileges, "subjectivizes" deictically the here and now, positing implicitly a psychological center. But, deictic markers are sometimes not culturally neutral: the "implicit" here-and-now in the word "here" in English is sited in an English-speaking context. The dichotomy of Us vs. Them is a convenient trope of every unscrupulous demogogue. To say, "此地" ("here", or "this place" in Chinese) bespeaks a different psychological center. It is not an ideological hegemony that functions here, but a linguistic hermeticism which is ultimately, for each and every language, self-referential. Even the unique feature of Japanese which is designated for specifically foreign words, katakana, does not speak of the foreign from the viewpoint of a object, but from the perspective of the subject. In katakana, the foreignness of the locution is marked, and the center of consciousness is unmistakably Japanese.

Post-colonialism has undoubtedly alerted us to the evils of colonial exploitation, of the evils of European ethnocentricity, and the denigrations by whites of brown, black, and yellow brethren. Yet, there is in much of post-colonial writers a sense of clever muckraking, as if the devious machinations of greedy imperialists were not quite subtle enough to deceive them. There is also a sense of piety in having exposed the selfish and inconsiderate, not to say cruel and inhuman, behavior of humans who exploit other humans. And there is little or no compassion for what they perceive as bourgeois bias and greed, and no suspicion that victims may be as complicitous in the dynamics of colonialism as victimizers.

The p-c writers — I use this deliberately ambivalent abbreviation to indicate a genealogical connection — are ruthless about other people's blitheness; they deplore the irony of imperial hypocrisies that conquer the world with good Christian intentions; and they abhor the civilities that give a lie to the most uncivil behavior. But in exploiting the plight of the exploited, they are alert to everyone else's blitheness but their own; in exposing the bourgeois hypocrisies, they manage to neglect their own; and in vilifying the piety of the imperial oppressors, who shoulder the "white man's burden", they overlook the white man's toleration — nay, celebration — of their anti-white vitriol. If the rejoinder to these animadversions is the banal observation that there are, in every race, whites included, some who are good as well as some who are evil, my response would be: "Precisely!" But you'd never glean that from any post-colonial diatribes. If the practitioners of p-c are right in tracing the imperialist dehumanization of the subalterns, their demonizing of the oppressors suffers no less from the same fault of stereotyping. It is easy to see humanity in the salt of the earth: what is difficult is to see the human in the scum of the earth.

The act of translation precludes these dogmas, for in confronting the hermeticism of the original, in facing the intractabilities, not to say the impossibilities, of rendering a work from one language into another, in transposing the meaning from one culture to another, one cannot escape the recognition that, within each language is its own rationale, and each language is intensely chauvinistic, inevitably hegemonic. Translations are necessary when one is restricted by monolingualism: it provides what I call "faute de mieux" benefits. The insights they offer are provisional, and deeply compromised by autochthonicity of language, i.e., the will in language to revert to its own soil in comprehending the world.

But translations purvey a subtle and subversive implication: they define the world in terms of the target language. The target language, inevitably, dictates the perspective, the point of view, and sees the world in terms of its own syntax, its own accent, its own phrasing. It recognizes as reasonable what makes sense on its own terms. It reverses the polarities of the native and the foreign. This is why post-colonial discourse in colonial languages must be generically ironic. For the language in which the protest against oppression is lodged is articulated in the language, and the logic, of the oppressor. The post-colonial is, then, defined, even in his or her protest, in terms of the hegemonic discourse. Even when it subverts that discourse, abrogates or appropriates it, it remains hegemonic. The greatest indictment I have of colonialism is that it has forced those who have opposed it to become either post-colonial, anti-colonial, or neo-colonial, when what is neglected is that ontological fact that before colonialism, these peoples and cultures did not care to be on any point in the colonial spectrum. In just the same way, there are billions in the world who do not remotely think of themselves as "non-Western", no more than most people think of themselves as "non-Eskimo." The vast majority of people that theorists characterize as "post-colonial" have no inkling of what that means, nor do they care.

In order to get past colonialism and post-colonialism, to eliminate the center-margin dilemma that is at the heart of any hegemonic situation, one must adopt a multiple perspective. As Ashcroft et al propose:

> The syncretic is validated by the disappearance of the "centre", and with no "centre" the marginal becomes the formative constituent of reality (104).

But how can we put this abstract ideal into concrete practice? Ashcroft et al propose a "polydialectical theory", which "reveals the performace of speakers, with all the variations"; it is this theory, they claim, which must be the true subject of linguistics" (47). They refer to the "polydialectical culture of the Caribbean" and suggest that "the view of language which polydialectical cultures generate dismantles many received views of the structure of language" (45). But the insights they claim for polydialectical cultures are already available in a close study of the practice and the theory of translation, and in the analysis, through translation, of the innate hegemony of language. In order to escape this innate linguistic hegemony and to get past colonialism, we need to contemplate a new mode of discourse to accommodate increasingly a biliterate audience. We must produce bi- and multi-literate books, i.e., books written in more than one language. This is not merely to accommodate a growing population of bilingual and biliterate populations, but to recognize the existence of a significant pool of readers who are already biliterate.[4]

Only by seeing from more than one center of consciousness, only by adopting the subjective stance in more than one linguistic milieu, can one hope to reshape one's thinking, to regard oneself from both the outside and the inside.

Which brings us back to the children of the pirate schooner that abducted the children off the good ship Clorinda in Richard Hughes' *High Wind in Jamaica*. At the outset, I highlighted the fascinating portrait that Hughes gives us of "wise innocence." But this is, after all, no fairy tale, no benign children's story. The narrative involves serious consequences, frightening developments: the children have been kidnapped: they are nearly shot by the pirates to force the captain of the Clorinda to reveal where he has hidden the cash box; one of them, John, the oldest, dies of a broken neck after falling forty feet from a parapet; another, Emily will survive a rape attempt and kill a Dutch sea captain. And yet, the attitude of the children is still one of wondrous curiosity, of unquenchable thirst for adventure, of severe self-criticism (usually reserved for a rival sibling). Their quarrels and squabbles, far from annoying are, appropriately, childlike, but far from infantile, they have a sageness and a perspicacity that sophistication knows nothing of. They are not hostages nor victims, despite their perilous plight. They even identify with their captors, and imagine future careers as pirates.

The p-c writers I have in mind can be seen in contrast to the children in *High Wind in Jamaica*: where the latter show a wise innocence, the former evince a naive cynicism. Post-colonial thought will always be self-defeating, because, in demonizing the other, it demonizes itself; by attacking the limitations of the hegemonists, it assumes the mantle of hegemony. They are clever in seeing the deceptions and the machinations of the oppressors, but in doing so, they outwit themselves, and become mirror images of the very opponents they despise. In seeing the deceptions of others, they miss their own self-deceptions. There is something about a good deal of p.-c. criticism that strikes me as intensely jaded: what's lacking is a sense of wonder; what they write is not tempered by tolerant humor. There's a know-it-all wariness in its rhetoric, a brittle cleverness in its logic. It is smart — intelligent, facile, fashionable — but it is not wise. For all its insights, it does not allow for the unexpected or the imponderable. Its fault, one shared by their mentor, Marx, is to confuse analysis with prophecy, theory with science.

We want to learn the lesson that the children in *High Wind in Jamaica* teach us, and say, imitating Harry, "These imperialist pigs, these colonial cockroaches, they're post-colonials themselves!"

---

[4]   It is interesting that while data on bilingualism is readily available, data of biliterate populations is difficult to come by.

7. "Here and Now" vs. "There and Then" in Translating Chinese Literature

To begin this discussion of a deictic concern with the self, and with indexical notions of immediacy and remoteness, I resort to an indifferent political joke:

> When, late in 1990, John Major succeeded Margaret Thatcher as Prime Minister of Great Britain, everyone was struck at how very quickly this relative unknown assumed a commanding presence on the world stage. President Bush, concerned at the time with his own second in command, and — according to reports — contemplating a replacement for Dan Quayle in anticipation of the 1992 elections, was naturally interested in Margaret Thatcher's methods for identifying a worthy successor. Thatcher told Bush that her method was simple. She merely posed the following riddle as a test of a candidate's suitability for leadership: "Who is your father's son who is not your brother?"
>
> Delighted at this litmus test for leadership, Bush eagerly sought out Dan Quayle.
>
> "Dan," he said, "I have a riddle for you to solve. 'Who is your father's son who is not your brother?'"
>
> To which Dan Quayle, with practiced guardedness, replied: "Can I get back to you on that one, Mr. President?"
>
> "Sure," the president said.
>
> Characteristically, Dan Quayle spent little time figuring out the answer, knowing the now well publicized limits of his intellectual prowess. He decided to call the smartest human being he knew. He called Henry Kissinger.
>
> "Say, Henry, I have a puzzle I'd like you to help me with."
>
> "What is it?" Kissinger asked.
>
> "Who is your father's son who is not your brother?"
>
> "That's easy," Kissinger responded, "It's me."
>
> Triumphant, Quayle called President Bush with the solution. "Mr. President, you know that riddle you asked me about? I have the answer."
>
> "Excellent," the President said, "Who is it?"
>
> "It's Henry Kissinger."

The confusion attributed to Dan Quayle in the joke points out the ambiguity of deictic markers, and of pronouns that function in a way that is radically different from the usual nominals. For unlike nominals, deictic markers are tied for their meaning to the speaker, and to the speaker's specific attributes, circumstances, and location.

What I propose to explore here are three types of deictic markers: markers of persona, markers of time, and markers of place. These will be normally recognized as indicators of the self, as indicators of the now and then, and as indicators of the here and there. These dimensional indicators are so subtle and transparent that we do not often notice them. They become crucial when Chinese, which often leaves tenses and subject indicators unmarked, is translated into languages with marked tenses and designated subject-agents.

To appreciate the significance of these deictic markers, let's look at the following poem by Wang Rong 王 融 (468-485)

> Forests break off, the mountains continue on;
> Islands disappear, the river opens up again.
> Amid cloud-scraping peaks, an imperial city rises,
> The source of the river, and of paulownia and cypress.

> 林斷山更續
> 洲盡江復開
> 雲峰帝鄉起
> 水源桐柏來

The self is not specified, nor is the time: it isn't important in the poem to know who the persona is, nor when the poem takes place. The thoughts reflected in the poem presumably occur in a present of the utterance. What is specified, and unmistakably, is place, although the prospect adduced in the poem is so vast as to become cosmic. The first three lines describe an almost ineffable invocation of geography, with no parti-cular location identifiable. The last line narrows the topography a bit, and fo-cuses on "the source of the stream" (水源) and on a spot where there are catalpa and cypress (桐柏). We see two of our three deictic markers un-specified; by contrast, the sense of space, of landscape (in the first three lines) and of location (in the last line) leaves an indelible impression.

In the following poem, the subject self is left unspecified, and the sense of location is pronounced, but while time and the seasons are invoked, there is no specified now or then. There is no immanent moment, no diegetic now in the description, only the now of the writing (and the reading) of the poem. It's Kong Zhigui's 孔稚珪 (448-501) "Trip to Mount Taiping" (遊 太 平 山):

> Precipitous rocks, the sky's face split;
> Forests interlaced, the sun's visage wanes.
> Brook in shadow, spring's splendor falls,
> On the cold crags, summer snows persist.

> 石險天貌分
> 林交日容缺
> 陰潤落春榮
> 寒巖留夏雪

The lineaments of the mountain are vividly described; its craggy promontories unforgettably dramatized; its forest face dappling the sunlight beautifully rendered. But we have in the last two lines reference both to the dissipating petals of spring flowers, the fading, as it were, of spring glory (*luo chun rong*) as well as the vestigial summer snow (*liu xia xue*). The effect is not of an actual landscape, but, despite its vividness, of an abstract composite that cuts across the seasons, a prospect that no naked eye can capture, but rather something only the mind's eye can visualize. The unspecified subject takes the description out of autobiography into generic tourism: the poem is virtually a poetic postcard with a spring and summer photograph of Taiping shan juxtaposed side by side.

We can contrast these persona-less, locative poems with the following generic *ziye* expression of personal and personified feeling, where the (anonymous) subject predominates over the landscape (like the Mona Lisa over the rivers and groves in the background). In this poem, both self and time are specified, but not place:

The flowers of spring's grove, how charming!
The sense of spring birds, how sad!
Spring winds, plaintive once again,
Ruffles open the hem of my skirt.

春林花多媚
春鳥意多哀
春風復多情
吹我羅裳開

The landscape is "peopled" but with one individual, the narrator-persona in the poem: spring is both the agent of the action and its setting, blowing open the silk robes of the narrator-persona (吹我羅裳開). It is also clear, from our knowledge of the usual ziye persona that the narrator-persona is a woman.[1]

There is an ingenuous licentiousness, even a natural eroticism, in this depiction of a seductive almost masculinized spring, whose groves are lovely (春林花多媚), whose birds are heartbreaking (春鳥意多哀), and whose winds stir one's feelings (春風復多情). The last line is not merely an innocent description of the flapping of a gown in a gust of wind: it depicts as well a woman yielding to "feelings of spring" (懷春).

Deictics of the Explicit and Implicit Self

Explicit self-references in Chinese need to be explored in greater depth than they have been, because the practice of translating many self-references in Chinese with the generic "I" or "me" results in the loss of a crucial dimension of implicit characterizations in Chinese discourse. At the very

---

[1] It should not be assumed, as modern imaginations might, that the only silk robes that would blow open in ancient times would be worn by women. However, other considerations make it clear that, while silk robes were not only worn by women, in this case, there is no doubt that the implied persona is female.

least, it misapplies Western grammar to the Chinese language. For example, the deictic markers for the self, such as *qie* 妾 meaning "I" when used by a traditional wife or concubine to her spouse, or *chen* 臣 meaning "I" when used by a minister addressing the emperor, or *gua* 寡, the "I" of a nobleman in ancient times, or *zhen* 朕, meaning "I" when used by an emperor — these are construed erroneously as first-person pronouns, and are often translated as such — disastrously, in my opinion.

Consider the losses of character and personification in rendering the following self-references in the *Shuihu zhuan* 水浒傳 all with "I" or "me": *an* 俺 or *sajia* 酒家 (which are specifically Shandong self-references); *xiaoren* 小人(which is a self-deprecation, as for example when Shi Jin addresses Lu Zhishen for the first time in Chapter 3 of the *Shuihu*: "Xiaoren dadan, ganwen guanren gaoxing daming? 小人大胆敢问官人高姓大名？); *laoshen* 老身 (another self-deprecation, used by an old woman); and *laoniang* 老娘 (a far from self-deprecating expression of insolence by a vixen ready to do battle).[2]

These markers clearly differ linguistically from pronouns, because they are not universal but particular: they can't be used by any interlocutor, any self, but only by certain selves in certain situations, when addressing certain individuals. They share with pronouns the feature that can refer to more than one person at a time (although, in the case of *zhen*, the emperor's self-reference, even that's not true); and they share with nouns a determinate, descriptive, categorical function. They are pronouns and they are not pronouns; they are nouns and they are not nouns. I like to think of them as "pronominals," i. e., names, rather than designations, for different "selves"; i.e., different terms of self-address for different people.

I find it fascinating and, to my knowledge, unremarked, that vernacular Chinese developed an abundance of self-references, particularly in the form of these pronominals, while literary Chinese, beginning with the Tang and ending only with the modern period, went precisely in the op-posite direction, of refining self-references out of existence. The reasons for this divergence may be sought in both semantic linguistics and in psycholinguistics. Clearly, spoken language needs more specificity and "redundancy" to avoid misunderstanding and to compensate for the often incomplete reception in oral discourse, whereas literary Chinese, more concentrated, more allusive, can achieve its effects more succinctly, without loss of clarity. As for the psychological aspect of the issue, one might surmise that the ethos of the literatus and scholar, unlike the bravos and the dahans 大漢 that populate vernacular literature, was one of verbal self-effacement and self-deprecation — a trait that remains familiar in modern Chinese notions of the protocols and the deferences of what one encounters as the ethics of the etiquette *keqi* 客氣

Implicit as self-references have tended to be in traditional Chinese poetry, one should not assume that they were in any sense vague or

---

[2]   For these and other examples, see GE Liangyan, "'So to Speak': Dialectic and Dialogism in the *Shuihu zhuan*, Ph.D dissertation, Indiana University, 1995.

indistinct. Self-references need not be explicit to be particular, as the familiar Tao Qian's "Drinking Wine" (飲酒) poem illustrates:

結廬在人境
而無車馬喧
問君何能爾
心遠地自偏
採菊東籬下
悠然見南山
山氣日夕佳
飛鳥相與還
此中有真意
欲辨已忘言

[I] thatch my hut among people,
Yet there's no sound of horse or carriage,
You ask, How can this be?
When the heart is distant, the place naturally seems far.
Picking chrysanthemums by the eastern hedge
In the distance, I see the Southern Mountain.
Lovely, the mountain air, the setting sun,
Flying birds, flocking together, return,
In this, there is a real meaning,
On the verge of explaining, [I] forget the words.

While there is no reference to self specified, a self is definitively implied by the poem, by virtue of the indirect second-person address in the third line (問君何能爾) and by the psychological introspection of lines four, nine and ten 問君何能爾 / 此中有真意 / 欲辨已忘言).

One must be careful to distinguish between poems that leave the self unspecified (as with the first *ziye* poems cited) from poems that only imply the self. For these implicit references to persona can be quite definitive, even if unstated. Take, for example, the following poem—"Crossing Jingmen to See a Friend Off" 渡荊門送別) by Li Bai (701-762):

[We] journey here to the land of Chu
Where mountains extend beyond the empty plain,
And the river enters into the great hinterland.
The moon sets, a mirror fleeing the sky,
Clouds emerge, form terraces above the sea.
How [I] grudge the river that takes [you] home,
And the miles and miles [your] boat will sail.

渡遠荊門外
來從楚國遊
山隨平野盡
江入大荒流
月下飛天鏡
雲生結海樓

Retreat at Mount Zhongnan" (終山別業):

仍憐故鄉水
萬里送行舟

The location is specified in the first two lines (渡遠荊門外 / 來從楚國遊); the time is specified after a fashion in lines five and six 月下飛天鏡 / 雲生結海樓), but there are no explicit markers of self: no "I" or "we" references in the entire poem. Yet, implicit though they may be, the very poignance of the poem lies in the fact that plural personae are implied in the first seven lines, and a single persona is implied in the final line (*wan li song xing zhou*). For the act of seeing a friend off is a transitive act: in this case, the contrast between the one who is sending off and the one being sent off is not obvious until the end of the poem, for Li Bai (let's assume an autobiographical self, for the sake of convenience) has traveled with his friend across Jingmen before they go their separate ways at the end of the poem. The poem enacts the stages of the experience of parting: lingering companionship ended by a final sendoff. (Notice that assuming a single persona rather than a double persona in the first seven lines would require that we understand the experience as a rendezvous at Jingmen to which Li Bai has travelled, which yields a reading that would be as preposterous as it would be pointless.)

The same technique of shifting implicit persona may be found in Wang Wei's 王維

> In my middle years [I] cherish the way,
> Later, [I] dwelt at the Southern Mountain,
> Whenever [I]like, [I]walk out alone:
> Transcendent things I alone know.
> [I] venture to the source of the stream,
> And begin watching the cloudlets form.
> From time to time, [I] meet the old man of the forest:
> [We] talk and laugh, with not one thought of home.

> 中歲頗好道
> 晚家南山陸
> 興來每獨往
> 勝事空自知
> 行到水窮處
> 生看雲起時
> 偶然值林叟
> 談笑無還期

Again, there is no marker of the self-persona, but it is clear that the poet is alone (獨往) through the first six lines; only in the seventh does he suddenly come upon an old man in the woods (偶然值林叟). The last line makes it clear, even if it's unspecified, that two people, not one, are laughing (談笑無還期). We can safely assume that a conversation (談) involves two interlocutors, and that, unless otherwise specified, one can assume both of them to be laughing.

Deictics of Place: Here and There

Du Fu's famous "Moonlit Night" (月夜) provides an apt illustration of the deictics of place. Indeed, markers of place are used as metonymies for subject-persona: Fuzhou as surrogate for his wife, Changan for himself.

Tonight, beneath a Fuzhou moon,
From [my] chamber looking out alone,
Missing [my] children so far away,
Who don't understand [my] being in Changan.
Fragrant mist dampens [my] cloud-knot,
Clear moonglow chills my bare arms.
When will [we] stand before the window,
And [see:] glistening on both our faces, tears evaporating?

今夜鄜州月
閨中只獨看
遙憐小兒女
來解憶長安
香霧雲鬟濕
清輝玉臂寒
何時依虛幌
雙照淚痕乾

The constant in the poem is the sense of now (今夜), and the locatives alternate from a sense of here and there. The first two lines are located here (今夜鄜州月 / 閨中只獨看). The next line is located in a here, but a here, with the homesick subject the implied I, that's very much thinking of there (遙憐小兒女) . The next line involves a there, with the implied subject his children, invoked at the end of the previous line, but the there in this line is very much mindful of here (來解憶長安).   The next two lines again alternate implied subjects and place markers: 香霧雲鬟濕 / 清輝玉臂寒. In the first line, the subject is the self, and the place, implied, is here; in the second line the subject is Du Fu's wife, and the place, implied, is there. The final couplet longs for their reunion sometime in the future — 何時依虛幌 / 雙照淚痕乾 — but the locative for this projected reunion, implied by the "empty curtain" (虛幌), is unmistakably there rather than here.

One of Du Fu's poems to Li Bai 李白 offers another example of a telling use of a deictics of place. In "Thinking of Li Bai, on a Spring Day" (春日憶李白), no first-person subject is designated (though it is unmistakable).

Li Bai's poetry is irresistible,
His soaring imagination is uncommon.
Clear and fresh, like Yü Xin;
Forceful and fluent, like Bao Zhao.
[Here] North of the Wei, spring trees flower;

[There] South of the Yangzi, the sunset clouds over.
When [will we] raise a cup of wine again
And discuss again the finer points of literature?

白 也 詩 無 敵
飄 然 思 不 群
清 新 庾 開 府
俊 逸 鮑 參 軍
渭 北 春 天 樹
江 南 日 暮 雲
何 時 一 樽 酒
重 與 細 論 文

The structure is very much like the "Moonlit Night" poem, and it also
ends with a wish for reunion. But the key lines, for our present purposes,
are the second *duilian* couplet, lines five and six: 渭 北 春 天 樹 / 江
南 日 暮 雲 "[Here] North of the Wei, spring trees flower; / [There]
South of the River [Yangzi], the sunset darkens". The sense of longing is
calibrated in the geographic distances, the sense of separation in the
remoteness between 渭 北 "North of the Wei" and 江 南 "South of the
River".

The remarkable economy of means in the poem is reflected in these
two phrases, which mark both place and person: it invokes touchingly
both here and there, both self and friend, Du Fu and Li Bai, in a depiction
of two contrasting landscapes which also implies a concern in the younger
poet (春 天 樹 "spring trees flower") about the possible decrepitude of
the older poet (日 暮 雲 "the sunset clouds over"). The distance, actual
and psychological, is erased in the final couplet with an interrogative wish,
that reflects both desire and apprehension: 何 時 一 樽 酒 / 重 與 細
論 文 "When [will we] raise a cup of wine again / And discuss the finer
points of literature? The last line reflects the joys of true literati,
discussing the finer points of literature (重 與 細 論 文 "And discuss
again the finer points of literature?"), but the opening two words — 重 與
"again together or again with [each other]") — sounds a note of reunion
both specifically — when shall we meet once more? — and generally —
when shall we be together. The distance invoked in the first six lines is
erased in this condensed emblem of intimacy.

The deictics of place can be adduced in any number of "homestead"
poems. Tao Qian's "Returning to the Fields and Gardens to Live" (歸
田 園 居) comes immediately to mind. But, since we're looking at
poems at Du Fu, I select his "A Guest Is Coming" (客 至):

South of the house, north of the house, spring freshets,
But look at the flock of geese that come by day after day,
Flower-strewn paths haven't been swept for the guest,
The thatched door is open today, just for you.
Far as we are from market, our food has no taste
Being a poor homestead, our wine is home-brewed.
To propose a toast with our old neighboor

We call across the fence, and empty a few draughts.

舍 南 舍 北 皆 春 水
但 見 群 鷗 日 日 來
花 徑 不 曾 緣 客 掃
蓬 門 今 始 為 君 開
盤 飧 市 遠 無 兼 味
樽 酒 家 貧 只 舊 醅
肯 與 鄰 翁 相 對 飲
隔 籬 呼 取 盡 餘 杯

The place is localized by virtually drawing a circle around it: both south and north of the house, there's spring freshets (舍 南 舍 北 皆 春 水; day after day, the gulls fly overhead (但 見 群 鷗 日 日 來). The paths have not been swept to admit a guest for some time (花 徑 不 曾 緣 客 掃), but "the thatched door" has been swung open today just for you (蓬 門 今 始 為 君 開). The phrase 蓬 門 "the thatched door" works not only as a deictic of place, identifying — self-deprecatingly — the home of the narrator-persona, it also functions as a deictic of self, 蓬 門 represents an idiomatic first-person reference to one's own domicile; and it is an index to character, since it is apodictic for a humble abode. Here is another instance where there is no first-person designation anywhere in the poem, but it is implied in this metonymy of 蓬 門, "my humble home."

The lineaments of the home are circumscribed by the fence (隔 籬) which by punning on *ge li* (隔 離) designates not only the physical divide between neighbor and neighbor, but also the psychological separation (we moderns would call it alienation) between neighbor and neighbor. As with the invocation of Li Bai across considerable distances in the previous poem, here the barriers between next-door neighbors are removed in the joy of having a guest. Comradeship breeds camaraderie.

Perhaps the most unerring sense of place occurs in Liu Zongyuan's (773-819) haunting 江 雪 ("River Snow"). First, one notices what is not specified: there is no personified "I", so there is no deictic marker of self; there is no indicator of an order in time, so there is no here and no there. What is contrasted is the vast perspective in the first two lines of the poem, and a specifically localized perspective in the last two lines. Here is this justly famous poem:

> In hundred mountains, the birds have flown off,
> On a thousand paths, footprints have been rubbed out.
> A solitary boat; an old man in straw cape and hat
> Fishes alone. Cold. River. Snow.

百 山 鳥 飛 絕
千 徑 人 蹤 滅
孤 舟 蓑 笠 翁
獨 釣 寒 江 雪

The first part of the poem adopts a panoramic — even cosmological —

view of things: 百 山 鳥 飛 絕 / 千 徑 人 蹤 滅. Over hundreds of mountains, the flight of the birds has been cut off; over a thousand paths, the traces of people have been rubbed out.   Against this nihilistic background, in a landscape where no birds sing, where no traces of human beings are to be found, one comes upon what seems at first an idyllic scene: 孤 舟 蓑 笠 翁 / 獨 釣 寒 江 雪. A solitary boat; an old man, in a cape and hat made from bamboo thatch fishing by himself in the wintry river snow.   The absences of the first part of the poem are now replaced by the vivid presences of the images in this simple but unforgettable tableau.   But the message of desolation, to our surprise, hasn't changed, and the second part of the poem merely echoes in concrete terms what in the first part of the poem was posited in the abstract.   One can only abstractly imagine the first part, but the second is concretely recognizable. The sharply etched scene contains harmoniously integrated images of loneliness, from the solitary boat to the schematic form of the fisherman, whose visual form is not human, but takes on the outlines of hat and raincape: the single fishing line dangles in the water, but neither the wintry cold nor the river snow promise anything. This "places" before the eyes of the reader a pictorial scene of unimaginable power: anecdotal at first glance, it achieves a metaphysical dimension after several rereadings. No self is posited; no here and now, no there and then. What remains in the poem is an unforgettable place, which we would misprise if we saw it merely as an emblem for the destitution of old age, and the ineffable reminders of extinction in cold and snow. For the very picturesqueness of the scene is its salvation: we see a serenity and a peace, and the absence of the cheerful chirping of birds, as well as of the comforting signs of human activity does nothing to undermine the repose of seeing this old man fishing alone in the icy water, unmindful of the snow.   The setting becomes the most unlikely locus amoenus (happy place) we can imagine.

Deictics of Time: Now and Then

Many Chinese poems are, in a real sense, philosophical reminiscences, not unlike *Le Temps Retrouvé*, the last book in Proust's *A la recherche de temps perdu*. But, whereas the modern narrative recounts the past vividly in order to annihilate the "pastness" of the past, traditional Chinese poets would freely modulate their preoccupations between the past and the present, making the past present, and the present past. A telling example is Du Fu's 登 高 "Climbing the Mount":

> The wind whirls, the sky's high, the monkeys scream mournfully.
> The islet is clean, the sands are white, the birds circle overhead.
> There's no end to trees soughing, shedding their leaves,
> Ceaseless, the roiling waves of the Long River.
> For thousand-league melancholy autumns, long a sojourner,
> A hundred lifetimes, sick, [I've] climbed this terrace alone,
> Travail and anxiety turn the hair at my temples white,
> Disheartened once again, [I] decline to drink the new wine.

風急天高猿嘯哀
渚清沙白鳥飛回
無邊落木蕭蕭下
不盡長江滾滾來
萬里悲秋常作客
百年多病獨登臺
艱難苦恨繁霜鬢
潦倒新停濁酒杯

If we look at the first four lines, the predominant setting is the present: the gibbons yelling mournfully (猿 嘯 哀), the birds flying back (鳥 飛 回), the rustling of trees shedding their leaves in the wind (落 木 蕭 蕭 下), the waters gurgling in the river (長 江 滾 滾 來). All these events occur in the now of the poem. The fifth line refers, however, to the experiences of the past: 萬 里 悲 秋 常 作 客 "For thousand-league melancholy autumns", while the matching couplet combines both the past (百 年 多 病 "A hundred lifetimes, sick") and the present (獨 登 臺 "climbed this terrace). And with the final couplets, past and present are virtually indissoluble: 艱 難 苦 恨 繁 霜 鬢 / 潦 到 新 停 濁 酒 杯 "Travail and anxiety turn the hair at my temples white, / Disheartened once again, [I] decline to drink the new wine". The hardships of the past continue into the present and produce the white hairs of old age; the defeats of bygone years, to say nothing of the dejectedness of the present, preclude taking up the cup. The brilliantly ambivalent phrase 新 停 ("stop anew") would at first suggest present action, but what is implied is that one has done this before. The line bears the mark of both a then and a now in equal prominence.

How differently the dimensions of time can be handled becomes obvious when we contrast these manipulations of temporal dimension with the timeless (in both senses) *jueju* 絕 句 of Wang Wei. For these "spots of time" (to borrow Wordsworth's phrase) not only capture a present that is immediate, they also record an experience that is both immanent and eternal:

Birds Singing at the Stream 鳥鳴溪

One's at leisure, the cassia flowers fall,
The night is still, spring mountains empty.
The moon rises, startling the mountain birds,
They sing now and then from the mountain streams.

人閒桂花落
夜靜春山空
月出驚山鳥
時鳴春澗中

Deer Retreat 鹿柴

97

Empty mountain, no one to be seen,
But there's the sound of something human.
Dappled reflections penetrate the deep woods,
And shine again on the green moss.

空 山 不 見 人
但 聞 人 語 響
返 景 入 深 林
複 照 青 苔 上

Bamboo Grove Abode　竹 里 館

Alone [I] sit in the dense bamboos,
Strumming my lute, humming long tunes,
Deep in the forest, which no one knows,
Where only the moon shines down [on me].

獨 坐 幽 篁 裡
彈 琴 複 長 嘯
深 林 人 不 知
明 月 來 相 照

If one looks closely at the markers of time, one notices that, unlike, for example, the Deng gao 登 高　poem of Du Fu we just examined, no contrast between present and past is invoked: everything occurs in what is familiar in narrative as an "eternal present." The present is capaciously self-sufficient, and endlessly fascinating. What is compelling is the presence of place, and the place in which we find ourselves present. But it is a present unlike our usual sublunary experience, for the present in these poems seem to transcend a mundane now. The quiddities of nature become metaphysical events that resonate beyond the present.

Self references in Wang Wei's best known *jueju* are sparse, as if the persona identity were "refining himself out of existence," in a Joycean epiphany. The focus is not on one's state of mind, nor on the memory, nor on self-as-object, for these are, in Wang Wei, and in the sect of Buddhism which he espoused, the poison which alienates us from the dharma, from the phenomena of existence. Indeed, one is led to believe that a consciousness of time and of its passing is itself a conventionalized irrelevancy, distracting us from, rather than pointing us to, life.

Conclusion

In exploring the deictic dimensions of self, time, and place, I hope I have made clear not only how useful these distinctions are, but also how this approach might begin to reveal the enormous richness and complexity of these poems. Further permutations await concentrated study. For example, if we hold constant the here dimension, and vary the now and then factors, we discover the genre of the huaigu 壞 古, in which the poem shifts from past to present on a specific historical site. Du Fu's *Chun wang* 春望 would be a perfect case of a here: now and then poem, for it achieves its effects precisely by contrasting the same places in ancient times and in the present. We can also identify poems that keep the now constant, and contrast the here and there. These are familiar as xiangsi, or homesick poems, or poems of longing: Du Fu's poems about his wife and of Li Bai fall naturally in this category. Then there are historical reconstructions, such as Su Dongpo's *Chibi fu* 赤壁賦, which privilege a place in the past, a there if you like, and contrast its character then and now. And lamentations for the past, of the decline of empire and of past glories are easily found in that genre known as *diaogu shi* 吊古詩.

I should like to end by looking at two very different texts: the first a vernacular folk poem; the second, a literary reminiscence in classic prose. They are worth our attention precisely because they complicate our notions of deixis. In these poems, our search for markers of self, time, and place cannot be so straightforward. This is one way of proving the usefulness of any theory, not by showing where the theory succeeds, but much more important, but by analyzing those instances where the theory fails, where its explanatory power is inadequate.

> Fragrance is what fragrance does,
> A charming face dare not presume;
> Heaven does not thwart one's desires,
> Which is why you should let me see you.

芳是香所為
冶容不敢當
天不奪人願
故使儂見郎

A charmingly modest poem, about a young lady who quails at first when confronted with a seductive swain, yet responds bravely, despite the instinctive 不敢當 "dare not presume", to take a full-face view of the seducer, this time, with the implicit sanction of heaven: 天不奪人願 / 故使儂見郎 "Heaven does not thwart our desires, / Which is why you should let me see you." Although this *ziye* 子野 ditty clearly posits the persona of a young girl: *lang* 郎 as the second-person denotes a male suitor. Yet the same poem can be read without significant distortion, if the *nong* 儂 were read in the Shanghai dialect, where it would mean "you" or in the Zhejiang dialect, where it is a third-person reference. "Heaven does not thwart our desires," the Shanghai version may be taken to mean, "Which is why you should take a good look at him!" "Heaven does not thwart our desires," the Zhejiang reader might take it, "Which is why she should take a good look at him." I am by no means proposing these alternate versions as the "correct" reading of this ancient poem: clearly, they are not. Yet, what fascinates me is the ability of the poem, if needed, to accommodate all three readings, with *nong* understood alternately as first-, second-, and third-person deictic indicators of persona.

What this poem suggests is that deictic indicators are not always as determinate as we might think them to be, nor are they always crucial to the meaning. We must take care to distinguish instances in which deictic markers are not so much undeclared (only implied) from deictic markers which are definitive but simply not specified.

The literary masterpiece I've chosen is Wang Xizhi's 蘭亭序 ("Orchid Pavilion"). This evocation of a gathering in the year 353, perhaps the most memorialized party in Chinese history, is clearly situated in chronological time. We know the people who were present, what they did, how they felt. Yet, the poem describes not the historical event, but the poet's own philosophical vista.

蘭亭

王羲之

仰視碧天際
俯瞰綠水濱
寥閴無涯觀
寓目理自陳
大矣造化工
萬殊莫不均
群籟雖參差
適我無非新

Looking up at the edge of the azure sky,
Looking down at the shore of the green waters,
Desolate silence; no horizon in sight,
Before [my] eye, the pattern reveals itself
How vast, the work of creation!
A multitude of differences, yet none out of place,
A host of sounds, even if irregular,
All suit me, and there's nothing that's not new.

The third line is revealing: 寥閴無涯觀[("Desolate silence; no horizon in sight,") can hardly be describing the convivial proceedings. The last four lines abstracts from the reality of even the brilliant occasion memorialized, and ascends into cosmological speculation: 大矣造化工 ("How vast! The work of creation!") / 萬殊莫不均 ("A multitude of differences, yet none out of place") / 群籟雖參差 / 適我無非新 ("A host of sounds, even if irregular / [All] suit me, and there's nothing that's not new").

In these lines, we are beyond differentiating between markers of persona, time, and place. There is a self-reference in the last line, to be sure, but there is nothing autobiographical, anecdotal, or self-conscious about this allusion to the first person, for it is genericized, and it becomes rhetorically powerful. The reader becomes the "I" / 我 of the poem; the reader assumes the role of one for whom "there's nothing that's not new." The reader becomes the poet in the act of reading the poem. And what might have started as an errant observation by one individual becomes an insight that anyone can share.

Time, either chronological or psychological, is not a factor in this poem, for it exists in the perspective of eternity, with infinite variety, and its endlessly fresh creativity. We would be amiss to conjugate these lines in terms of past, present, or future, for the distinctions do not apply here. Nor is place an issue for there is no particularized location: the blue horizon of the sky (碧 天 際), the green of the waters (綠 水 濱), gazing at a sparse, desolate, horizonless landscape (寥 闊 無 涯 觀), and staring intently on the principle of things as they unfold (寓 目 理 自 陳) — these acts of wisdom can be accomplished anywhere.

As a result of this poem, we see life afresh, and the phenomena we encounter wherever we are, which the poet has "defamiliarized" for us, becomes the source of fresh wonder.

Theories

8. Déjà lu:
Recurrence, Allusion, and Plagiarism in Translation

Translations presuppose a previously read text. However, many translations, consciously or subconsciously, are influenced by the reading of previous published translations. These instances of *déjà lu* may be divided into three categories: (1) recurrence, where one translation builds on, or incorporates, other versions; (2) allusion, where one translation complements another translation (or other translations); and (3) plagiarism, where one translation pretends to be a different and original translation. I offer as an example of the first, recurrence, the King James Version of the Bible; as examples of the second, allusion, Waley's translations and Pound's versions of the Shijing, the Chinese classic of songs, as well as the Waley and the Seidensticker versions of *The Tale of Genji*; and as an example of the third, plagiarism, Stephen Mitchell's compositely borrowed renderings of the *Tao Te Ching*. In the process of analysing these instances of *déjà lu*, I hope to illuminate the differences between (1) intertextuality, which is creative license; (2) influence, which is creative opposition and apposition; and (3) imposture, which is uncreative theft.

The King James Version (KJV) of the Bible has remained a masterpiece for more than three centuries, though it may surprise modern readers that it encountered "plenty of criticism" (Greenslade, 168), a fate that greeted many subsequent translations as well. The modern admiration for the KJV has created the virtually universal myth that it was instantly accepted. Actually, it was two generations before the KJV assumed its place as the supreme English translation of the Bible. The Geneva Bible, and not the King James Version (or Authorized Version), was the most popular version for at least a generation after the appearance of the KJV — indeed, Lancelot Andrewes, one of the most prominent revisers on the KJV "commonly used the Geneva Bible for his sermons, as did other bishops" (Greenslade, 168). Nor did the KJV discourage other versions from appearing. However, no translation, not even the KJV, challenged the Geneva Bible (Greenslade, 188). And, as for the plausible but erroneous claim that the KJV version was decisive on Milton,[1] that is belied by the fact that Milton read from the original Biblical texts on a daily basis. According to his biographer, William Riley Parker, "He was especially fond of hearing the Old Testament in the original Hebrew at the beginning of the day" (Parker, I:577); "And every Sunday, Milton read to [John and Edward Phillips] a chapter of the Greek New Testament, explicating it with learning and with piety" (Parker, I: 209); "From his youth onwards Milton had constantly studied the Old and New Testaments in their original tongues, and his memory was excellent" (Parker, I: 481).

---

[1]   For example, about the KJV, Douglas Robinson writes: "Every great poet in the English language beginning with Milton has tapped its poetic power" (224)

While it is true that Milton owned a copy of the KJV, he "also owned a Hebrew Bible. . . and a Geneva Bible" (Parker, II:704, fn. 32).

Indeed, the King James Version was not exactly an original composition at all, but merely the product of an editing enterprise by a complex arrangement that involved "certain learned men, to the number of four and fifty" (Greenslade, 164). The group reviewed existing versions, and adopted whichever rendering they found most suitable. (I avoid the word "faithful" in this context, because it can be shown that some choices were clearly not guided by fidelity to the original.) The KJV is, among other things, a compendium of the versions that the KJV committee had read, and it reflects the taste of the committee as editors as much as it displays the originality of the committee as translators. Indeed, many translations of the Bible, as one nineteenth-century commentator put it, "were, in fact, not so much new versions as revisions of one another; and this, so true of them, is emphatically true of that of King James; though, as to qualities not denied it, so often and strangely admired, like . . . the bird in the fable, for borrowed plumage, and praised, as if an independent translation, for virtues not its own" (Dabney, 1)

The opening of the Gospel of St. John (Chapter 1, Verses 1-5) offers a representative example of the provenance of the KJV:

> In the begynnynge was that worde, and that worde was with god: and god was thatt worde. The same was in the begynnynge wyth god. All thynges were made by it, and with out it, was made noo thinge: that made was. In it was lyfe. And lyfe was the light of men. And the light shyneth in darcknes, and darcknes comprehended it not. (Dabney)

In the King James Version, discounting variations in orthography and spelling, we find something almost identical:

> In the beginning was the Word, and the Word was with God, and the Word was God. The same was in the beginning with God. All things were made by him; and without him was not any thing made that was made. In him was life; and the life was the light of men. And the light shineth in darkness; and the darkness comprehended it not. (The Holy Bible).

There is a helpful clarification of the syntax in the third verse: "All thynges were made by it, and with out it was made noo thing: that made was" emerges, in the KJV, as "All things were made by him, and without him was not any thing made that was made." A slight awkwardness, however, remains in the last segment: " . . . was not any thing made that was made."

The pre-existence of previous translations, far from discouraging subsequent efforts, often inspires them. Arthur Waley's three-volume version of *The Tale of Genji*, published in 1925-1933, held sway for nearly half a century, unchallenged for its unforgettable evocation of a bygone era. His version was leisurely, ornate, and, befitting the taste of the time, almost Jamesian — a combination of Lampedusa's *The Leopard* and Proust's *A la recherche de temps perdu* set in Heian Japan. The opening of Waley's version reads as follows:

> At the court of an Emperor (he lived it matters not when) there was among the many gentlewomen of the Wardrobe & Chamber one, who though she was not of very high rank was favoured far beyond all the rest; so that the great ladies of the Palace, each of whom had secretly hoped that she herself would be chosen, looked with scorn and hatred upon the upstart who had dispelled their dreams. Still less were her former companions, the minor ladies of the Wardrobe, content to see her raised so far above them. Thus her position at Court, preponderant though it was, exposed her to constant jealousy and ill will; and soon, worn out with petty vexations, she fell into a decline, growing very melancholy and retiring frequently to her home. (7)

The traits of this style are familiar: an expository tone, a suggestive manner, an Olympian point of view. There is a modesty in the tact and the locution that bespeaks elegance and discretion. To enter this world is to participate immediately in an atmosphere of nuance and implication, of inference and indirection. Certainly, anyone familiar with the Heian world would find this style congenial to the Jamesian "incidents" that comprise the plot of *The Tale of Genji*, which seem to involve not so much actual events as turns of mind and changes of heart.[2] For readers at the middle of the twentieth century, there is even a sense of the appropriately archaic in Waley's somewhat Edwardian English, redolent of the end of empire, a post-Victorian sensibility that seems to match Murasaki's prose elegy a thousand years earlier for a vanishing Heian court culture.

But elegance and refinement have their cultural faces. There are different kinds of elegance and different premises undergirding notions of elegance in different contexts. To take examples from but one country, we can consider different paradigms of elegance in English literature. The height of elegance in the Elizabethan period and the subsequent seventeenth century — with Shakespeare in poetry and Sir Thomas Browne in prose as exemplars — tended to be loquacious and oratorical: "Time which antiquates antiquities," Sir Thomas Browne wrote, relishing the sound of the syllables more than the semantics of his words; "a consummation devoutly to be wished" is Shakespeare's version of circumlocution and inversion as oratorical flourish. By contrast, the wit and elegance of the neo-classic writers, the poetry of Pope and Dryden and the prose of Addison and Steele, pursued a leaner aesthetic of elegance, epitomized by Pope in his aphoristic, and paradigmatic quip: "Brevity is the soul of wit." The combination of spareness and balance constituted a

---

[2]   English readers have the benefit of Ivan Morris's *The World of the Shining Prince* in getting a corroborative glimpse of this world.

standard of elegance that was found perhaps a generation earlier in France, in the plays of Jean Racine.

What makes *The Tale of Genji* rare if not unique is that it is a vernacular fiction about nobility. Its discourse, unlike the crude and often gruffly masculine accents of most vernaculars, is refined and feminine, even if it isn't formal. It is stylized without being artificial, ceremonious without being stiff. The aesthetic of the Heian period tended toward what Morris characterizes as the "unmanly": "the picture of the average Heian aristocrat . . . ." he writes, "is likely to strike many Western readers as effeminate" (156), and the challenge of the translator of the *Genji* for English readers of the last quarter of the 20th century was to provide a glimpse of this world in the sinewy and succinct prose that was epitomized in mid-century by Hemingway. The challenge to a modern translator is to capture the character of the *Genji*, uncommon in patrician literature, as a vernacular narrative that idealizes its characters. In this sense, it bears an affinity with the genre of romance, traditionally respectable, but which has fallen on hard times in the modern era.[3]

What Seidensticker attempted in his 1976 version was a succinct and sinewy style, one with a Gary Cooper sense of the laconic, but capable of Jamesian nuance. His version is easily less than half as long as Waley's, yet it is not abridged. The subtlety of the unstated, the implied, and the omitted — this is the effect Seidensticker pursued. The indirection is not, as is the case with Waley, circumlocution; Seidensticker's indirection, on the other hand, is terse implicitness. What is "too deep for words" remains unelaborated, unanalyzed. Seidensticker's version of the *Genji* is like the novels of Henry James without the interior monologues: it is briefer by far, but no less evocative. The subtlety that Seidensticker pursues is slightly Hemingway-esque. Unlike Waley (and Henry James), its nuances and convolutions are left to the reader's imagination. Seidensticker renders the opening of the novel as follows:

> In a certain reign there was a lady not of the first rank whom the emperor loved more than any of the others. The grand ladies with high ambitions thought her a presumptuous upstart, and lesser ladies were still more resentful. Everything she did offended someone. Probably aware of what was happening, she fell seriously ill and came to spend more time at home than at court. (3)

Seidensticker's rendering of the opening passage in the *Genji* is not merely a corrective to Waley,[4] not just a replacement of a faulty version, but a complement to it. At half the length (67 vs. 131 words), it lacks the detail (the distinction, for example, between the "great ladies" and the

---

[3] At the Nobel symposium, where an early version of this chapter was first offered, Margaret Mitsutani reported that Royall Tyler of Australian National University is working on a new translation; cf. "The Sea Girl and the Shepherdess" in *Currents in Japanese Literature: Translations and Transformations*, ed., Amy Bladeck Henrich (New York: Columbia University Press, 1997), pp. 205-222.

[4] There *are* instances in which Seidensticker corrects Waley's mistakes, but that is not our concern here.

"minor ladies", between the Wardrobe and the Chamber) , but there is
nothing lost in subtlety or panache.   The blunt summariness of
"Everything she did offended someone" has an unerring aptness that can be
found nowhere in the Waley.   There is an immediate sympathy for
Kiritsubo, a sense of exasperation on her behalf, that can only be guessed
at in Waley's elaborate circumlocutions.   The social historian will
appreciate the explicit identification of classes Waley's Wardrobe,
Chamber, and Court in the Waley, but the lay reader might appreciate the
swifter identification of generic envy that one finds in Seidensticker.

Let us to turn to an oft-cited passage in the *Genji* for a further
illustration.   That's the passage in which Genji comments on the
monogatari   — whether one translates that term as "narrative",
"romance", "novel", or "fiction".   The expressive need to record one's
experience is what Genji sees as the impulse behind *monogatari*.   In
Waley's version, it comes out like this:

> Genji continued: "So you see as a matter of fact I think far better of
> this art than I have led you to suppose. Even its practical value is
> immense. Without it what should we know of how people lived in
> the past, from the Age of the Gods down to the present day? For
> history-books such as the Chronicles of Japan show us only one
> small corner of life; whereas these diaries and romances which I see
> piled around you contain, I am sure, the most minute information
> about all sorts of people's private affairs . . . . " He smiled, and went
> on: "But I have a theory of my own about what the art of the novel
> is, and how it came into being. To begin with, it does not simply
> consist in the author's telling a story about the adventures of some
> other person. On the contrary, it happens because the storyteller's
> own experience of men and things, whether for good or ill — not
> only what he has passed through himself, but even events which he
> has only witnessed or been told of — has moved him to an emotion
> so passionate that he can no longer keep it shut up in his heart.
> Again and again something in his own life or in that around him will
> seem to the writer so important that he cannot bear to let it pass into
> oblivion. There must never come a time, he feels, when men do not
> know about it." (501).

There is a conversational ease about this passage, a leisurely,
contemplative pace that has nary a doubt about the reader's patience, or the
reader's fascination with what is being said. Though the parsing of the
sentence is immensely stylized, the writing is clear and limpid.

Now, we turn to Seidensticker:

> He laughed. "I have been rude and unfair to your romances,
> haven't I? They have set down and preserved happenings from the
> age of the gods to our own. The Chronicles of Japan and the rest are
> a mere fragment of the whole truth. It is your romances that fill in
> the details.
> "We are not told of things that happened to specific people

> exactly as they happened; but the beginning is when there are good things and bad things, things that happen in this life which one never tires of seeing and hearing about, things which one can not bear not to tell of and must pass on for all generations. . . ." (437)

The remarkable thing about Seidensticker's version is how little it loses, even though it has less than half the verbiage of the Waley (114 vs. 254 words).   What is missing is Genji's self-references, which are only implied; they seem, in any case, superfluous.   Yet, one cannot say that Waley's is overwritten: for its style and by the standards of elegance for its time, his version can hardly be faulted for excesses of rhetoric. Reading the Seidensticker immediately after the Waley, one can't help but sense that the Waley is somehow being heard in the background, that it infuses the Seidensticker with unstated reminiscences of an earlier evocation. To read them side by side is — surprisingly — to appreciate them both.

We are not dealing here with something as simple as influence — whether positive or negative — but of allusion. Seidensticker's version may be said to allude to the Waley; and Waley's, despite the reverse chronology, alludes proleptically to the Seidensticker. The strict "billiard-ball" theorist would insist that it is impossible for a work to allude to another work produced half a century later; but for the reader of both, and in the contemporaneity — the intertextuality — of the reading experience, chronology is immaterial.

As readers, we are the richer for having access to an ancient and obscure original[5] in two voices in English, and from two points of view.
A similar case can be made of the two versions of the ancient Chinese classic, the *Shijing*, which Waley titled, *The Book of Songs*, and which Pound referred to as *The Confucian Odes* or, more pedantically, *The Classic Anthology as Defined by Confucius*. Pound was certainly aware of the Waley, though he avoids, studiously, any mention of it in his translation.   The two versions are separated by almost a quarter of a century: Waley's version appeared in 1937, whereas Pound's was published in 1955. But where a case can be made that Seidensticker's version of the *Genji* profited from the scholarship on the text that developed after the earlier version, the same cannot be said about Pound, despite his conspicuous efforts to learn Chinese, and the intriguingly permissive consultation of the Korean-American Harvard scholar, Achilles Fang. Pound's versions are "liberties" taken with the original, or — more

---

[5]   The Heian text of the Genji is as remote to modern Japanese as it is us: indeed, they rely on translations into modern Japanese (Tanizaki's has been popular), including Waley's version in English.

exactly — liberties taken with Waley's rendering.[6]

In their translations of the 305 poems in the *Shijing*, there is a remarkable consistency in the *dis*similarities between Pound's version and Waley's. Mere chance might have produced at least a few translations where the original meaning was so determinative that two translators might have come up with similar versions — despite the vagaries of errant translation and idiosyncratic interpretations. Yet one is hard-pressed to find a single Shijing poem in which Pound's version could be confused with Waley's. It was as if Pound wrote "anti-Waley" versions of the Chinese classic.[7]

Here's one of Pound's more outrageous complements to Waley:

> Yaller bird, let my corn alone,
> Yaller bird, let my crawps alone,
> These folks here won't let me eat,
> I wanna go back whaar I can meet
> the folks I used to know at home,
>   I got a home an' I wanna' git goin'.
>
> Yalla' bird, let my trees alone,
> Let them berries stay whaar they'z growin',
> These folks here ain't got no sense,
> can't tell 'em nawthin' without offence,
> Yalla' bird, lemme, le'mme go home.
>   I gotta home an' I wanna' git goin'.
>
> Yalla' bird, you stay outa dem oaks,
> Yalla' bird, let them crawps alone,
> I just can't live with these here folks,
>   I gotta home and I want to git goin'
>   To whaar my dad's folks still is a-growin'.

(#187)

Where Waley tried to make his poems as remote, as "Chinese" as possible (his 1917 volume was titled *Chinese Poems*), Pound wants not merely to "Anglicize": he wants to "Americanize" the ancient folksong. His recreation is, of course, very dated now, and one suspects that even hillbillies in the U. S. A. no longer talk quite the way Pound has them talk, or as he imagined them talking in the fifties. But, awkward as the attempt may be, Pound's effort makes clear that his sympathies were to "naturalize" rather than to "barbarize" (to use James J. Y. Liu's

---

[6]   Eliot Weinberger quite correctly points out that Pound relied on Bernhard Karlgrens' *Glosses on the Book of Odes* as well as on Achilles Fang. And he reminds me that I offer no documentary evidence that Pound actually read Waley. Still, Waley's renderings were available to Pound for eighteen years, and it is not plausible that he did not consult them, especially since, as I argue, we do not find even one accidental resemblance between any of the two versions of the same 305 poems.

[7]   A clear instance of what Anna Balakian, a generation ago, identified as "negative influence."

terminology), that is, to make (to American readers) the strange and obscure original as familiar and as transparent as possible. The irony is that, through the rapid changes in modern American English, his recreation of a dialect that might have been contemporary forty years ago seems as remote as Waley's more circumspect version of sixty years ago. Waley's folk ballad seems the more accessible:

> O oriole, yellow bird,
> Do not settle on the corn,
> Do not peck at my millet.
> The people of this land
> Are not minded to nurture me.
> I must go back, go home
> To my own land and kin.
>
> O oriole, yellow bird,
> Do not settle on the mulberries,
> Do not peck my sorghum.
> With the people of this land
> One can make no covenant.
> I must go back, go home
> To where my brothers are.
>
> O oriole, yellow bird
> Do not settle on the oaks,
> Do not peck my wine-millet.
> With the people of this land
> One can come to no understanding.
> I must go back, go home
> To where my own men are.

> (Waley #103 [#187])

Elsewhere, I have characterized Waley's approach as more of a "contingent" translator, i.e., one who was trying to provide an aide to students of ancient Chinese poetry, whereas I saw Pound as attempting what I called "co-eval" translations.[8] The pre-existence of the Waley translations precluded Pound from composing what I have identified as "surrogate' translations, i. e., translations intended to replace the original for the target language reader, although Pound's would certainly have preferred his own version for a Chinese-less reader.[9] Still, his translations are doubly "co-eval": they are enhanced if read alongside the original as well as alongside the Waley version. Indeed, in many instances, Pound's version must be read co-evally, in conjunction with a second text, if one is to make any sense out of them, or else one is going to be scarcely aware that the originals were in Chinese, and in a language that's very ancient.

---

[8]   See my *The Transparent Eye: Translation, Chinese Literature, and Comparative Poetics*, chapter 8.

[9]   Waley's version is not a "virginal" translation either, because he was familiar with Legge's translations and commentary, and he had access to Bernhard Karlgren's literal expositions and his glosses.

The Waley and Pound versions of *Shijing* 23 provides an illuminating instance of the dynamics of *déjà lu* for both translator and the reader of translations.[10] Waley preserves the balladic eleven-line form, reflecting the folkloric nature of the original. The guileless repetitions of the ballad underlines the theme and tenor of the poem:

> In the wilds there is a dead doe;
> With white rushes we cover her.
> There was a lady longing for the spring;
> A fair knight seduced her.
>
> In the wood there is a clump of oaks,
> And in the wilds a dead deer
> With white rushes well bound;
> There was a lady fair as jade.
>
> "Heigh, not so hasty, not so rough;
> Heigh, do not touch my handkerchief.
> Take care, or the dog will bark" (60-61)

Waley characterizes the principal character as a "lady" (Legge had specified "a young lady") and the narrative involves a seduction in which the "lady" is the victim (Legge described the ballad as "A Virtuous Young Lady Resists the Attempts of a Seducer"). Pound's version is far more subtle, and more realistic:

> Lies a dead deer on younder [sic] plain
> whom white grass covers,
> A melancholy maid in spring
>
> > is luck
> > for
> > lovers.
>
> Where the scrub elm skirts the wood,
> be it not in white mat bound,
> as a jewel flawless found,
>
> > dead as doe is maidenhood.
>
> Hark!
> Unhand my girdle-knot,
>
> > stay, stay, stay
> > or the dog
> > may
> > bark. (10-11)

Pound converts the eleven lines of the ballad to sixteen more condensed distichs with half lines consisting of a word or two, in the manner of e. e.

---

[10] My earlier consideration of the translations of this poem, in *The Transparent Eye*, dealt with the generic differences between these two versions: here I wish to concentrate on their lineage, and on the connections between them.

cummings or Marianne Moore. His version converts the situation to a victimization not of the "lady", not even of the "melancholy maid", but of her virginity. Metaphorically and metonymically, "dead as doe is maidenhood", and we realize that the funeral lament of the first stanza — "Lies a dead deer . . . whom white grass covers" — is for virginity, for maidenhood, and not for the maid.

The symbolic embodiment of what is lost is epitomized by the last line of the second stanza: "There's a girl like jade". In the original, the metaphor is sensual and sensuous, jade referring to the white, flesh-colored smoothness of a maiden's skin. Waley translates this literally as "There was a lady fair as jade" but Pound transforms this into "as a jewel flawless found". Pound loses the sensuousness of the original, but Waley's literal version distracts the reader if it does not confuse him entirely — since, for most Westerners the association of jade is green, and not white. Pound finesses this semantic problem metonymically by characterizing the virginity of the maid, her maidenhood, as perfect and "flawless".[11] The "flawlessness" is precisely what is violated in the act of love. But in Pound, what is clear (as it is not in the Waley or the Legge) is that the maid is complicitous in the loss of her own maidenhood. The last stanza, encompassing both entreaty and warning, is not resistance (as Legge would have it) so much as circumspection.

Pound has clearly benefitted from a reading of his predecessors: his choices are refinements, not in accuracy, but in poetic imagery and dramatic rhetoric. He avoids both Legge's Puritanism and Waley's literalism in fashioning a lyric of lost innocence that is unforgettable. His versions complement earlier versions by their attempts to be — correctively — more poetical.

To the instances of creative licence we examined in the King James Version, and the examples of creative opposition and apposition that we found in the Seidensticker version of the Genji and the Pound version of the *Shijing*, we now come to examine a case of uncreative theft: Stephen Mitchell's popular version of the Dao De Jing (Tao Te Ching).

Mitchell's contribution was published in 1988, with much fanfare. Having broken through as a best-selling author with his versions of Rilke and his rendering of the Book of Job, Mitchell's proposal to translate the Dao De Jing — whose translations in English number in the hundreds — attracted an offer of $130,000 from Harper & Row, and even merited press coverage in the *New York Times* (February 16, 1988). Mitchell's authority derives not from his knowledge of Chinese or of the text (according to the *New York Times*, "Mr. Mitchell does not read or speak Chinese"), but presumably from three facts: his marriage to a Chinese-American wife, his study of Zen Buddhism, extending for some 14 years, and his having meditated "on the book for many years, and in a sense living it for many years." "That's what allowed me." Mitchell is reported to have said, "to translate it in two months" (*New York Times*). Despite his ignorance of Chinese, "He said he worked with a text that contained every Chinese

---

[11]   Legge seemed to sense this problem as well, since he genericizes "jade" into "gem".

character, as well as their English equivalents." Curious expenditure of meditative energy, to pore over the Chinese characters that one admits one cannot read.

With this non-linguistic access to the wisdom of an ancient text, one might have expected something truly fresh. Claiming to be "A New English Translation," Mitchell's version has, alas, something very stale about it. One can even document that staleness in part. Here are some excerpts with his versions compared with a previously published version (a more extensive selection is included in the Appendix):

> Return is the movement of the Tao.
> Yielding is the way of the Tao.
> All things are born of being.
> Being is born of non-being.

> (#40, Mitchell)

> Returning is the direction of the Tao.
> Yielding is the way of the Tao.
> The ten thousand things are born of Being
> and Being is born of Nonbeing.

> (#40, McCarroll)

*   *   *

> For governing a country well
> there is nothing better than moderation.

> (#59, Mitchell)

> For governing others and serving heaven
> there is nothing better than moderation

> . (#59, McCarroll)

*   *   *

> My teachings are easy to understand
> and easy to put into practice.

> (#70, Mitchell)

> My words are easy to understand
> and easy to put into practice.

> (#70, McCarroll)

*   *   *

> The Tao never does anything,
> Yet through it all things are done.

> (#37, Mitchell)

> Tao never does anything,
> And everything gets done.

(#37, Maurer)

*   *   *

> Without looking out your window,
> you can see the essence of the Tao

(#47, Mitchell)

> Without looking out of the window
> You can see heaven's way.

(#47, Maurer)

One is reminded of Samuel Johnson's assessment of a second-rate work: "Your manuscript is both good and original," he told a would-be writer, "but the part that is good is not original, and the part that is original is not good." Not having to wrestle with the intractibilities of the original text nor being confronted with problems of translating Chinese into English, it is no wonder that Mitchell was able to accomplish his "new translation" in two months.

The similarities between Mitchell's translation and other versions can scarcely be coincidental, given their frequency. (An examination of the numerous translations of *Tao Te Ching* would indicate very few instances where two translations would resemble each other as closely as the excerpts included here.) It may be argued that the appropriations that Mitchell makes of other versions differs in no way from the appropriations made by the "four and fifty" learned men who prepared the King James Version. The rephrasings, the verbatim borrowings, the only slightly different parsings, are, indeed, comparable. There are, however, three crucial differences between Mitchell's enterprise and that of the KJV revisers: one involves literary value, another involves remuneration and profit, and a third involves, ironically, authorization. Whatever the provenance of the KJV translation, there is no disputing the literary judgment of the revisers: their choices were unerring, and the text they produced is of undoubted literary value. As for remuneration and profit, there is no record that, in responding to the commission of King James, the KJV revisers received any remuneration; they were clerics and scholars supported by their respective academies and parishes.[12] Ultimately, the commission to the KJV revisers came from the King himself (even if the translation itself, was, despite its designation as "The Authorized Version", never actually

---

[12] Emanuela Tandello reminds me that the attitudes toward plagiarism were, of course, different: the notion of copyright and of intellectual property based on Romantic notions of originality is a post-Romantic development.

authorized, neither by any secular or ecclesiastical body).[13]

The KJV revisers were not exploiting previous work, but were bent on improving previous translations, creating "out of many good ones, one principal good one" (Greenslade, 167): they were empowered by virtue of their expertise as scholars and divines, as well as by the sanction of the king, and not by their previous success in attracting readers. (Mitchell, on the other hand, expressly denies being a scholar; he is not an ecclesiastical authority or Taoist cleric — although he does offer the less than relevant credential of being a Zen enthusiast.)

With the phenomenon of *déjà lu*, we must ask whether the sense of having "already read" something resides with the translator (as in the case of recurrence and of allusion) or the reader (as in the case of plagiarism). The first involves intertextuality, which is the salient presence of other texts; the second involves influence, which is the salient effect of another author or translator; and the third involves imposture, which is the salient borrowing of someone else's creativity. I will restrict myself merely to the literary aspects of intertextuality, influence, and imposture. In order to explore these questions, I choose to examine a fascinating controversy that puts into relief differences between literary value and originality. The controversy was enshrined in an exchange of letters in the *Times Literary Supplement* centered on the eminent Scottish poet, Hugh MacDiarmid (a. k. a. Christopher Grieve). This curious episode counterposes two seemingly contradictory conclusions: (1) that there is a verbatim correspondence between a published work by Hugh MacDiarmid and a previously published work by someone else; and (2) that there was no question of plagiarism, or literary theft. There is also the generic question of whether prose translated into verse constitutes the creation of an entirely different work, the verbatim correspondence between the two specimens notwithstanding. The poem in question is titled "Perfect":

> I found a pigeon's skull on the machair,
> All the bones pure white and dry, and chalky,
> But perfect
> Without a crack or a flaw anywhere.
> At the back, rising out of the beak,
> Were twin domes like bubbles of thin bone,
> Almost transparent, where the brain had been
> That fixed the tilt of the wings.

What is undisputed is the fact that these words (except for the first line) were written by one Glyn Jones "as prose in a volume of short stories entitled 'The Blue Bed' and published by Cape in 1937" (*TLS*, 182) MacDiarmid's version was published in 1944. Jones wrote to note the correspondence between his work and MacDiarmid's, but his letter was not

---

[13] "Strictly speaking," Greenslade has written, "the Authorized Version was never authorized, nor were parish churches ordered to procure it" (168). It is, perhaps, not sufficiently appreciated that the KJV derived from a secular authority, who, by virtue of his position as king, following Henry VIII, possessed institutional authority over the "Church of England".

a hostile remonstrance. At the end of his letter, he wrote, pointedly: "I ought to add that I have no personal quarrel with Hugh MacDiarmid at all and that I have long been an admirer of his poetry." Nor was there any denial from Hugh MacDiarmid, who conceded the inadvertent borrowing of the lines: "I have made the necessary explanations and apologies to Mr. Glyn Jones and he has generously accepted these. The poem will of course not appear again over my name" (*TLS*, 183). Explaining the coincidence, MacDiarmid wrote: "I have used quotations from many books in some of my poems but have always been careful to attribute such quotations to their sources when I know these. . . . I automatically memorized it and subsequently thought it my own, or wrote it into one my notebooks with the same result." "Any plagiarism," MacDiarmid concluded, "was certainly unconscious."

This exchange provides an intriguing case of unconscious intertextuality, even if it is not a clear case of plagiarism. Indeed, several of the distinguished commentators side with MacDiarmid in warranting that this was not a case of plagiarism, despite the exact correspondence (except for the first line, and the fact that one is in prose and the other in verse) of the two texts.[14] As for copyright considerations, no one apparently made any claims on the matter. From the point of view of literature, however, not only does MacDiarmid not consider himself culpable, he positively insists on the appropriateness of his borrowings, invoking in his own defense both T. S. Eliot and Ezra Pound and insisting that "copyright is a legal matter and not a literary one. As Mr. T. S. Eliot said, 'Minor poets borrow, major poets steal'[15] and my own practice in much of my later work has been like that of Mr. Ezra Pound who, in one of his essays, says he takes his material from wherever he can find it and endeavours to transform the assemblage into an artistic unity, the test being that in the upshot the whole. . . is more than the sum of the parts" (*TLS*, 194). The implications of this are fairly clear: MacDiarmid considers himself a major, not a minor poet, and he sees his literary appropriation as stealing, not borrowing. In other words, he confesses to a felony even as he vaunts himself as a poet.

But we can return with profit to Eliot's original formulation, which reads as follows:

> Immature poets imitate; mature poets steal; bad poets deface what they take, and good poets make it into something better, or at least something different. The good poet welds his theft into a whole feeling which is unique, utterly different from that from which it was torn; the bad poet throws it into something which has no cohesion (Eliot, 155).

---

[14] Commenting at the Nobel symposium, Seamus Heaney pointed to the period in MacDiarmid's life when collecting bits and snatches from his reading was a fact of his creative life. In his Oxford Lecture (*The Redress of Poetry*, [London: Faber and Faber, 1995]), Heaney wrote, "he was born in Synthetic Scots in 1922 and reborn in English sometime round 1933" and it was in this period that "the plagiarist too readly gained an upper hand over the poet" (116, 117).

[15] MacDiarmid misremembers the quote, as will be clear from what follows.

An interesting aspect of the exchange on MacDiarmid's appropriation of Glyn Jones's prose passage into one of his own poems is the contention that, by seeing the same words as a poem, MacDiarmid transformed it. In this regard, MacDiarmid's poem acquires the status of a collage; he "framed" a found object, as it were, and made it his own.[16]

Another apposite example, which, curiously, also emerges out of the exchange on MacDiarmid's creative practices, would be Chinese calligraphy. It is a tradition of Chinese calligraphy to "quote" calligraphically a previous piece of calligraphy. This is often misconstrued as a copy of the original. In the case of apprentice work, copying is a form of technical training, but when a master calligrapher calligraphs the text of an earlier master (as Bada Shanren, in the late 17th century, recreates the calligraphy of Wang Xizhi of the early 4th century), it is matter not so much of copying as of re-creation. Curiously, the model of Chinese calligraphy supplied the metaphor for another instance of creative appropriation:

> When a Chinese calligrapher 'copies'
> The work of an old master it is not
> A forged facsimile but an interpretation
> As personal within stylistic limits
> As a Samuel or Landowska performance
> Of a Bach partita.

This pastiche, as well as others, found their way into the MacDiarmid corpus: its relevance to our discussion is not that it exemplifies the "borrowing" we are exploring, but that the very text borrowed in this instance addresses the issue of creative license.[17] Hugh Porteus, the original author of these lines, argued in favor of liberal expropriations of this kind in the interests of poetic creation, even at his own expense: "It is, surely, a valid extension of our own traditional poetic licence." He compares MacDiarmid to T. S. Eliot and insists, on behalf of both: "When a borrowing is enhanced, by a twist or a fresh context, surely plagiarism is justified?" He praises MacDiarmid's ability to "transmogrify" his sources, "even if [compared to T. S. Eliot] they are not always so frankly acknowledged or else so well hidden" (188).

From this perspective, perhaps it might be useful to return to the case of Stephen Mitchell's "translation" of the *Dao De Jing*. Is not his case commensurate with, if not equivalent to, the case of Hugh MacDiarmid? Leaving aside the legal issue (which, in MacDiarmid's case, was uncontested, even if the "victim" refused to claim damages), might Mitchell's version not be a case of laudable literary larceny? Such a claim

---

[16]   As one correspondent to the TLS, Edwin Morgan, wrote: "Can prose become poetry through typographical rearrangement? I rather think it can . . . ." (184). MacDiarmid's biographer, Kenneth Buthlay, refers to MacDiarmid's "life-long practice of designing mosaics with pieces taken from his reading" (184).

[17]   TLS, 187.

is certainly possible. But, by the same token, it would entail the recognition that Stephen Mitchell is, like MacDiarmid, a major poet, and the admission that what he did was to steal rather than "borrow" the lines from lesser-known authors.

We are now prepared, I think, to address more closely the question of plagiarism from the perspective of literature, which may differ from, even contrast with, the question of plagiarism in the eyes of the law. The problem has been insightfully explored, in a playful bit of Derridean deconstruction, by Douglas Robinson, in his book, *The Translator's Turn* — a book which, among other things, is a comprehensive semantic pun on translation as turning and twisting and changing directions. Robinson dispels the myth of transparent translation, where the translator is merely a window through which the original is perceived, with more or less clarity, more or less accuracy.[18] Better admit the phenomenologist's truth at the outset, Robinson would insist, that no one can possibly escape the subjectivity of perception, and therefore, it is impossible for any translator to be absolutely neutral, nor is it possible ever to be "faithful" to the original. In this regard, translation, like literary composition, must be an act of deliberate literary appropriation, where something quoted or alluded to is made one's very own. To use the implicit logic of Eliot's formulation of borrowing and stealing, the major poets re-possess the text as their own, whereas the minor poet leaves traces of its previous possessors.

From a literary point of view, the fault in Mitchell's translation of the *Dao De Jing* is not that he borrowed someone else's literary property, but rather that he failed to make it his own. The examples of MacDiarmid, Eliot, and Pound indicate that one's fault is not in appropriating someone else's work: in a sense, every author (not to mention every scholar) does that. Rather, the fault lies in failing to take creative control of what one has appropriated. The gentlest remonstrance on plagiarism I've ever encountered was made by a student of mine. When confronted by the presentation of another student who had clearly plagiarized her work, the first student, more by way of encouragement than criticism, said: "There's not enough *you* in your work." My version for the would-be plagiarist would be: "Take what you like, but do something with it." Make sure there's enough *you* in your version.

Doing something with what we take, in life as in literature, is the difference between something of value and something that is worthless.

---

[18]   The implicit paradigm of transparency underlies several familiar tropes on translation: when one speaks of translation as "seeing through a glass darkly" or "kissing a bride as through a veil" one is — consciously or unconsciously — adopting the image of translation as a window.

9. "I lose something in the original": Translation as "Enhancement"

The late incomparable James Thurber once met a fervent French admirer. "I am fortunate," said the admirer, "because I speak English well enough to appreciate — and to love — your stories. But," he went on, "I have also read them translated into French and, believe me, they are even better in French." Thurber, with his usual modesty, gave an understanding nod. "I know," he said, "I tend to lose something in the original"[1]

The preponderant majority of analyses of translation usually highlight the failures and the frustrations of translators in matching the literary and stylistic quality of the original. "Poetry," as Robert Frost has often been quoted as saying "is what gets lost in translation." It is axiomatic to believe that translations can never approach the original, much less exceed them. Yet, familiar as the misconception is, one wonders at the paradigm that assumes that the job of translation is to duplicate one work in another language. Indeed, given the uniqueness of outstanding works, it is a surprise that exact clones in another language would even be considered possible, much less normative. Underlying this "original as perfection" / "translation as imperfection" notion is an assumption, popular especially with the New Critics of half a century ago, that an original work has its own inviolable integrity and its uncontested inevitability. However, despite our admiration for outstanding works of literature, and our tendency to deify their authors and to enshrine their compositions, we should not forget that we are dealing not only with the intractabilities of language, but also with the genius and the versatility of language. Translation is literary creation of a special kind: its difficulties — unlike those involved in "writer's block" — are not those of the blank page, the horrific challenge to creation from the void, but those of a prompted challenge, to achieve the palpable objectives embodied in what the author has already achieved. In one sense, the literary creation involved in translation is both easier and more difficult than the literary creation of original composition. Translation does not afford the freedom of original composition, which makes it more confining; but that very restriction provides a focus, a point of concentration, that often prompts a more efficient imagination. In the first case, the objective is often obscure, and — tantalizingly — manifest only at the end; in the second case, the objective is all too annoyingly present, and declared at the beginning.

In this chapter, I want to examine those instances when a text has generated another text which is, "believe me, better" in another language. These are indeed the instances when the author, if confronted with a successful translation, might well say, along with Thurber, "I tend to lose

[1]   Moura Budberg, "On Translating from Russian" in *The World of Translation* (New York: Pen American Center), 1971, 1987.

something in the original."

I will start with: "Yea, though I walk through the valley of the shadow of death" — perhaps the best known and most beautiful line of Bible translation, the fourth verse of the 23rd Psalm, composed initially by William Tyndale, and adapted by the translators of the King James Version. When compared with the Hebrew original, the exact equivalent of which would be, "Even though I should walk in the midst of total darkness" (Dahood, p. 145), this line glows. The "shadow of death", as brilliant a conceit for the "total darkness" of the original may be, is, nevertheless, unwarranted lexically, for the Hebrew does not mention either literal or metaphorical death. The beauty of the rest of the Psalm remains as much in the original as in the English translation, but in this one detail, and in this one line, something definitely "gets lost in the original".

Another instance of a text being improved in translation would be Baudelaire's version of the poetry of Edgar Allen Poe.

The first stanza of Poe's "The Raven" sets the tone for the poem. It would be cruel and unusual punishment to inflict the poem on the reader in its entirety. The doubled rhymes, the portentous tone, the archness of the diction — the ominous features which so distinguish Poe's stories and fill them with dark foreboding become ponderous and ludicrous in its poetic rendering. We leave aside the "scientific" explanation behind the structure of this poem, meticulously explored in Poe's famous "The Philosophy of Composition."[2] Whatever principles it may or may not illustrate, this is by any account a not very successful poem. That it continues for another seventeen stanzas makes it all the more insufferable. By at least midway through the poem, the rhymes "Lenore / more / Nevermore" begin to pall, and the English reader may be forgiven if he abandons an interesting but tedious artifact of literary history.

Baudelaire, in an interesting claim of anti-chronological imitation, suggested that Poe had proleptically copied from him: "The first time I opened one of his books, I saw with terror and delight not only subjects that I had dreamt of, but sentences that I had written and that he had imitated twenty years before."[3] This curious bit of Baudelairean ontology, which places the imitation before the original, and sees the translation as authentic, and the original as imitation, is in some ways vindicated by his version — or vision — of the same poem.

Let's take a look at the first verse.

> Once upon a midnight dreary, while I pondered, weak and weary,
> Over many a quaint and curious volume of forgotten lore —
> While I nodded, nearly napping, suddenly there came a tapping,
> As of some one gently rapping, rapping at my chamber door.

---

[2] Paul Valéry didn't much like the poem and cared even less for the commentary on its composition: "'The Raven'" he confessed, was not greatly to his liking, while the narrative of its genesis was unworthy of Poe" (Lawler, 106).

[3] Baudelaire to Théophile Thoré, *Correspondance générale* (4:277);quoted by Lawler(97).

> "'Tis some visitor,' I muttered, 'tapping at my chamber door —
> Only this and nothing more.'

We can easily sympathize with Daniel Hoffman's comment that "one of the chief powers exercised upon me by the poems of Edgarpoe [sic] is the power to make me wince" (p. 75). And the *explication de texte* that Poe provides in "The Principles of Composition" scarcely enhances our appreciation of the poem. T. S. Eliot's judgment is hard to dismiss:

> It is difficult for us to read that essay without reflecting, that if Poe plotted out his poem with such calculation, he might have taken a little more pains over it: the result hardly does credit to the method.

Both Baudelaire and Mallarmé provided translations of "The Raven" in French, both in blessedly fluent prose. There is not much to choose between them,[4] so we'll focus on Baudelaire's:

> "une fois, sur le minuit lugubre, pendant que je méditais, faible et fatigué, sur maint précieux et curieux volume d'une doctrine oubliée, pendant que je donnais de la tête, presque assoupi, soudain il se fit un tapotement, comme de quelqu'un frappant doucement, frappant à la porte de ma chambre. "C'est quelque visiteur, — murmurai-je, — qui frappe à la porte de ma chambre; ce n'est que cela, et rien de plus." (p. 115)

The first impression on reading this prose translation is the unerring sense that this would have been an excellent opening to one of Poe's eerie, haunting narratives. The opening reminds one of the stock opening of the line of the generic opening of melodrama (enshrined in the annual Bulwer-Lytton awards): "It was a dark and stormy night." We are properly in the realm of narrative rather than poetry: even as a ballad, "The Raven" seems to be uncomfortable. It does not exploit the generic strengths of the ballad form, its refrain is more annoying than haunting, its development is more chronological than emotional, its diction is more scholarly than vernacular, and its metrics more expository than vocative. Baudelaire, the poet, produces a translation that — tellingly — captures Poe the superior storyteller rather than Poe the inferior poet. "The Raven", T. S. Eliot has written, "is . . . far from being Poe's best poem"; in commenting on Poe's achievement as a poet in general, Eliot refers to "the effect of an incantation which, because of its very crudity, stirs the feelings at a deep and almost primitive level" (p. 333, 332). But there is no doubt in Eliot's mind that Baudlaire's version is a decided improvement: " . . . it is true

---

[4]   Mallarmé's version (pp.190-193) differs only marginally from Baudelaire's, the most glaring difference is that he omits the line, "C'est quelque visiteur, — murmurai-je, — qui frappe à la porte de ma chambre.. " towards the end. The other departures are these (B/M):   pendant que je méditais / tandis que je m'appesantissais; précieux et curieux / curieux et bizarre; d'une doctrine oubliée / de savoir oublié; pendant que je donnais de la tête, presque assoupi / tandis que je dodelinais la tête, somnolant presque; un tapotement / un heurt.

that in translating Poe's prose into French, Baudelaire effected a striking improvement: he transformed what is often a slipshod and a shoddy English prose into admirable French" (p. 336). Even if one maintains,[5] that the oratorical and declamatory tradition exemplified by "The Raven" (as well as Whitman's "Captain, My Captain") is not much in favor in American poetry, one might observe that Baudelaire's version is not lacking in oratorical and declamatory force.

It might be argued that almost any translation of Poe's "The Raven" would be an improvement, but that certainly cannot be said of the plays of Shakespeare, yet even here, we can cite a famous instance of "something that gets lost in the original." I refer to the translations that were begun by August Wilhelm Schlegel, and continued by Ludwig Tieck and his daughter, Dorothea, with the collaboration of Graf Baudissin. One scholar has written: " . . . it has never ceased to gratify its admirers and to substantiate claims that thanks to Schlegel/Tieck the 'German Shakespeare' is an improvement upon Shakespeare himself, a conviction that was to become a nationalistic topos . . . ." (Habicht, 47).

As an illustration of this seemingly preposterous claim, many excerpts can be cited, but the following passage from *Hamlet*, Act III, Scene i, will have to suffice.

> And thus the native hue of resolution
> Is sicklied o'er with the pale cast of thought (III.I.84-85)

is rendered in German as:

> Der angebornen Farbe der Entschliessung
> Wird des Gedankens Blässe angekränkelt.

The multisyllabic German may appear to an English reader to reflect more aptly Hamlet's indecisive mood than Shakespeare's more monosyllabic, definitive, abrupt and — one might almost say — decisive locution, especially in the second line. The German seems to embody the wavering shifts of thought, whereas Shakespeare describes it with counter-expressive exactitude. The last line is particularly interesting because it alternates an open "a" in "Gedanken" and "angekränkelt" with a closed "ä" — the umlauted "a" — in "Blässe" and "angekränkelt".[6]

By contrast, Shakespeare alternates the open and close a-sound only once in "pale cast".

I am not unmindful of the difficulty of what I am attempting here, of arguing the literary merits of a German version of a beloved line from an English classic, and doing it, moreover, in English. However persuasive my argument may or may not be, normative linguistics cannot dispute at least one respect in which the German is superior to Shakespeare, and that

---

[5]   As both Seamus Heaney and Emanuela Tandello did at the Nobel symposium.

[6]   One could also hear a near equivalent to the "ä" sound in the *ge* in "an*ge*kränkelt".

is, its accessibility to modern readers. Shakespeare has an arcaneness — in such a locution as "Sicklied o'er" — that is missing in the German, which is easily comprehensible to any contemporary speaker of German.[7]

The early nineteenth century reader of German, in all probability, found the Schlegel-Tieck rendering of Shakespeare more accessible than the English reader of the same period would find Shakespeare's Elizabethan and Jacobean texts.[8]

Another instance of "translation as enhancement" would be the translations of Western texts that Lin Shu 林 舒 (1852-1924) produced of such writers as Alexandre Dumas, fils, Harriet Beecher Stowe, Aesop, H. Rider Haggard, Charles and Mary Lamb, Sir Walter Scott, Daniel Defoe (2 works), Jonathan Swift, Washington Irving (3 works) , A. Conan Doyle, Charles Dickens (5 works). His method of translation was time-honored, dating back to at least the seventh century, when the celebrated Hsuan-tsang (Xuanzang 玄 奘) brought back thousands of Buddhist scriptures from India, and organized translation teams to prepare the Buddhist canon in Chinese. There is no great mystery as to how Lin Shu's translations were done. Lin knew no foreign languages; he worked in every case with an assistant or collaborator who was familiar with the original language and who orally rendered the text into spoken vernacular for him. Upon hearing the oral version, he put what he heard into his own words on paper. He did so with a remarkable facility: it was said that as soon as his collaborator stopped speaking, his pen stopped as well, having already written down all that was said (Compton, p. 94). His published work exceeds 20 million Chinese characters; he estimated that "he turned out between 1500 to 2000 characters per hour in translation, 5000 to 6000 characters in a normal four-hour day" (Compton, p. 95). The remarkable irony is that, in introducing Western works to the Chinese, and contributing thereby to the modernization, or at least the westernization, of China, Lin Shu was an arch-conservative, who wrote in the most traditional form of classical literary Chinese. The presentation of fiction, a notably vernacular form of literature, in a classical idiom, particularly one that tends to be condensed and elliptical where fiction is expansive and digressive, may be viewed as an anomaly, perhaps even as an infidelity, but it is generally recognized as the primary factor behind the huge success in China of Lin Shu's versions.

It would be easy to focus on Lin Shu's translations of lesser writers (many of whom are entirely unknown today) to show that he made silk's purses out of sow's ears, but that would scarcely constitute a challenge.

---

[7] The contemporaneity of the Schlegel-Tieck version, almost two hundred years after their composition may be attested by the fact that "Of the almost three hundred Shakespearean plays performed on Austrian, Swiss, and West German stages from 1987-1983, nearly seventy-five — that is, roughly speaking, one quarter — still follow the classical Schegel-Tieck version" (Wenzel, p. 318).

[8] Inga-Stina Ewbank quoted George Eliot at the Nobel Symposium: "sometimes the German is as good as the English — the same music played on another but as good an instrument" (*The Leader*, 7, 20 October 1855, 1014-1015); cf. "Shakespeare Translation as Cultural Exchange" *Shakespeare Survey* 1995, 1-7..

What is more interesting is to suggest that Lin Shu improved on the work of undoubted masters, like Charles Dickens. Indeed, no less a scholar and translator as Arthur Waley has written of Lin's translations of Dickens:

> . . . I have compared a number of passages with the original. To put Dickens into classical Chinese would on the face of it seem to be a grotesque undertaking. But the results are not grotesque. Dickens inevitably becomes a different and to my mind a better writer. All of the overelaboration, the overstatement and uncurbed garrulity disappear. The humor is there, but is transmitted by a precise, economical style; every point that Dickens spoils by uncontrolled exuberance, Lin Shu makes quietly and efficiently (p. 111).

There are some who have objected to these "improvements",[9] but most commentators tend to agree with Waley. Some scholars have praised these efforts, and anticipated the objections by regarding them as literary adaptations rather than as strict translations:

> . . . the alterations and omissions often had the effect of improving the text for Chinese readers, who were able to feel that they were reading an elegant classical tale which recounted the strange but interesting lives of the people of the West. In many cases Lin's versions of Western literary works may be considered imaginative adaptations rather than closely worked translations (p. 385).

Cheng Chen-to 鄭 振 鐸 has testified that:

> If one reads the original in one sitting, and then reads the translation, the feeling of the author is retained without the slightest change; sometimes even the humor, which is most difficult to achieve, is nevertheless captured in Lin's translations. Sometimes even clever phrasings are maintained in his translations (p. 114). [10]

This would seem to belie the need for the exculpation that would characterize Lin Shu's work an "imaginative adaptation" rather than a "strict translation". Certainly, if the humor and the wordplay are preserved intact, one can hardly claim that the "spirit and style of the original" has not been faithfully served.

We might sample an instance of literary enhancement. Thanks to Qian Zhongshu 錢 仲 書, no mean wordsmith himself, we can provide not only the original translation in Chinese but also an English equivalent — a retro-translation, if you will — so that the reader innocent of Chinese can compare an approximation in English of Lin Shu's literary version with Dickens's original text, which is an excerpt from Chapter 17

---

[9]   C. T. Hsia has written: "Granted that Lin Shu's 'precise, economical style' makes better reading than Dickens's 'uncontrolled exuberance,' shouldn't a translator's primary duty be fidelity to the spirit and style of the original" (p. 606).

[10]   Translated by Compton (p. 266).

of Nicholas Nickelby.

> 那格。。。始笑而終哭，哭聲以謳歌。「嗟夫！吾來
> 十五年，樓中咸謂我如名花之鮮妍」－歌時，頓
> 其左足，曰：「嗟夫天！」又頓其右足，曰：「嗟夫
> 天！十五年中未被人輕賤。竟有騷孤奔我前，辱
> 我，令我肝腸顫！」

Qian's translation of this Chinese translation into English is a bit verbose, and does not quite capture the succinctness and brevity of the Chinese, but he tries to convey the antic pomposity in the Chinese:

> Knag . . . began by laughing out loud and ended up crying in a sort of sing-song tone. "Alas!" she said. "I have been here fifteen years and everybody in this establishment respects me as a most honored flower" — so chanting, she stamped her left foot, exclaiming "Alas, my Heaven!" then, stamping her right foot, she exclaimed, "Alas My Heaven! In all these fifteen years, I have not once been an object of contempt. To think that this saucy vixen should have got ahead of me and humiliated me, it is enough to rack my heart!" (p. 12)

There is, if possible, a greater wit in the precise and concise formulations of these ridiculous actions in literary Chinese than in an ambling and leisurely vernacular, somewhat resembling the effect of a clerical description of clownish behavior. Qian's translation, unfortunately, has its clunkers, like "enough to rack my heart" — for the conventional phrase 令 我 肝 腸 顫！means, literally, "make my liver and intestines tremble", but which has the idiomatic meaning of being "heartbroken": the colloquial equivalent in English might be, in this case with exaggerated self-pity, "it's enough to break one's heart!"

Dickens's original reads as follows:

> . . . Miss Knag laughed, and after that, cried. "For fifteen years," exclaimed Miss Knag, sobbing in a most affecting manner, "for fifteen years have I been a credit and ornament of this room and the one upstairs. Thank God," said Miss Knag, stamping first her right foot and then her left with remarkable energy, "I have never in all that time, till now, been exposed to the arts, the vile arts of a creature, who disgraces us with all her proceedings, and makes proper people blush for themselves. But I feel it, I do feel it, although I am disgusted.

Not to put too fine a point on it, but Dickens nods a bit in this passage as well: the reference to "this room and the one upstairs" seems gratuitous; and the expression "exposed to the arts, the vile arts of a creature" does reflect a haste in composition; and the last line, "But I feel it, I do feel it, although I am disgusted" sounds limp (the Chinese is much more theatrically melodramatic). Indeed, if we were to compare these three versions, Dickens' original, Lin Shu's Chinese translation, and Qian Zhongshu's English rendering of Lin Shu's translation, Lin Shu's version is clearly the best, in verve, in economy, in directness.

Qian Zhongshu's argument is decidedly ambivalent: on the one hand, he condemns Lin Shu's unauthorized embellishments, but on the other hand, he envies Lin Shu's instinct for literary creation. "Based on his own standards of good writing," Qian writes of Lin, "he would act as 'best friend and severest critic' to the original author, confident that he has the right, and even the duty, to do what is necessary to turn dross into gold" (p. 17).

In all the examples cited so far, we lack the perspective of the author toward the translation of his own work into another language. What would the original Psalmist have said about Tyndale's rendering of the 23rd Psalm into English? What would Poe have thought of Baudelaire's French version of his "Raven" or Mallarmé's — assuming he lived long enough, and could read French? How would Shakespeare, if he knew 19th-century German, have reacted to the popularity of the Schlegel-Tieck version of his plays? And would Dickens have been offended by the admiration reflected in Lin Shu's attempts to make "gold" out of his "dross"? To find testimonies of this kind two conditions must be fulfilled: (1) the translation must be contemporaneous with the author, and (2) the author has to be bilingual.

In our time, we do have at least one instance where an author, far from denigrating the attempts to render him into other languages and assuming — like Frost — that something must always be lost in translation, maintains the superiority of a translated version over his original. Speaking of Gregory Rabassa's English translation of *One Hundred Years of Solitude*, Gabriel García Márquez, according to Alastair Reid, "insists that he prefers the English translation to the original." Reid transmutes this to what is already high praise and considers García Márquez's compliment to be "tantamount to saying that [the translation and the original] are interchangeable — the near-unattainable point of arrival for any translator" (p. 199).

But García Márquez was not merely conceding equivalence between his original and Rabassa's translation: he was insisting that he preferred Rabassa's version to his own. Reid's immediate dilution of this claim, which he takes as gestural generosity toward an excellent translator, reflects the reluctance of theorists and commentators on translation to entertain the possibility that, exceptionally, the translation can surpass the original. Earlier, Reid has said, "Obviously, [*One Hundred Years of Solitude*] was not being lost in translation . . . ." (p. 199), and he points out that the Spanish text "raises no insurmountable technical problems." "The challenge," Reid maintains, "lies in reproducing the extraordinary running rhythm of the original." And then he concedes, "where the rhythm is concerned the English translation, by Gregory Rabassa, is something of a masterpiece, for it is almost matched to the tune of the Spanish, never lengthening or shortening sentences but following them measure for measure." Reid is firm in his claim that Rabassa's version is the equal of the original, but García Márquez suggests that it is better. Like Thurber, García Márquez might, with less irony than Thurber, admit that he "loses something in the original."

In the same essay, Reid makes an astonishing point about the English translations of Borges. "Borges learned English as a child, read voraciously in English," Reid writes, "and has been influenced in the formal sense more by English writing . . . than by Spanish literature. . . . Indeed, translating Borges into English often feels like restoring the work to its natural language, or retranslating it." In other words, translation is not always merely translating from an original, it can be an act of restoring the precursor to an original.

In considering these several — and rare — examples in which a translation does, in some respects, surpass the original, our purpose is not to contradict the contention that translation is an enormously difficult enterprise. However, these instances do suggest that the *ne plus ultra* of translation as equivalence to the original may be misconceived. In certain circumstances, an original can be exceeded. In what way, then, may one contend that an original has been surpassed? There is the assumption that to surpass an original is as much a mistranslation as failing to match the original. But as I intimated at the outset, there is an ontological difficulty in this conception that an original can only be approached and never exceeded. The idea of equivalence is, itself, very problematic — particularly with works of indisputable literary merit. Whatever the disagreements in judging the value of a literary work, there is one criterion that is accepted by all theories of literature, i.e., that a literary work is a unique creation that cannot be replaced or duplicated. Ironically, unlike living things (sheep named Dolly, for example) a unique work of literature cannot be cloned. If that is true, then, by definition, there can never be an exact equivalent to a work whose very quality inheres in its uniqueness.

The question of a translation being "superior" to an original raises questions as to what that "superiority" consists of. In one respect, a more recent translation may be said to be "superior" to an ancient original. One genre of translation that is generally neglected is the translation of a work from an archaic form to a modern form in the same language. Modern renditions of Chaucer in English, contemporary versions of *The Tale of Genji* in Japanese; "exegeses" of classical poetry in vernacular Chinese — all these are translations in the same language for enhanced accessibility. Same-language translations, for the most part — the modern Chaucer versions in English and the Chinese vernacular explications of traditional Chinese poetry, for example, fall into the category of what I have called "contingent" translations, i.e., translations which provide access to the originals: they do not replace them (as with "surrogate" translations), or compete with them (as with "co-eval" translations), and do not aspire to separate literary status.

Indeed, we have the interesting anomaly, that among the most accessible modern versions of the Genji for the Japanese are the English translations, first, the Waley and now the Seidensticker.[11] This would not be the first time that a literary work depended for its survival on its rendering in a foreign tongue. The Hebrew and *koine* Greek of the Bible, which survived through first the Greek of the *Septuagint*, the Latin of Jerome's Vulgate, and then the multifarious vernaculars, most notably Luther's version in German and the King James Version in English; ancient Greek, which survived in English through the versions of Dryden, Pope, Chapman, and E. V. Rieu before the present era, and which has seen no less than three renderings — the Richmond Lattimore, the Robert Fitzgerald, and the Robert Fagles versions — in our lifetime; the medieval Persian of Omar Khayyam, which is principally known throughout the non-Persian world in Edward Fitzgerald's Victorian retelling; the Sanskrit and Pali originals of the Buddhist canon, which is accessible to more readers today, including adherents, in their Chinese and Japanese renderings — none of these would be familiar as classics today if they had not been preserved, in however a distorted form, in translation. The only thing anomalous about the case of the *Genji* is that the modern Japanese reader finds one of their ancient texts more accessible in a foreign language than in their own. It would be as if readers of English were to find a French version of Chaucer more accessible than the original, or any modern retelling.

The question of accessibility is what lies behind the need for a new translation every generation: as language changes, translations themselves become obsolete, and must be replaced, or they become as obsolete as the original. By the criterion of accessibility, every contemporary translation is superior not only to the obsolete original, but to every previous translation. Indeed, one might say that, unless a translation is superior to the original in accessibility, it has no reason for being. That is why I have a particular brief against some translations which are more arcane and more esoteric than the original ever was in its own day (see Chapter 4); some "contingent", scholarly translations are, if possible, even less accessible as comprehensible texts, much less as literature, than the originals which they purport to explain.

There is an ontological mistake here: what these textual obfuscators are preserving is not the original in some modern guise but the arcaneness of the original, as if outdatedness were a generic trait of the work rather

---

[11]   But some of the modern versions of the Genji (including the Yosano Akiko and Junichiro Tanizaki versions in Japanese, and the Waley and the Seidensticker renderings in English) may be rivals to the original Heian text (for those few who can manage both eleventh-century Japanese as well as modern Japanese and English): in any case, unlike the "contingent" versions, these translations do aspire to literature, but far from replacing any previous texts, they may actually actually allude to them, as the Seidensticker alludes to the Waley (cf. Chapter 7).

than a phenomenological accident. Few works (with perhaps the sole exception of Spenser's *Faerie Queene*) tried to be arcane and esoteric at the outset.

But superior accessibility is not all that motivated Thurber's bilingual fan to prefer the French version to the English original. Nor is accessibility the sole reason why a quarter of the modern productions of Shakespeare in German still use the Schlegel-Tieck version, when numerous versions more contemporary exist. Nor would accessibility be a reason for Gabriel García Márquez to prefer Rabassa's English translation to his own original in Spanish. Surely something else is involved besides the currency of the language in the translation.

If we abandon the concept of the original as an ideal to be approached, and remember that, even in the most exalted examples, we are dealing not with a sacred text but with a human construct,[12] we may yet find an answer. It is a commonplace of artistic judgment to invoke perfection as the hallmark of value, but it is quite misleading and beside the point, for perfection involves a static construct in a static context and presupposes a static ideal. It is abstract and immutable, whereas language, and the use of language, is concrete and dynamic. Perfection invokes notions of a Platonic ideal which sublunary language can only approximate and allude to, but never achieve. Literary works, however, no matter how divine, are, at bottom, human: they derive their energy and their imagination from human experience, their meaning can only be certified by human readers, and they have no other value other than their inherent humanity. As human nature is variable, and as the language that humans use is idiomatic if not idiosyncratic, the concept of a "perfect" work of art and of translations that attempt to duplicate that "perfection" involves an ontological error. As no work is "perfect"; it would be pointless to judge translations in terms of the degree to which they fall short of perfection.

We might posit an iconoclastic definition of literary value, based not on its putative perfection, but on its organic vitality, one that sees the value of a literary work in terms of its capacity to renew the language and to generate new versions of itself. If we apply this metric of evaluation, certainly the Bible would, on the basis of its seemingly infinite translatability, qualify as one of the greatest works every composed, if not the greatest story ever told. Far from being diminished in literary value by being surpassed by later versions, the *sine qua non* of literary value of durable work may lie precisely in its generative powers. It is this quality that Walter Benjamin, in his perversely seminal essay, "Die Aufgabe des Übersetzers", referred to as "*übersetzigkeit*" — translatability — by which he meant not the ease with which a work can be translated, but its generative power in inspiring translation. In one sense, this is obvious: if "imitation is the sincerest form of flattery," the attempts of translators to "imitate" an original in another language are a form of flattery, which reflect admiration and esteem. But at a deeper level, one might look for

---

[12] It is only superficially ironical that even "sacred" texts sometimes inspire superior translations.

the capacity of a work to generate superior translations as a reflection of its own superiority.

This framework would provide a basis for removing the discomfort that we experience when we encounter the possibility that Shakespeare might have been improved upon in German, or that Lady Murasaki is now better served in English than in Heian Japanese, or that the Bible has been enhanced in English by the King James Version or in German by Martin Luther. Indeed, the enhancements are a testimonial to rather than a denigration of the original's worth. James Thurber might also have said, not just ironically, "I tend to lose something in the original", but earnestly, and without false modesty, "I tend to gain something in translation." Thurber's bilingual French admirer was not, in fact, insulting the master, he was paying a greater tribute than merely appreciating his work; he was expressing a gratitude that Thurber had, indeed, enriched the French language, just as Shakespeare has enriched the German, just as Jerome's Vulgate enriched all the romance languages, just as the Sanskrit and Pali scriptures have enriched Chinese, and just as Chinese, in turn, has enriched Japanese. There is a Chinese expression that captures this sense of achievement, whereby a teacher is surpassed by his or her student: 青 出 於 藍. which may be rendered, "Azure stands out in blue" or "A blue that's bluer than blue." To be surpassed is not to be put to shame, but is rather a reflection of one's crucial importance and genius.[13]

Scientists have no problem with this notion of "A blue that's bluer than blue" — for progress in science involves precisely the student surpassing the teacher, in the same way that Copernicus went beyond by correcting Ptolemy, as Galileo went beyond and corrected Copernicus, as Tycho Brahe went beyond and corrected Galileo, as Newton went beyond and corrected Galileo, as — in our time — Einstein has gone beyond Newton by replacing Newton's clockwork world with a universe of relativity.[14]

The issue is not whether any human endeavor offers a perfect answer: the holocausts of the twentieth century should remind us about the dangers inherent in the absolutism of any "final solutions"; the issue is whether a human endeavor has contributed to significant progress in human understanding. The irony is that human understanding is evinced only in the recognition of the inadequacy of previous understandings.

We may now venture a different taxonomy of literary works: (1) those which are not worth translating; (2) those which, however difficult to translate, attract adherents in other languages; and (3) those which, impressive as they may be in the native language, have an even greater success abroad. The works in the first category are, of course, legion; those in the second category are numerous as well; but those in the third

---

[13] Guy Davenport, writing of Proust surpassing Ruskin, says something similar: "Proust and Ruskin are an example of pupil and teacher wherein the pupil took, with splendid comprehension, everything the teacher knew, paid the teacher the highest gratitude, and then remade all that he had learned into a matter wholly his own" (338).

[14] Cf. Michael Polanyi, *The Tacit Dimension* (Gloucester: Peter Smith, 1966, 1983).

category are very few and they are worth looking at closely. We have to ask cross-culturally whether these works may have a value that natives cannot appreciate, and that require a foreign reader to discern. Edgar Allan Poe's poetry would be one such example; the success of the Cold Mountain poet — Hanshan 寒 山 in Chinese — in both its Japanese and English translations is also worth contemplating, as are the successes of John Steinbeck in Russian, and Jack London in Hungarian and Polish. Is it possible, indeed, that there are some works with literary merits that are obscure to native readers but that are apparent to translators and to foreign readers of their translations? We are reminded of Eliot's sensible cautionary advice, in discussing the esteem in which Baudelaire, Mallarmé, and Valéry held Edgar Allan Poe:

> Now, we all of us like to believe that we understand our own poets better than any foreigner can do; but I think we should be prepared to entertain the possibility that these Frenchmen have seen something in Poe that English-speaking readers have missed. (p. 328)

These are not negligible questions in an intraworldly poetics, where neither nationalisms nor linguistic chauvinisms can be the final arbiter of literary value.

10. Translating as a Mode of Thinking, Translation as a Model of Thought

It is by now axiomatic that translation, far from being a peripheral enterprise in human discourse, may lie at the very core of our understanding, not only of language, but of understanding itself. George Steiner has insisted that there is intralingual translation as well as bilingual translation, involving no less pervasive an activity than our effort to understand each other. No human communication is spared the subjective tendency to distort (as we are reminded by the childhood game of 'telephone', in which a story whispered through a series of 'communicants' ends up being virtually unrecognizable to the original narrator. And if we accept Franz Mauthner's formulation, seconded by Wittgenstein, that all philosophy is linguistic criticism ["Alle Philosophic ist Sprachkritik"], then a study of the ways in which meaning is transmitted between languages — a critique of different languages, a "Sprachenkritik" — may very well constitute a form of comparative philosophy. Finally, if, along with André Lefevère, Joseph Lau and others, we accept that "translation is interpretation," we are not far from the proposition that a study of translation may provide clues to the way in which we understand and the way in which we think. A hermeneutics of translation may constitute a heuristics of thought and an aesthetics of thinking.

The work of George Lakoff, Mark Johnson, and Mark Turner on metaphorical paradigms and image schemata is extremely apt in an analysis of the implicit preconceptions of language reflected in schools of translation. It is now clear that we really do make cognitive connections and draw conclusions on the basis of our underlying metaphorical systems" (Johnson 1987: 101). If, as Johnson suggests, "understanding does not consist merely of after-the-fact reflections on prior experiences", and if "it is, more fundamentally, the way (or means by which) we have those experiences in the first place . . . the way our world presents itself to us" (p. 104), then the way we translate reflects not only our view of the original text, but also our view of the relationship between language and the world. There is in these relationships a double perspective: the original work is the author's view of the world, and comprises the way in which the world presents itself to him or her; and the translation reflects the translator's view of the world, and the way in which the world presents itself to him or her.

First we must examine the various approaches to translation and discover ways in which they reflect different assumptions about the relationship between language and reality. For, if we can adduce errors about our conceptions of that relationship, it follows that parallel assumptions about the relationship between the translation and the 'original' may be inherently flawed, if not entirely fallacious. I shall concentrate here on the theoretical underpinnings of my argument, and on the ramifications of insights for actual translations.[1]

Traditionally, there have been two major approaches to translation: the "word-for-word" method and "free rendition." These may be compared to the twin extremes of philosophical positivism sometimes termed "deflationary" and "inflationary". The impulse of the first extreme is to reduce the proposition to its irrefutable, essential elements; the impulse of the second extreme is to confer 'categoricalness' on all versions of the original. "Deflationary" strategies attempt to define one absolute meaning; "inflationary" strategies admit any meaning as valid. Berlin points out that both positions harbor the same fallacy: "What is common to both methods and equally fatal to either is . . . the correspondence model" (68). The correspondence model, as Berlin explains, is "fallacious because all words are not names, and meaning is not a species of correspondence with a . . . formally analysable structure" (75). There is, in other words, neither a category of 'good propositions' against which every proposition can be meaningfully tested, nor are all 'propositions' equally valid. Applying these conceptual paradigms to the notion of translation means that there is neither one 'correct' version of an original, nor are all versions of the original equally 'correct'. The analysis is similar to the subtle notion of poetry as plurisignification (Empson's "ambiguity"): to say that there is more than one meaning in a particular poetic discourse is not the same as saying that a poem contains all meanings. In poetry as well as in translation there is more than one single valid meaning, but — even if the number of valid meanings in a poem or translation remains indeterminable — the number of those interpretations is finite, not infinite. It is the lazy mind which equates plurisignification with infinite possibilities of meaning: that is tantamount to assuming in mathematics that anything greater than one must be equal to infinity. This misunderstanding of plurisignification, this semantic anarchy, assumes that just because there is more than one meaning to a sentence, that sentence can be construed to mean anything. 'Everything is relative', is the popular formulation of this misunderstanding.

A concern with translation involves some consideration of a theory of meaning. Here again, Mark Johnson is helpful:

> The key to an adequate 'cognitive semantics' will be the nature of the theory of understanding upon which it relies. To ask about the meaning of something (whether it be an experience, a word, a sentence, a story, or a theory) is to ask about our understanding of it. In short, a theory of meaning is a theory of how we understand things (of whatever sort). And we have seen that this is not merely a matter of how some individual might happen to understand something but rather about how an individual is embedded in a (linguistic) community, a culture, and a historical context

---

[1] Roberts (1992) also discusses the function of the translation and the relationship between a translation and the original but does not explore the problematics of the ontology of the original.

understands. In other words, we are concerned here with public, shared meaning (Johnson 1987: 190).

The aptness of these speculations to a theory of translation can be seen when we ask ourselves the following questions:

(1) What view of the original is reflected when we read a translation? Is it a fixed masterpiece for which an exact counterpart is sought? Is it a dynamic work, of which the text is only one verbal clue?
 (2) Is the language into which the original is translated, the language of an individual, a coterie of individuals, or 'an individual as embedded in a . . . community, a culture, and a historical context'? Is the language of the translation 'public', a 'shared meaning'?
 (3) Does the literary translation (especially of poetry) reflect the translator's view of the original as an imaginative enterprise, or does the translation reflect the view that the original is merely a document for which a counterpart in the target language must be sought?

Examples of various kinds of translation come easily to mind if we characterize them in the following way:

(1) texts as codes to be deciphered;
(2) texts as catalysts for literary inspiration; and
(3) texts as documents from which history is to be reconstructed.

The first kind presupposes that there is a correct message to be deciphered: codes are amenable only to unambiguous messages. In the language of codes, an ambiguous message is a faulty message. "Let's meet at 1700" is more precise than "Let's meet at 5 o'clock" — although few would meet casually at 5:00 in the morning. In the second kind, it is assumed that a text is whatever one makes of it: any meaning is correct provided it makes sense to the translator. "He ate the frankfurter with relish" could mean either that he ate the unaccompanied hot dog with particular delight, or he ate the hot dog with relish as the condiment — rather than, say, with sauerkraut. In the third kind, it is assumed that the historical presence can be recaptured, that the contemporaneity of a past era is recoverable, and the meaning of a document is recuperable. Pascal's "If the nose of Cleopatra had been shorter, the whole face of the earth would have been changed" "Le nez de Cléopâtre: s'il eût été plus court, toute la face de la terre aurait changé" (*Pensées*, #162) is an example that not only evokes the contemporary physiognomy of Cleopatra, but also the ruminations of Pascal.

Each of these assumptions bespeaks a view of reality that is paradigmatic and, in a sense, arbitrary. The view of translation as code-breaking, and of language as meaningful only if unambiguous, may be suited to direct action or to scientific discourse, but it is certainly inadequate to semantic exchanges between languages that inhabit different cultural contexts and therefore reflect different realities. The view of translation as catalytic is, on the other hand, plausible as an explanation of literary creativity — it would not be difficult to write a book detailing the inspirational role of translations in both Western and Chinese literature — but it skirts the issue of relevance and interpretation and neglects the intersubjective factor in any human exchange.

Finally, the view of the text as a recoverable historical document, while useful as a concept for archaeology and for history, cannot address the ambiguities of literary discourse, which specifically preclude the reconstructibility of any occasion, the recoverability of any discourse (cf. Gadamer's "radical historicity"). We must first establish the ontology of the original before we can adequately address the shortcomings of various views of translation.

Most traditional discussions of translation focus on the accuracy or fidelity with which the original is transformed into another language. Little or no thought is given to the problematic ontology of the original: this has been especially true in the last two generations, first with the primacy of New Critical ways of thinking, which regarded the text itself as totally self-sufficient and autonomous; then with deconstructionist notions of textuality and intertextuality; and, finally, with poststructuralist theories of 'writerly' (*scriptible*) and 'readable' (*lisible*) texts. The ontology of the text was, however, most prominently called into question by *Rezeptionsästhetik*, most notably in the work of Wolfgang Iser and Hans Robert Jauss, which was anticipated by Roman Ingarden, in particular. Ingarden's notion of the concretization (*Konkretizierung*) of a work of art — which I interpret as the reader's (or the spectator's or the listener's) 'realization' of a work of art — is crucial to an understanding of the ontology of the original 'text'.

If the ontology of reality itself has been problematic in philosophical discourse for centuries, and if, as the phenomenologists remind us, no objective reality can be asserted except through what individual subjects have perceived as 'real', then the unchallenged ontology of the original in a translation seems odd. Our assumption as to the fixity of the text stems from the stereotypical concept that there is an original, and that any original is, by its very nature, more authoritative than any subsequent version. Yet, priority is no sufficient guarantee of authority, as can easily be adduced by examples from all the arts: it may be that the final version has as good a claim to authority as any earlier version (Henry James' New York edition and the Folio editions of Shakespeare represent but two examples of authority being invested in later rather than early versions). The notion of a 'variorum' edition also privileges one 'correct' version, to which all variants are considered inferior. But this vision of certitude cannot be sustained even in the Variorum Shakespeare.

More than a generation ago, Fredson Bowers pointed out that there is good textual evidence that the most famous speech in all of English literature, Hamlet's "Oh, that this too, too solid flesh would melt, / Thaw, and resolve itself into a dew," should actually read: "Oh, that this too, too. sallied [meaning, 'sullied'] flesh would melt, / Thaw, and resolve itself into a dew" (Bowers 1956). The fact that some academics would disregard this as a trivial problem, preferring the conventional reading of the line, does not alter the serious ramifications of this anomaly (and others like it), for the consideration of the 'original text' as the ultimate authority. Nor is it reassuring for our assumption that primary sources are the last, irrefutable word on what the 'original text' really is. We do not have to go as far back as Shakespeare to encounter disparities between what we accept as the incontrovertible 'original' and what is actually the primary source. Even a poet as seemingly spontaneous as Walt Whitman is not immune to problems concerning the ontology of the original. Our preconceptions of Whitman as an untrained genius are belied by the extant manuscripts which show him "casting and recasting his lines six and seven times, trying out words in different combinations in layer after layer of revision" (Bowers 1959: 37).[2] "One of the difficulties facing the serious critic of American literature," Bowers writes, "is the unpredictability of the primary source materials on which textual and literary investigation must depend" (Bowers 1959: 35). The same difficulty may be encountered, indeed, in the serious study of texts in other literatures as well.

If the exact nature of reality is a question for philosophers, and the exact nature of the object being rendered in a different language is not always as definitive as translators (as well as most theorists of translation) suppose, one may well wonder at the claims to accuracy made by various schools of translators. Accuracy to what? Fidelity to what? It makes a difference if one conceives of the object to be translated as a communication to be transmitted, a code to be broken, an experience to be reconstructed, or an impulse to be passed on. Each of these paradigms is, for the translator of literature, inadequate, yet each is subsumed implicitly in one or another approach to translation.

Communication has as a primary desideratum that a specific meaning be transmitted without distortion from sender to receiver. This presumes a determinate unmistakable message, not subject to deviant interpretation. Indeed, composers of these messages (like those who used to send cables and telegrams) must take pains to eliminate all ambiguities, to disambiguate forcibly. Communication follows the model of explicit instruction: a clear and unambiguous series of directives must be formulated. Anything that might admit of mis-interpretation, or of plurisignification, must be resolutely eliminated. Consider how exasperating, for example, a set of instructions would be if they were written with all the suggestiveness, the allusiveness, and the ambiguity of a poem. But clearly, literature — even didactic, moralizing literature — does not merely communicate: factors that are extraneous, or even inimical to, communication are important to literature — such as tone, style, metaphor, rhythm, and imagery. What is pared away in precise communication is precisely that which makes literature literature. "Yet any

---

[2]   William Carlos Williams put it this way: "Whitman didn't have the training to construct his verses after a conscious mold which would have given him power over them to turn them this way, then that, at will. He only knew how to give them birth and to release them to go their own way" (as quoted by Bowers 1959: 23).

translation which intends to perform a transmitting function", Walter Benjamin wrote, "cannot transmit anything but information, hence something inessential. This is the hallmark of bad translations" (1968: 69). The communication model, to say nothing of the communication theory model, cannot be the paradigm for effective literary translation.

Nor can the original work of literature be viewed as a code to be broken, because one of the essential traits of a work of literary art is precisely its accessibility to the audience for which it is intended. The difficulty arises from the disparity between the audience for the translation and the audience for the original.

One of the most neglected factors in the difficulty of translating Chinese literature, especially literati literature, is the problem of conveying a literati experience clearly to an egalitarian audience. The obscurity that results in that transfer is extraneous to the text but is a function of differences in the historical, cultural, and linguistic mindset between the audience for the original and for the translation. The pity is that a translation which conveys that difficulty, however real, to a reader in the foreign language, constructs an obstacle that never existed for the original audience. The reader of this translation encounters an exasperation quite the reverse of the delights of spontaneous insight experienced by elite readers of the original. Translators who want to be faithful to the original reading experience cannot ignore the phenomenology of reading. If every language is a code then the code must be transparent to the native user. A code may not be a cipher for the native user, but a non-native user must resort to deciphering in order to attain understanding. However necessary this act of deciphering, it undercuts the ease of access which native readers expect in a work from their own tradition. The translator who 'breaks the code' of the original yields to the reader not a living work of literature, but a disassembly of meaningless parts, like a dissected cadaver. The student may have the dubious pleasure of solving a crossword puzzle, but he will have missed "that sense of sudden growth, which," according to Pound, "we experience in the presence of the greatest works of art" (1935: 336).

If a text is not a message to be delivered, nor a code to be broken, is it an experience to be reconstructed? This is a particularly vexing question because of the seemingly strong autobiographical element in Chinese poetry. Traditional Chinese poets seem to encourage this act of reconstruction when they append specific headnotes, long epigraphs, to their poems about the occasion that inspired the poem.[3]

Are we, then, required to recapture all the historical detail before we can fully appreciate the poem? Must we know the complete biography of the poet before we can begin to appreciate his or her poem? Aside from the obvious difficulties in historical reconstruction, only partly addressed in Wimsatt and Beardsley's key article on 'The Intentional Fallacy", we

---

[3]   These headnote citations deserve close study. They are often misconstrued in translations as 'titles' which are formal labels for ease of reference in published material; they actually perform an altogether different function, somewhere between a personal prompt and the establishment of an impersonal mood.

would be confronted with the dilemma of monolithic meaning, or the diachronic version of the same dilemma, which Gadamer has dubbed "radical historicity". It is impossible to fully reconstruct a moment in the past, just as it is impossible to fully recapture the music of earlier eras, despite the 'Early Music Societies', and the reconstruction and use of period instruments: the point is that no matter how authentic the reconstructions are, we, the modern listeners (and readers), are not antiques. The best (or the worst) we can be are 'pseudo-antiques'. And if we accept the notion of the absolute authority of a particular experience, we are left with no other choice but to assign the ultimate reality in the poem to the moment which occasioned the writing of it, and to restrict our reading to rerunning that moment, in an act of antiquarian nostalgia.

To some extent, this notion of historicity is inevitable. Every act, no matter how trivial, has the tincture of its time; every statement, every expression of emotion, is redolent of the circumstances that prompted it. Still, a total reconstruction of a historical moment, however ingenious our efforts, would be as chimerical as it is pointless. There is no archaeology thorough enough to excavate all the details of a particular point in time, no metempsychosis powerful enough to enable a modern reader to be reborn in a historical period. If reconstruction of the original experience were the only valid and meaningful way of reading a poem, then only the Bridey Murphys and the New Age Shirley MacLaines — those who believe themselves reincarnations of former lives — would be qualified readers of poetry. These 'reconstructions' are, in Benjamin's words, "the cause of another characteristic of inferior translation, which . . . we may define as the inaccurate transmission of inessential content" (1968: 70).

A somewhat mystical notion of translation, as an impulse to pass on, or a life force that persists from one version to the next, animates Walter Benjamin's notion of "translatability" [*übersetzigkeit*]. In his sense, "translatability" does not refer to the ease with which a work can be translated. Quite the contrary. Otherwise, some of his 'apodictic' remarks would seem puzzling rather than self-evident. Benjamin writes, for example: " . . . the translatability of linguistic creations ought to be considered even if men should prove unable to translate them" (1968: 70). This would be self-contradictory, if by "translatability" Benjamin refers to that character of a work which lends itself easily to being rendered in another language. The key to the meaning of Benjamin's sense of "translatability" is provided by the recurrent metaphor of life and afterlife in his protean essay, 'The Task of the Translator'. The relationship between the original and its translation "is a natural one, or, more specifically, a vital connection". Later, Benjamin writes, " . . . a translation issues from the original — not so much from its life as from its afterlife" (1968: 71). "Translatability", then, involves an impulse to life, to survival. But its survival does not take the form of preservation, but of transformation. "For in its afterlife — which could not be called that if it were not a transformation and a renewal of something living — the original undergoes a change" (73). Benjamin's notion of "translatability" reminds one of Dawkin's notions of 'the selfish gene'. The notion of the 'selfish gene' suggests that living organisms are merely the vessels for genes to continue their existence in one transformation after another. "We are", so this theory goes, "merely the gene's way of making another gene". By analogy, a translation is merely a means for the "translatability" in the original to survive the demise of the original. The factor of "translatability" subsumes Benjamin's notion of "pure language": "it is the task of the translator," Benjamin insists," to release in his own language that pure language which is under the spell of another, to liberate the language imprisoned in a work in his recreation of that work" (1968: 80). The implicit metaphor in this statement reminds one of the image of the soul leaving the dying body.

Is translation the manifestation of this impulse, the realization of Benjamin's "translatability"? We are perhaps closer to the mark, but we are still beset with problems. If the act of translating is to make explicit the "vital connection" between the original and a secondary version, the relation being as life is to afterlife, then translation might be regarded as in some measure causing, at the same time, a death and a birth. The translation has the capacity to kill the original (to replace it ontologically), even while it gives the original new life (perpetuating it in another language). But this is definitely not the case with all translation. Good translations are not killed all at once by new translations. Translations of Homer have not undermined interest in the original epic, the oral nature of which has been exhaustively explored in the last two generations; nor have the now classic translations of Dickens by Lin Shu replaced the originals, even in China;[4] and the irreplaceable versions of Shakespeare in German by Schlegel and Tieck have done nothing to 'kill' Shakespeare in English. Clearly, the life impulse model, while helpful, is not completely adequate in defining the act of translation.

It is perhaps easier to reject some models implicit in certain assumptions about translation than to reject them all. For one can hardly deny that literary works, and especially Chinese texts, carry a message that might be characterized variously as moral, or cosmological, or humanitarian, or aesthetic. Nor would any translator deny the fact that the act of translation involves an effort to "figure out" what is being said in the text, which in effect is an attempt to "break a code". Historical exegesis is also essential to any conscientious attempt to translate a text, particularly a traditional text. One cannot assume the total equivalence of experience in past periods with our contemporary experience. Although total historical reconstruction is not possible, an ignorance of history in rendering the masterworks of the past is also unacceptable, and no meaningful translation can be achieved without some knowledge of the historical background. We have not emered from the triumphs of New Critical theory into a "new historical" era to retract the gains made or to

---

[4]   Cf. Eva Hung, "The Introduction of Dickens in China" and Wang Ning, "Translation study in a context of comparative culture studies" in Perspectives: Studies in Translatology, 1996:1, 29-42, 43-52.

repudiate the insights we have recently acquired. And, as for the notion of translation as the passing on of life impulses, of "vital connections", we are mindful of the need to distinguish between the undoubted fecundity of translation as a stimulus to literary creation (particularly in the modern period), and the unquestioned importance of translation as a means of preserving the multicultural heritage of the past.

What happens in translation? What is involved when we translate? Each of the paradigms we have explored has proved either wrong or inadequate. Yet even while we recognize the pitfalls in each conception, we have to admit that translating involves some aspects of the models we have rejected, and that there are, despite what seems to be insuperable obstacles, successful translations. Translation is not merely communicating a message or deciphering a code or reconstructing a historical experience or passing on a literary impulse to capture the vital force of "pure language" — it is a combination of all of these. We may judge the value of a translation by the degree to which it has accomplished each of these objectives, not just one of them; conversely, we may recognize the limitations of any translation if only one of these objectives is effectively served.

I have now indicated the inadequacy of each paradigm at the same time that we have recognized its relevance. We can therefore address the second part of the thesis put forward in my title, 'Translation as a model of thought'. By using the word 'model', I mean the word both in the sense of a standard to be imitated and in the sense of a provisional construct to facilitate understanding. If we accept translation as a model of thought, and if my analysis of ways in which translations may be judged is valid, then we can proceed to explore the implications of using translation models as representative of the ways we think, and of using optimum models of translations as paradigms for the full exercise of our minds. For if translating involves (1) communicating; (2) decoding; (3) reconstructing; and (4) transforming, then we can posit counterpart behaviors to the process of thought, which would then involve: (1) transmitting and receiving; (2) deducing; (3) inferring and intuiting; and (4) interpreting, imagining and inventing.

Each of these activities presuppose inadequate models of reality: the world is not a single-valued set of objects with determinate meanings and messages; nor is it merely a mathematical construct which can be calculated; nor is it totally whimsical and arbitrary; nor is it a figment of our imaginations, a product of our subjective will that we can shape and fashion to our own purposes. Yet if the world is none of these things, it is, in large measure, a composite of all of these things.[5]

It is only the Gradgrinds of the world who insist that reality is "facts" and only facts and who therefore regard meaning as determinate and single-valued. Logical positivists are only slightly more sophisticated: they contend that only phenomena which can be demonstrated are relevant in

---

[5]   Juliane House has a similar argument although she focuses on functions rather than on models and paradigms (p. 36).

the search for truth. It is an irony that among adherents of the communication model we must also include the radically pious, whose hold on truth, i.e., the Word of God, is so unshakable that any deviation is heresy — the work of the devil. "Truth" as a "message" characterizes missionaries and proselytizers who are resistant to a dialectic model of knowledge: they are interested primarily in effective means of transmitting the Word without distortion.

The idea of meaning as a code to be broken reflects a determinate vision of the world and of meaning. Reality is relegated to unchanging Platonic forms: mathematical, geometric, and algebraic relationships that apply equally to all situations. Reality is not to be experienced but to be solved. The intractability of some translator exegetes reflects a pseudo-mathematical view of a discourse which is distinctly unmathematical and definitely imprecise. In their world there is no room for ambiguity, ambivalence, or fuzziness: in their view the fuzziness of things is controlled by assigning a particular word, preferably an unusual one, which gives precision to something we see only 'through a glass, darkly'. One must subscribe to the orthodox nomenclature, even when it is obscure.

The view of meaning as random and haphazard poses the problem of semantic anarchy. If something can mean anything, then it is also clear that everything can be taken to mean nothing. Benjamin offers us a suggestively paradoxical formulation: ". . . no case for literalness can be based on a desire to retain the meaning. Meaning is served far better — and literature and language far worse — by the unrestrained license of bad translations" (78). Again, I would insist that to recognize that there may be more than one meaning in a statement is not to claim that the meanings are infinite. Rigor must still be exercised to determine a finite yet underdetermined number of meanings; the intellectual demands are, perhaps, greater than in the search for, and the insistence on, one irrefutable meaning.

The Golden Mean requires that one eschews either the pointlessness of infinite interpretation (anything goes) or the dogmatism of only one meaning (preaching the Word). The ironies of life would suggest that the univalent view of the world can capture but a segment of what passes for reality. It is often the indeterminate factors in life that affect us most; it is foolish to expect predictability — whether mathematical or scientific — in everything real. The variables in an equation are often as meaningful as the constants. But even chaos has a pattern, and disorder may refer not to the inherent nature of things — whether conceived of as entropy or as synergy — but to an order yet undiscovered. There is a difference between absolute chaos and the premise that "chaos" is merely our word for describing what we do not understand — that attitude reflects more on the limitations of our comprehension than on the nature of reality.

The emphasis on originality and on the individual, which has developed in Western civilization since the Renaissance and has received special impetus from German idealist philosophy and English Romanticism, lies behind the view that the world is merely a prompt for the inspirations of genius. But this view of the artist as the source of all meaning, a Prospero who can conjure up realities and who can shape the world to his will, is a misunderstanding of the original notion of 'genius'. As the etymology of the word reminds us, genius is not the exclusive endowment of the individual, but the accumulated patrimony of the collective. The passing on of the impulse to language, Benjamin's "vital connection", is not an unbroken chain of masterpieces passed down from one individual author to another through the ages, but rather the transmission through traditional cultures of a generic force and power that individual "geniuses" tap. The world at large supplies our individual imagination. No genius was ever created in a vacuum; no inspiration was ever elicited without a sense of audience (actual or implied). That is why the Chinese word *xing* 興, normally and inadequately translated as "evocation" or "inspiration", causes such confusion in Western discussions of Chinese poetics. That's because, whereas the word "inspiration" is author-centered, and "evocation" is normally audience-centered, *xing* comprises both the heightened sensitivity of the author at the moment of composition "inspiration") and the heightened interest of the reader responding to the text ("evocation").[6]

In my view there are three kinds of translation, which I have labeled 'surrogate', 'contingent', and 'co-eval'. The 'surrogate' genre designates such works as European translations of *The Arabian Nights* or the *Bible*, translations in which the reader is not expected to have any access to the language of the original. The translation, in effect, stands in for the original, and there is a definite bias in favor of the target language.

We may say that surrogate translations are an extreme but natural form of solipsism, which accords reality only to objects within one's field of comprehension, i.e. in one's own language.[7]

The 'contingent' category includes the scholarly translations produced in the last generation and which are of enormous assistance and use to students of philology and literature. These are the editions with extensive word-for-word glosses, and which do not attempt to make the translation exist independently in the target language. Examples would include Nabokov's extensive, but unreadable translation of Pushkin's *Eugene Onegin*. Nabokov would have doubtless approved if the reader of his translation decided, in exasperation, that it would be easier to study Pushkin in the original. In this case, the objective reality of the original is all important, and there is no permissible variability in reading: one must assume that all Russians read Pushkin in exactly the same way.

The third category of translations, which I have called 'co-eval',

---

[6]   In general, the central confusion in comparing Western with Chinese poetics stems from an inadequate appreciation of the differences between the character of the author and that of the audience in both traditions.

[7]   This bias is reflected in the practice of some American departments of English, who teach works not originally composed in English on the premise that, having been translated into English, these works have become part of the canon of English literature. This position may be defensible with Edward Fitzgerald's translation of the Rubaiyat of Omar Khayyam (1859), but it cannot be applied with validity to, say, the plays of Strindberg and Ibsen.

includes so-called 'imitations'. It is pointless to compare translations of the Bible with various eighteenth-century translations of Homer, such as Pope's, Dryden's or Chapman's. In the first case, the audience would not know the source text, whereas the audience of the latter translations was expected to be conversant with the original. Pound's 'Homage to Sextius Propertius' is one of the last instances of a poet assuming that his audience knew Latin. A similar logic applies to Robert Lowell's translations from the French, which he titled *Imitations* (1961): he assumed his readers would know French.

These categories of translation reflect three different views of reality: 'Surrogate translations' privilege the subjective world and consider the objective world as something to be 'replaced', 'contingent translations', on the other hand, deny the validity of any subjective interpretation, and point the reader — by paraphrase, gloss, exegesis — toward the original as the only reality. 'Co-eval translations' presume both premises: they suggest that the source language version and the target language version are ontologically on a par, even if the source language has chronological priority. In this perspective, the Authorized Version of the Bible is not inferior to the Masoretic texts. Chronological priority is not always a guarantee of literary superiority.[8]

We can now entertain a heuristics of translation. In early encounters between two cultures, surrogate translations will predominate, because the "other" does not exist unless it is completely absorbed in the native medium. FitzGerald's Rubaiyat of Omar Khayyam is the most conspicuous example. In the next phase, when curiosity about the "other" prevails, contingent translations become popular aids to students who want to acquire native command of a foreign medium. In this perspective, translations will always be inferior, simply because they are not the original. Nabokov's fussy and meticulous, but ultimately unreadable version of *Eugene Onegin* would constitute an example. And finally, in a multicultural context, when the self and the other co-exist, and the audience may be, in some measure, familiar with both mediums, co-eval translations become possible, for now there is an audience which can appreciate literary quality in both the original and the translation. Pound's brilliant, but linguistically wayward translations in his *Cathay* volume of 1915 would be an important example. Questions of 'fidelity' will no longer be assumed, because the object of fidelity — a determinate text, an indeterminate historical moment, a discrete meaning in the original — can no longer be taken for granted. We have come to realize that the ontology of the original is extremely problematic.

The ontology of the translation is no less complex. Before we can judge the quality of a translation we must recognize its different functions, the different audiences for which it is intended. A surrogate translation may be criticized for not being readable in the target language, but

---

[8]   These notions are discussed extensively in Eoyang 1993. Sager devises similar categories, but the distinctions between his Type B and Type C are not as clear-cut as the differences between my 'contingent' and 'co-eval' categories (Sager 1983: 121-123).

concerns with its accuracy will be irrelevant. Contingent translations will not read much like literature, but inaccuracies will be fatal, for if it is not a reliable conduit to the original, what other value can it claim? Co-eval translations are doubly exigent: they must, on the one hand, read as if they were original in the target language, yet they must bear the "flavor" of the original: the reader with access to both original and translation will marvel at both, each the more remarkable in light of the other.

It will be noticed that this scheme is resolutely non-categorical. Versions need not fit exclusively in one or the other category (though contingent translations will be conspicuously different, at least in form, from both surrogate and co-eval versions). Ezra Pound's "The River Merchant's Wife: A Letter", first published in 1915 as a surrogate translation in a collection of Chinese-style poems, turns out a generation later to be a superior "co-eval translation" which scholars familiar with both traditional Chinese texts and modern American poetry have come to appreciate (Yip 1959: 88-94). Arthur Waley's attempt at a translation (Waley 1919), while more literal (and perhaps more reliable as a contingent translation), falls far short of Pound's version as poetry. Pound's version of *Shih Ching* # 23, which begins, in his rendering: "Lies a dead doe . . . " (we analyzed it in a previous chapter) is another instance of a translation intended to be a 'surrogate', but which is also relished by 'co-eval' audiences. In the discourse on translation, insights have been challenged because of a pervasive insistence on categorical systems, on mutually exclusive genres, on clear lines of division between functions. But the study of translation involves all forms of intellectual activity, such as deduction, analysis, inference, and intuition. The sinological dogmatist wants to impose an absolutist vision of the world, and forgets that while meaningful discourse cannot be read in any way that one wants to, anything that is worth rereading can usually be read in more than one way. This is a call not for intellectual permissiveness, but for a critical and scholarly imagination as disciplined and as creative as that of the genius that inspired the original composition.

In recent years computers have eclipsed human computational skills with their aptitude for digital thinking. With megabyte data bases, CD-ROM's, and silicon chips, we are no longer as impressed with human computers as in the past. [9] We require human insights which a computer cannot deliver. Clearly, decoding and deciphering can be done more efficiently by artificial intelligence; to the natural intelligences among us falls the not entirely onerous burden of matching the creativity of original composition with the creativity of sensitive interpretation. In 1992, a patent was issued to two scientists who have developed a technique that enables computers to avoid "digital" thinking and to adopt "analog" ways of figuring out or divining incoming signals of light or sound, thus processing information "through something like flashes of recognition".

---

[9]   It is interesting that individuals who could perform miraculous feats of mental calculation were considered geniuses a generation ago: they are now called "idiot savants"; cf. *The New York Times*, November 30, 1992, C2.

If machines have mastered deduction and analysis, and are now making inroads into recognition, then human researchers must learn to exercise even more the faculties of inference, intuition, and imagination. To explore the processes involved in translation is, by analogy, to probe the way we come to understand something. Our understanding of translations and of translation theory cannot make significant progress unless we understand how we understand. The objective in translation studies is nothing less than to test the adequacy of our thinking, and to assess the quality of our thought.

Divertissements

11. Peacock, Parakeet, Partridge, "Pidgin":
An "Ornithology" of Translators

The title of this chapter should in no way mislead you into thinking that I'm an expert on ornithology, nor do I profess great wisdom about translators. What I'm attempting here is a metaphorical foray into a descriptive taxonomy, using popular images of birds to characterize certain practitioners of the art of translation. It isn't important whether my comparisons are apt, nor is it my suggestion that a translator can be found to fit the description of each bird in existence — although it would not be difficult, if a little malicious, to find translators who might be revealingly identified with buzzards, cormorants, or dodoes. My "conceit" — different species of bird representing different kinds of translators — is flighty, but not, I hope, entirely frivolous.

I choose as a specimen of the translator "peacock" the redoubtable Edward Fitzgerald. His memorable quatrains, not so much translations as embroideries and a patchwork of different texts, are not always easy to trace to their originals, but their gaudy, spectacular display is undeniable:

> A Book of Verses underneath the Bough,
> A Jug of Wine, a Loaf of Bread — and Thou
> Beside me singing in the Wilderness —
> Oh, Wilderness were Paradise enow![1]

A less flambuoyant version would read as follows:

> I need a jug of wine and a book of poetry,
> Half a loaf for a bite to eat,
> Then you and I, seated in a desert spot,
> Will have more than a Sultan's realm.[2]

Notice that in the more faithful version there is no singing, and there is no subtle, unspoken inference — as there is in the FitzGerald — that the companion is a woman, so ardently invoked by the phrase " . . . and Thou." FitzGerald erases the Sultan and all his wealth and universalizes the earthly pleasures in the deliberate archaism of "Paradise enow!" What is striking is that the original appears not to involve a wilderness at all: it is a "desert spot," in one version, a "desert place" in another. What, indeed, would a wilderness be doing in Arabia Deserta? FitzGerald has so completely transformed the poem into a northern setting, forested it with

---

[1]   *Rubaiyat of Omar Khayyam*, translated into English Quatrains by Edward FitzGerald, edited by Louis Untermeyer (New York: Random House, 1947), p. 58. [Hereafter: FitzGerald].

[2]   *The Ruba'ijat of Omar Khayyam*, translated by Peter Avery and John Heath-Stubbs (London: Allen Lane, 1979), p. 71. [Hereafter: Avery and Heath-Stubbs]

wilderness, Christianized it with the notion of "Paradise," archaicized it with obsolete diction, and sexualized it with an implied female companion. But the most subtle transmogrification in FitzGerald is his manipulation of case, changing the speculatively conditional to the willfully subjunctive, from "I need . . . then you and I . . . will have more than . . . . " to the very presently indicative enumeration of the first three lines: ". . . Wine. . .Bread . . . singing . . . wilderness" concluding with the wish-fulfillment of the "were" in "were Paradise," which is neither past nor present, but ideally and contingently indicative. The final touch, archaic though it may seem at the outset, but necessarily paranomasic, is the use of the word "enow," in ". . . Wilderness were Paradise enow!" — meaning not only "enough" but carrying with it phonetically more than a hint of "now," meaning present. Where the original is a plain statement of what one hopes for, FitzGerald presents not only the ardent prospect of paradise, but, subjunctively and indicatively, a present "Paradise enow!"

Consider the following literal rendition of another quatrain from Omar Khayyam:

> The characters of all creatures are on the Tablet,
> The Pen always worn with writing 'Good', 'Bad':
> Our grieving and striving are in vain,
> Before time began all that was necessary was given. [3]

These are certainly thoughtful, even philosophical ruminations, but they are, for the most part, an abstract delineation of a familiar predeterminism. These drab formulations flash into color under FitzGerald's dramatic eye:

> The Moving Finger writes; and, having writ,
> Moves on: not all your Piety nor Wit
> Shall lure it back to cancel half a Line,
> Nor all your Tears wash out a Word of it. [4]

Never has allusion been used more effectively or more ironically, for with the simple phrase, "the Moving Finger," FitzGerald transports us to Belshazzar's feast, as recorded in the *Book of Daniel*, when "Immediately the fingers of a man's hand appeared and wrote on the plaster of the wall of the king's palace . . . .and they saw the hand as it wrote" (5:5). We are told "the king's color changed; his limbs gave way, and his knees knocked together" (5:6). And we recall that Daniel is brought in and asked to gloss the words penned by the "moving finger":

> MENE, MENE, TEKEL, and PARSIN. This is the interpretation of the matter: MENE, God has numbered the days of your kingdom and brought it to an end; TEKEL, you have been weighed in the balxances and found wanting; PERES, your kingdom is divided and given to the Medes and Persians. (5:25-28)

---

[3] Avery and Heath-Stubbs, p. 44

[4] FitzGerald, p. 94.

Belshazzar honors Daniel, but it is too late: "That very night Belshazzar the Chaldean king was slain. And Darius the Mede received the kingdom . . . ." (5:30). For the purposes of exploring the irony of FitzGerald's translation of a Persian poem, perhaps one should not forget the end of Chapter 7 of the Book of Daniel: "So this Daniel prospered during the reign of Darius and the reign of Cyrus the Persian" (6:28).

The import of these expositions is now obvious: aside from the irony of FitzGerald transposing a Persian poem so richly into a Christian context, so that it would appear almost as if Omar Khayyam were commenting on the *Book of Daniel*, there is the further irony that the victim of the prophecy of the "moving finger" should be a Chaldean who is replaced first by a Mede, and later by a Persian. FitzGerald has led the translation full circle, from the Persian to the Christian, back to Daniel and the Chaldeans, who are in turn conquered by the Medes, who are succeeded in the end by the Persians.

FitzGerald's liberties can be faulted as inaccurate interpretations of the text, yet he never fails to realize the fully potential of the poetry. What we read in him is more FitzGerald than Omar Khayyam, and it is clear from his own comments that he suffered from no lack of vanity with regard to his sources. Like a peacock, he preened about his own dazzling display: "It is an amusement for me to take what liberties I like with the Persians, who (as I think) are not Poets enough to frighten one from such excursions, and who really do want a little Art to shape them."[5]

Where the peacock preens proudly in its own glory, the parakeet borrows someone else's glory. By mimicking the sounds precisely, it makes us almost believe that a bird is saying something human. This uncanny effect is found in a genre of translation that might be characterized as "translatophony," i.e., rendering the phonetics of an original in one language with approximations in another language. The result is "phony," of course, in another sense, since the semantics of the words used in the second language do not correspond to the semantics in the original, yet they constitute — by several stretches of the imagination — their own somewhat coherent meaning. This genre dates back at least to the nineteenth century, but I will share a modern example, from the so-called *Mots d'Heurcs: Gousses, Rames: The d'Antin Manuscript*, delightfully "discovered" and annotated by Luis d'Antin Van Rooten. Lest we are rusty on our Mother Goose rhymes, let me refresh your memory with the original before proceeding to the "translatophony" version:

> There was a little girl, and she had a little curl
> Right in the middle of her forehead;
> When she was good, she was very, very good,
> And when she was bad, she was horrid.[6]

---

[5]   From a letter written to E. B. Cowell in 1857, quoted by André Lefevere, in *Translation / History / Culture: A Sourcebook* (London: Routledge, 1992), p. 80.

[6]   *The Oxford Dictionary of Nursery Rhymes*, edited by Iona and Peter Opie (Oxford: Clarendon Press, 1951), pp. 187-188. [Hereafter: *Oxford Dictionary*]

Van Rooten, the human parakeet, mimics the English of the rhyme almost perfectly in French:

> Amboise élite gueule, chic à d'élite écoure-le
> Ratine d'émis de l'eau va fort raide.
> Oing chinois goutte, chinoise béribéri goutte
> Beau doane chinoise batte, j'y vais aux rides. [7]

With Gallic drollness, Van Rooten offers an exegesis of these lines which confirms their status as translatophony:

> The poet reveals his feelings quite clearly anent the élite. He finds
> their elegance disgusting and their red clothing with a high nap
> stiff and uncomfortable. Their taste for Oriental ointments, fancied
> exotic maladies and childish attempts to smuggle their purchases
> makes him grow old before his time. The high moral tone of these
> fragments precludes the assumption that it might be just envy.

Still, deviant as these expositions might first appear, the spirit of this version does not depart markedly from the mock innocence, the ironic worldliness of nursery rhymes in general. Hearing this French parakeet with ears accustomed to English, it is almost like hearing two nursery rhymes, the original recited with a heavy French accent, and a translation with a different meaning in French.

Next we turn to the couple who complemented each other in their eating habits:

> Jack Sprat could eat no fat,
> His wife could eat no lean,
> And so between them both, you see,
> They licked the platter clean. [8]

The French translatophony version does not involve cultural prejudice against the Chinese, although it mentions them, along with a sauce chef named Jacques, an alcoholic and an aficionado of Arab music, who nevertheless believed the earth was flat.

> Jacques s'apprete coulis de nos fetes,
> Et soif que dites nos lignes.
> Et ne sauve bédouine tempo y aussi,
> Telle y que de plat terre, cligne. [9]

Voice recognition systems are now fairly sophisticated, but I wonder if a computer could deduce the meaning of these lines accurately from these

---

[7]   Luis d'Antin Van Rooten, *Mots d'Heures: Gousse, Rames* (New York: Viking, 1967), #12. [hereafter: *Mots d'Heures*]

[8]   *Oxford Dictionary*, p. 238.

[9]   *Mots d'Heures*, #7.

sounds. What program would the computer apply: interpreting accented English? Or translating authentic French?

To indicate how limp it might be to produce a non-"phony" translation of this rhyme into non-rhymed French, I offer this effort, composed by a probably pseudonymous A. M. Nitramof, of Warsaw, in 1872:

> Jacques Spras
> N'aimoit pas le gras,
> Sa femme le maigre détestoit:
> Ainsi, que ses deux
> Rien au monde n'alloit mieux,
> Et rien sur la table ne restait.

This gets the sense of the original nursery rhyme across, but not the nonsense.

Finally, we consider Humpty Dumpty, emblem of the globe, and of the egg, and of chaos:

> Humpty Dumpty sat on a wall,
> Humpty Dumpty had a great fall.
> All the king's horses
> And all the king's men,
> Couldn't put Humpty Dumpty together again. [10]

Van Rooten's version is equally simple in structure, yet it far exceeds the original in allusive complexity:

> Un petit d'un petit
> S'Étonne aux Halles
> Un petit d'un petit
> Ah! degrés te fallent
> Indolent qui ne sort cesse
> Indolent qui ne se mène
> Qu'importe un petit d'un petit
> Tout Gai de Reguennes.

The commentary that Van Rooten supplies is as ingenious as it is droll: of the line "S'Étonne aux Halles" ("Overwhelmed by Les Halles"), Van Rooten writes, "The subject of this epigrammatic poem is obviously from the provinces, since a native Parisian would take this famous old market for granted." Alas, even this remark needs itself further to be emended, since Les Halles has been torned down since this sentence was written. Indeed, a Parisian today would be "S'Étonné" if he saw Les Halles restored to its former state in the middle of Paris — where the Centre Pompidou (Beaubourg) now stands.

We have observed the inferential instinct of the human mind when hearing these translatophony lines. Whatever sounds we hear, we're

---

[10]   *Oxford Dictionary*, p. 213.

inclined to make sense out of them. This genre of translation is a perfect example of what I have called "co-eval" translation, which involves readers familiar with both the source and the target languages. The pleasure is enriched when one sees the similarity of sound in tension with the dissimilarity of meaning. If one is familiar with only one language, the jest would be lost.

Translator parakeets may not mimic sounds as accurately as their avian counterparts, but they know what they mean.

We turn next to the partridge. The Oxford English Dictionary tells us that "In former British Colonies and U. S.," "partridge" is "popularly applied to . . . the Ruffed Grouse." One can, therefore, hardly be blamed for attributing to this species of bird the tendency to complain and to grumble. I don't think anyone would dispute my claim that among the complainers and grumblers to be found in the fraternity of translators, none surpasses Vladimir Nabokov in his ill-tempered vituperation. In citing the four "metrical translations" which he examined in 1964, and which were, he lamented, "unfortunately available to students."[11] "The clumsiest literal translation," he insisted, famously, "is a thousand times more useful than the prettiest paraphrase."[12]

As if to prove the usefulness of his own version, Nabokov produced the following lines with which to end Chapter One of *Eugene Onegin*:

> Of the plan's form I've thought already
> and what my hero I shall call.
> Meantime, my novel's
> first chapter I have finished;
> all this I have looked over closely;
> the inconsistencies are very many,
> but to correct them I don't wish.
> I shall pay censorship its due
> and to the reviewers for devourment
> give away the fruits of my labors.
> Be off, then, to the Neva's banks,
> newborn production!
> And deserve for me fame's tribute,
> false interpretations, noise, and abuse![13]

It is perverse for Nabokov, who is such a superb stylist himself, to produce drivel like this in the name of a "clumsy literal translation," so that he can be "a thousand times more useful." In an astonishingly self-contradictory dictum, Nabokov enjoins translators to render the very text itself. How this might be done in another language is impossible to imagine, because surely Nabokov would agree that the text that is worth translating is hardly

---

[11] *Eugene Onegin: A Novel in Verse by Aleksandr Pushkin*, translated from the Russian, with a Commentary, by Vladimir Nabokov (New York: Bollingen Foundation, 1964), vol. 2, p. 3.

[12] Quoted in *Theories of Translation*, edited by Rainer Schulte and John Biguenet (Chicago: The University of Chicago Press, 1992), p. 127. [Hereafter: *Theories of Translation*]

[13] *Eugene Onegin*, vol. 1, p. 122.

"clumsy" in the original, as almost any literal translation must be. "The person who desires to turn a literary masterpiece into another language," Nabokov writes, "has only one duty to perform, and this is to reproduce with absolute exactitude the whole text, and nothing but the text." [14]

Quite clearly, Nabokov fails to follow his own injunction which, if taken literally, would have discouraged him from venturing forth with a translation at all, for reproducing "with absolute exactitude the whole text" means nothing less than an exact replica of the original in another language, which is neither semantically nor phenomenologically possible.

There is irony in Nabokov's position: proud as a peacock as he may be as an author, he becomes a grouse when it comes to translation, especially the work of other translators.

Finally, we come to "pidgin," which, as you may have already guessed, is not even a bird, but merely sounds like one. According to the OED, "pidgin" is a "Chinese corruption of Eng. business, used widely for any action, occupation, or affair. Hence, pidgin-English, the jargon, consisting chiefly of English words, often corrupted in pronunciation, and arranged according to Chinese idiom, "orig. used for intercommunication between the Chinese and Europeans at seaports, etc., in China, the Straits Settlements, etc.[15]

"Pidgin-English" is a jargon familiar enough, but I should like to sample a bit of "Pidgin-Chinese" to illustrate the disastrous consequences of following Nabokov's advice, of rendering with "absolute exactitude" the original text. Here are a few examples, some rather surprising to natives, most amusing to bilinguals:

小 心	"small-heart" / Take care
馬 上	"horse-on" / right away
生 意	"grow-meaning" / business
點 心	"dot-heart" / dim sum (dumplings)
天 花	"heaven-flower" / smallpox
客 氣	"guest-air" / polite(ness)
赤 足	"red-foot" / barefoot
虛 字	"empty-word" / grammatical particle
那 里	"that place" / where?
那 里 那 里	"where? where?" / (modestly deflecting compliment)
人 山 人 海	"people mountain people sea" / a big crowd
馬 馬 虎 虎	"horse horse tiger tiger" / sloppily

Clearly, absolute word-for-word translation (or even compound-for-compound — see "Where? "Where" example) cannot capture the sheer idiomaticity of language, its gestalt structures of meaning, which refuse to be disassembled, like a machine, into its constituent parts, to be conveniently reassembled on foreign soil. That's why the import-export <u>model for translation is</u> so faulty, because the commodities that can be

---

[14]   *Theories of Translation*, p. 134.

[15]   *The Oxford English Dictionary*, Second Edition, (Oxford: Clarendon Press, 1989), vol. XI, p. 789.

shipped from a source to a destination, carefully handled, usually arrives intact. Language, however, is no commodity, and is inchoate material: with a life and a personality of its own, it can scarcely be shipped without some loss in meaning or nuance. Like some wines, language does not "travel well": it carries the original soil of its provenance.

Our aviary of translators permits us the perspective of taxonomic clarity. We can differentiate between species of translators, and will not need to muddy the waters by venturing apples-and-oranges comparisons. We can ask, more precisely, which peacock is the more colorful; which partridge the grousier, which parakeet the more skillful, which "pidgin" the more ridiculous. Tellingly, each of the four avian counterparts emphasises a different sense: the peacock is clearly visual, and graphic; the parakeet is definitely aural, and phonetic; the grouse is, by instinct, olfactory: he knows when something smells; the "pidgin" is a groper and has only a clumsy tactile sense of words as objects, not as abstractions.

Having strained my original premise, perhaps I should escape by way of conclusion. When asked which bird I aspire to when I translate, my response is: none.

I try to emulate the chameleon.

12. Primal Nights and Verbal Daze:
Puns, Paronomasia, and the People's Daily

On March 20, 1991, a poem appeared in the People's Daily which was clearly a nationalistic, chauvinistic poem. It expressed a longing for home, a gratitude to the People's Republic of China for supporting the poet's life abroad, presumably to study, and it intimated a particular nostalgia for the homeland at the onset of spring. The poem was titled, Yuan Hsiao ("Primal Night"), which marks the end of the Chinese New Year's celebration, and the beginning of spring. It is the time of the Lantern Festival. The poem in the original Chinese reads as follows:

元宵

留美學生朱海洪

東 風 拂 面 催 桃 李
鶬 鷹 舒 翅 展 鵬 程
玉 盤 照 海 下 熱 淚
游 子 登 台 思 故 城
休 負 平 生 報 國 志
人 民 育 我 勝 萬 金
憤 起 急 追 振 華 夏
且 待 神 州 遍 地 春

After its publication, readers in the People's Republic and elsewhere noticed that there was a hidden message in this eight-line regulated (*lü-shih*) form. If read transversely, from the last word in line one to the first word in line seven, the poem spelled out tile following message: 李鵬下台平民憤. I decided to render this poem in English, and my first attempts came out like this:

Primal Night

by Zhu Haihong, Overseas Student

The east wind blows and hastens plum to bloom,
The hawk unfurls its wings and flies a thousand miles.
The silver disk of a moon shines down, sheds hot tears,
The sojourner mounts the lookout and thinks of home.
I must stop disappointing my motherland in this life,
The education she's given me is worth millions.
There's anger and unrest at home
As the good earth awaits the spring.

This versions captures the sentiments in the poem: devotion to country, gratitude for his blessings, homesickness, but there is nothing explicitly or implicitly subversive about it. I then tried to render the poem and at the same time to preserve the hidden, transverse anti-government message. It came out like this:

> East Wind urges plum to flourish its petals, soft as DOWN;
> The hawk unfurls its wings, soars far away WITH the wind.
> The moon shines, sheds tears on the LI-ward sea,
> And a sojourner in the PENG-hu islands thinks of home.
> I'll strive to the END and realize our hopes for the motherland.
> The PEOPLE'S gift to me is worth more than millions.
> RAGE, impetuous rage, invigorates the good earth,
> As we wait for spring to spread all over the land. [1]

The challenge of the poem, I soon realized, was not merely to embed the seditious message in the first seven lines, but also to "disguise" the lines effectively so that one could imagine a hard-pressed editor being impressed by the surface meaning even while he missed the "poisoned pill" in the acrostic.

The native reader will have noticed that the translation pares down the *t'ao-li* 桃 李 ("peach and plum") trope for spring by concentrating on the "plum." This has the net effect, if one remembers the meaning of the Li in "Li Peng," of a first line that flatters the prime minister even more than in the original: 東 風 拂 面 催 桃 李 "East Wind urges plum to flourish its petals, soft as DOWN." In an earlier version, I had the East Wind "blowing the peach and plum blossoms down." Now, while it is true that spring winds do blow flower petals off until they fall down, the convention of seasonal imagery mandates that blowing petals down suggests gusty "West winds" of autumn, rather than the gentle breezes of spring. That this is mere convention and not sound meteorology can be evinced by the recurrence of tornadoes in springtime. But, more to the point in this connection, surely an editor, even one with minimal literary sensibilities, might suspect a line that makes a point of the East Wind blowing petals down. So the strategy of disguise suggested (the conversion of "down" as adverb to "down" as noun). In a certain sense, the choice of "down" was unavoidable, since the hidden acrostic had to read naturally like a slogan calling for action. That required the "Down with . . . ." formula: anything else would seem unnatural.

The third and fourth line posed the greatest challenge. While it is easy in Chinese to talk about "plums" and surreptitiously mean a man whose surname is Li and one could cite a mythical bird, the *p'eng* 鵬 and designate at the same time the Prime Minster's given name, to render these as "plum" and "the *p'eng* bird" in English veers too much toward disguise. There is no way in English to recognize "Plum, the *p'eng* bird" as paronomasia for Li P'eng. To present a recognizable name, one was bound to use the familiar English transliteration, Li P'eng. The problem now became one of disguising what would otherwise be too obvious: how <u>might one camouflage "Li" and "P'eng"?</u>

---

[1] Published on the "Op-Ed" page, *New York Times*, April 30, 1991.

Fortunately, the next line 玉 盤 照 海 下 熱 淚 "The jade plate [the moon] shines on the sea, sheds hot tears" offered some latitude, although "hot tears" was perhaps more conspicuous in English than it would be in Chinese. It was necessary to finesse the trope of "the jade plate" as signifying the moon, not only because it would involve lengthy explanation and circumlocution, but also because the Western mind is not accustomed, as the Chinese are, to thinking of jade as white. Hence, "a jade plate," imagistically viewed as a "green plate," is not likely to conjure up the moon even in the most fertile Western imagination. I decided to opt for simplicity in this instance and use the denotation, "the moon." But how to smuggle in Li P'eng's family name in English?

The "sea" invoked in line 3 suggested waves and wind and sailing, and so the play on words, "LI-ward", presented itself naturally, and accommodated the imagery in the line. One considered disguising the pun on "Li" by spelling "LI-ward" as "leeward." But even though LI and LEE are phonetically equivalent, the reader of English is not likely to see in LEE an equivalent to the family name of the Chinese Prime Minister (even though LEE is a frequently encountered transliteration for 李. As for P'eng, there was no phonetic equivalent discoverable in English, so I hit upon a happy accident. Using a different grapheme for "*p'eng*" one could posit the "*P'enghu tao*" 澎 湖 島, the Pescadores Islands. Since these were offshore, they would be a natural location for a sojourning Chinese thinking of home, particularly poignant because it was, in a sense, so close to home yet so far away. The longing for home from someone across the Taiwan Straits was an apt counterpart for the original line, which read: 游 子 登 台 思 故 城, "The sojourner mounts the lookout and thinks of the ancient city." A Chinese reader could be imagined to miss the conjunction of "Li" with "P'eng" when these words are so naturally embedded in such moving reminiscences.

The second half of the poem is a series of platitudinous expressions of resolve, determination, as well as gratitude for the nurturing support of the motherland. As a student studying abroad, presumably with the financial support of the Ministry of Education, the poet-narrator does not appear to be like so many Chinese students abroad, critical of the government and seemingly ungrateful to the homeland. On the contrary, the claims that the education received from the people is worth more than ten thousand pieces of gold: 人 民 育 我 勝 萬 金 "The PEOPLE'S gift to me is worth more than millions". The seventh line is perhaps the only place in the poem which is not piously pacific: 憤 起 急 追　　　 振 華 RAGE, impetuous rage, invigorates the good earth". The binome, *hua-hsia* 華 夏 , a literary reference to China, is a term used by Chinese to indicate their homeland. To translate this phrase as "China" would be to trade connotation for denotation, and to confuse the deictic point of reference from that of an insider to the vantage point of an outsider. "China" is a neutral term that can be used by anyone; but *hua-hsia* 華 夏 is what I call an endotropic term, i.e., it is a term used by insiders. Just as intimates do not refer to themselves by their full name, so one's reference to one's motherland will be different from the terms that outsiders use. The problem for the translator is to capture this allusion and these suggestions, without violating the natural fluency of the original. The vigor of the imagery in the line suggested that a concrete nominal would be better than an abstract reference. "The good earth" recommended itself, not only because it carries out the theme of the world in spring, but also because, for the reader of English, "the good earth" will almost certainly — after Pearl Buck's famous novel — remind the reader of China. Another self-referential nominal occurs in the last line: *shen-chou* 神 州, which is an ancient name for China. Here, again, it seemed advisable to avoid the alienating reference to China: one was content to allow context to determine that the "land" mentioned in the line was unmistakably China.

What struck me about this poem were the ironies. The very nationalistic ardor of the original poem is what probably attracted the attention of the editor of the *People's Daily*, looking for appropriate items from all the submissions that are received unprompted and unsolicited. The aptness of the piece for a particular seasonal festival was obvious, and no one could question the inclusion of the poem if published around *yuan-hsiao*. And one could hardly blame a loyal bureaucratic sub-editor who, wishing to ingratiate himself with the authorities, publishes a poem from an overseas student that, far from criticizing his homeland, extols it in the most heartfelt way. The traditional nature of the form also spoke in favor of the poem: written in the classical *ch'i-yen lü-shih* 七 言 律 詩 form rather than a more modish and modern free verse, this verse was a reaffirmation of uniquely Chinese values, evidence that not all students were irrevocably influenced by the West. Surely the publication of this piece would be a coup for all those involved, an occasion for self-congratulation, a reassuring reminder that not all youth were rebellious or disloyal. Indeed, one can hardly imagine a more "patriotic" poem to mark the auspices of spring.

Had the editor been more literary, he might have noticed that the poem was — at the lexical level — almost totally without ambiguities: there appeared to be no obvious resonant ironies. The meaning was unmistakable: each line celebrated the season and the devotion to one's country. A more exigent literary reader might have dismissed the poem as too platitudinous, too trite, altogether too obvious — even if he were to miss the fatal diagonal acrostic.[2]

It is semiotically important, of course, for Chinese readers that the acrostic is diagonal *hsieh* 斜 — because in the contrast between *hsieh* and *cheng* 正 — is the contrast between not only the oblique and the straight, but also between the heterodox and the orthodox. Here, from the viewpoint of those who disapprove of the government, what is heterodox is orthodox, and what is orthodox is heterodox, or to borrow the

---

[2]   When I presented a seminar on this poem at the University of Vienna in 1994, my friend Richard Trappl discovered that the "complete" set of *The People's Daily* 人 民 日 報 in the University's library was missing the issue for March 20, 1991. Evidently, the error was discovered before the overseas edition was sent out.

formulations from the *Hung-lou meng* (variously rendered in English as *The Dream of the Red Chamber* or *The Dream of the Red Mansions* or *The Story of the Stone*): "when the false is taken for true, the true is false": 假作真時真作假

Even for a traditionalist culture, the poem might have been suspected of banality. In this connection, one might think that all nationalistic poems are banal, and indeed it would be hard to avoid that conclusion. But there are many great poets who are not nationalistic in any meaningful sense, including Goethe for the Germans, and Tu Fu (Du Fu) for the Chinese. What differentiates national poetry that is banal from national poetry that is not banal? I think there is a simple answer: banality discourages fresh insights; it encourages smug atavisms; it is inimical to thinking. The trouble with clichés is not that they are wrong, but that they do not stimulate the mind. As Donal Henahan of the New York Times once wrote, "Clichés are simply truths rubbed so smooth they deflect thought."[3] What the editor of the People's Daily saw was a poem that was well-meaning; a poem that he thought meant well. He saw only the sentiments that he recognized, and looked no further. The irony is that if the sub-editor was arrested he was arrested for political impropriety and not for bad taste in literature. (Fortunately or unfortunately, bad taste in literature has never been a criminal offense, although some might consider it at least a misdemeanor.) Yet the editor's political instincts were surely correct. How many politicians can be expected to look behind the slogans, how many are sensitive to the ironies behind the shibboleth, to be suspicious about "politically correct" sentiments which may be as insincere as they are "correct".

A further irony is that the embedded message is a political slogan, and hardly poetic at all. "Down with Li Peng; End People's Suffering!" or, in a more literal version: "Li P'eng Step Down; Mollify the Anger of the People!" can hardly be viewed as very literary. The message is straightforward; the rhetoric forceful. Indeed in the translation it was the unambiguous slogan which set the constraints on rendering, for whatever else was achieved the diagonal acrostic had to come across as a believable political slogan. Hence there was latitude in everything else —— the imagery, the rhythm, the diction — but the key words in the acrostic were set: they allowed for very little deviation. Slogans admit of no circumlocution. "Li P'eng, Step down from the Platform" might be literally a more faithful rendering of 李鵬下台 but it is far from plausible as a rude remonstrance from the rabble.

This incident, as well as the exercise of translating the original poem in such a way as to preserve the hidden acrostic, has provided concrete insights into the notion of nationalism and the essence of literature. The moral of the story is that nationalism is, on the whole, only political and rather superficial, and patriotism is, indeed, the last refuge of the scoundrel. One's allegiance to culture may be more important than one's allegiance to a polity. And I don't mind saying this on both sides of the

---

[3]   March 2, 1980, Section 2, page 33.

Taiwan Straits. When politics runs counter to culture, when ideology undermines the search for the multifaceted, dynamic truth, then the cretins and the Philistines have taken over. Any time anyone, whether Nationalist politician or Communist cadre, whether American patriot or Chinese loyalist, appeals to my emotions at the expense of my intelligence, then — yes, even if it were to celebrate motherhood and apple pie in America, or the sacredness of tradition in China — I want no part of that kind of chauvinism. My chauvinism is a chauvinism of humanity, embodied in the Confucian notion of *jen* 仁. And anything that undercuts that notion of humanity, that subdivides and categorizes and specializes to such a degree that the promontory of humanity is forgotten, and the sight of the continent is obscured, is mischievously ignorant and misguided.

In America, the fearful consequences of the Persian Gulf War and the horrified reactions to September 11, 2001 have unleashed a torrent of blind, flag-waving, yellow-beribboned patriotism that makes a mockery of true patriotism. It is ironic that Americans who support the students involved in the June 4, 1989 Tienanmen Incident should become increasingly intolerant of dissenters from the decision to go to war for a nation of desert shieks in Kuwait and Saudi Arabia or to accept "collateral" damage in the "War on Terrorism". Evidently, the freedom to disagree, in the eyes of some, is more supportable when it occurs in another country than in one's own.

That, in the end, may be the most interesting lesson of the fiasco of the *Yuan-hsiao* 元 宵 poem in the *People's Daily*. The ability to read a text, to read it as literature is an intensely subversive act. The literary imagination is — unlike the political intelligence — intensely self-critical and ironic. Literature has, within itself, a sort of "self-correcting ribbon," a "fault-proof" computer program, which doubts even as it asserts. Good literature will have this creative tension, which the now-old "New Critics" called ambiguity. There is, unfortunately, a negative formulation that privileges clarity and that assumes the definitiveness of declarative meaning: it suggests that something that is neither here nor there is ambiguous. There is even a hint of moral cravenness in being unable to decide between right and wrong. But the truth is dialectical, ironic, and self-reflexive 正 言 若 反 "The Truth appears to be its opposite", the *Tao Te Ching* reminds us, and we must read through the lines, between the lines, and, in the case of the *Yuan-hsiao* poem, across the lines.

As a literary scholar, I cannot help but see the whole incident as a recuperation of the value of critical discernment. Perhaps the editor at the *People's Daily* would have survived politically if he had been a more sensitive reader of literature, for the banal message in the original poem had nothing of the richness, either of literature or of life. Literary judgment (even without political vigilance) would have advised against the publication of the poem with the "poison pill."

Perhaps the moral of the story is that politicians should know something about literature, after all.

13. Hong Kong Place-Names:
Colonial or Postcolonial?

In Brian Friel's play, *Translations*, a team of British army engineers visit Ireland to survey the local geography with the express purpose of making a new map, "to see that the place-names on this map are . . . correct." When a local citizen remonstrates, asking, "What's 'incorrect' about the place-names we have here?", he is told, "Nothing at all. They're just going to be standardized." "You mean," says the local, "changed into English?" He is told: "Where there's ambiguity, they'll be Anglicised" (i, p. 32).

In surveying a map of Hong Kong, it is clear that no such team of British army engineers ever visited Hong Kong to "Anglicize" its place-names, or, if they had, they made, as the British would say, "a rum job of it." And it is also clear that in the many instances in which ambiguity exists, Anglicization was not always the solution. In fact, there appears to be no consistent principle at all in the way Hong Kong place-names are established or in the ways that they are presented.

What I offer here is a brief excursus into Hong Kong onomastics, viewed from the perspective of a translator, a cultural tourist, and a bicultural resident. I do not pretend to any great expertise in linguistics, or in geographical etymology, and my knowledge of Hong Kong is limited to the years I've lived there. My overall purpose is to use translation, and specifically translation of place-names, as a prism to refract the spectrum of the colonial and post-colonial character of Hong Kong.

But before we proceed to examine the colonial and postcolonial implications of Hong Kong place-names, we might review some of the axioms of recent postcolonial theory relating to questions of authenticity, particularly as it relates to translation, which involves the expropriation of foreign words as well as the imposition of foreign identities, on the local terrain. A defining dictum of postcolonial thought might be the following:

> In the early period of post-colonial writing many writers were forced into the search for an alternative authenticity which seemed to be escaping them, since the concept of authenticity itself was endorsed by a centre to which they did not belong and yet was continually contradicted by the everyday experience of marginality. The eventual consequence of this experience was that notions of centrality and the 'authentic' were themselves necessarily questioned, challenged, and finally abrogated. (Ashcroft et al, p. 41)

The Manichaean either/or formulation of these anti-centrist sentiments is, in my view, one of the major flaws of early postcolonial criticism. What is posited is a hegemonic authenticity, against which one needs to construct, presumably, an anti-hegemonic "alternative authenticity." Scarcely considered is a phenomenon that one will find pervasively familiar in Hong Kong — the emergence of not so much an alternative authenticity as alternative authenticities.

Another tenet of postcolonial criticism is that "colonialism and translation went hand in hand" (Susan Bassnett: Bassnett and Trivedi, p. 3). Bassnett quotes Eric Cheyfitz's statement "that translation was, and still is, the central act of European colonization and imperialism in America" (Cheyfitz 1991:104). Tejaswini Niranjana is pointedly skeptical of translation: "Translation as a practice shapes, and takes shape within, the asymmetrical relations of power that operate under colonialism," adding, ". . . in presenting particular versions of the colonized, translation brings into being overarching concepts of reality and representation." "These concepts, and what they allow us to assume," she concludes, "completely occlude the violence that accompanies the construction of the colonial subject" (p. 2).

Note that in these dicta the translation that is assumed is one-way, from the coloniz*ed* language into the coloniz*ing* language. In such words as "occlude", "violence," "assymetrical", there is more than a hint of injustice, duplicity, and — of course — hegemony. What is overlooked in the imperial myopia of this point of view is the translation that occurs in the other direction, from colonizer to colonized. Surely, in this process, there is, presumably, less occlusion, violence, assymmetry and violence.

Let us examine the realia of Hong Kong place-names in the light of this theory.

At the southern tip of the Kowloon Peninsula is the area called, in Cantonese, Tsim Sha Tsui 尖 沙 嘴[1]. pronounced Jian Sha Zui in Mandarin (the Cantonese locution is heard often, the Mandarin rarely if ever). This transliteration, Tsim Sha Tsui, has taken on a life of its own, and is now virtually an abstract marker for a commercial district that attracts tourists. Its etymology is, however, much more picturesque, and means, literally, "Point Sand Mouth." While no exact equivalent in English suggests itself, the topography of the original setting that inspired Tsim Sha Tsui might be captured by the designation "Promontory Point" (the notion of "sand" would, of course, be lost, but then there is, by now, no sand left in Tsim Sha Tsui.[2]

One doesn't know which to prefer: the phonetic exoticism of "Tsim Sha Tsui" (the original meaning of which has, perhaps, faded — even for Cantonese ears) or the euphonious romance of "Promontory Point". Certainly, the vistas of Victoria Harbor, and the view of Hong Kong Island across the bay would be more obviously evoked from "Promontory Point"

---

[1]   The word used is calligraphically simpler, combining 口 and 且.

[2]   By the same token, there is no sand left (except on a beach here and there) in Sha Tin 沙 田, "Sandy Fields" in the (eastern) New Territories, or in Cheung Sha Wan 長 沙 灣 "Long Sands Bay" on the Island. It is interesting to note that the topographic meaning of the Chinese word for "mouth" 嘴 refers to a land formation, whereas the topographic English connotation of "mouth" usually refers to a body of water, as in "the mouth of a

than from "Tsim Sha Tsui". In a sense, the English translation would preserve at least some of the topographic sense of the original, whereas the transliteration is merely a cipher, with no semantic mnemonic. If one assumes that the British occupied the northern shore of Hong Kong Island and the southern tip of the Kowloon Peninsula, one might expect that the primary landmarks in that area would be Anglicized, either English nominals or English translations. The persistence of Tsim Sha Tsui in its untranslated, non-anglicized form, flies in the face of what one might have expected. And if, as postcolonial theory suggests, "the choice of leaving words untranslated in postcolonial texts is a political act, because while translation is not inadmissable in itself, glossing gives the translated word, and thus the 'receptor' culture, the higher status" (Ashcroft et al, p. 66) — this means that Tsim Sha Tsui must have been "demoted" in the eyes of the British. What is said in post-colonial theory about "interlanguages" is, on the other hand, "bang on," as the English would say: "The use of untranslated words as interface signs seems a successful way to foreground cultural distinctions, so it would appear even more profitable to attempt to generate an 'interculture' by the fusion of the linguistic structures of two languages" (Ashcroft et al, p. 66). Surely, this reference to an area that is "even more profitable" by providing a "fusion of the linguistic structures of two languages" could not fit a district in Hong Kong more accurately than Tsim Sha Tsui!

The designation of the peninsula where Tsim Sha Tsui is situated, named Kowloon 九 龍 (Jiu Long in Mandarin — a collocation that one does encounter) may be offered as another form of linguistic bi-polarity. The etymology of this place-name is more accessible, meaning, as it does, "Nine Dragons". The Chinese propensity for designating mountain ranges as "dragons" might suggest that the characteristic of Kowloon that initially attracted attention was its mountainous terrain. Yet, even this accessible translation is rejected for a locution certainly more opaque to the Westerner — Kowloon. This may, indeed, be an instance of what the postcolonial theorist posits as *différance*: "The use here of untranslated words is a clear signifier of the fact that the language . . . is an/Other language" (Ashcroft el al, p. 64).

But if these post-colonial observations are true, surely they must be true, whatever the language. Let us consider reverse transliterations, not of Chinese names into English, but of English names into Chinese, as in Kin Nei Tei Sheng 堅 尼 地 城 whose Chinese characters ("firm", "nun", "place" "city") are misleading, because the first three words are mere phonetics, and only the last character "city" is used as a semanteme — yielding, "Kennedy Town". Similarly, 佐 敦 道 doesn't mean, as the Chinese characters might suggest, "assist", "candor" "road", but is merely the very close phonetic approximation in Cantonese, *Jor Dun Dao*, or, Jordan Road. Ma Gei Sin Gap (Mandarin: Ma Ji Xian Xia) 馬 己 仙 峽 doesn't mean "Horse", "Self" "Sage" "Gap" as the Chinese characters might suggest — but is the Cantonese way of referring, phonetically, to

Magazine Gap.[3]

What do these "untranslated" names signify? Is it a matter of conveying the sense of "an/Other language"? Or is it something less portentous and more pragmatic, i. e., merely a phonetic aid to the non-English speaking native as to how to approximate the pronunciation of "Kennedy Town", "Jordan Road," or "Magazine Gap Road" in Cantonese? We will see later on that even this rationale may not be warranted.

Actually, there is a third mode of handling place names in Hong Kong, involving neither transliteration nor translation: this class of counterparts might be called "co-eval" names, where both the English and the Chinese exist separately, and separate nominalisms designate the same location, with no lexical or phonetic relationship to each other. Repulse Bay, for example, with its very British connotation of discrete obduracy, is unrelated to the more descriptive oceanographic name in Chinese, which by contrast to the adjacent bay is called: "Shallow Water Bay" Qian Shui Wan 淺 水 灣, pronounced by Cantonese as Chin Shui Wan . And the Chinese version of the designation for the racecourse, Pao Ma Tei 跑 馬 地 (Mandarin: *Pao ma di*), literally, "a place where the horses run", is pretty straightforward, but it has nothing of the Elysian overtones of "Happy Valley," its designation in English. "Castle Peak Road" may sound a bit more gothic and medieval than 青 山 路, which may be more prosaically rendered as "Dark Mountain Road" or "Blue Mountain Road" or "Black Mountain Road" — depending on how one translates 青.

Is there any significance to the disparity between the Chinese and English versions of Hong Kong's sixteen-seat vehicles, which is 小 巴("Small Bus" in Chinese), and "Maxicab" — ("大的 士" in English)?

There are anomalies like 金 鐘 ("Gold Bell") for Admiralty, which is neither a transliteration nor a translation, though one can speculate that the Chinese and the English reflect two different associations of the original site, which, presumably, housed the British Naval headquarters, and where, again presumably, a large bell was routinely struck to mark the watches. A more difficult conundrum occurs with Causeway Bay and 銅 鑼 灣. The third word in each name is equivalent: 灣 / Bay. But 銅 鑼 means "Copper Gong" — not Causeway. Was there a Golden Bell in Admiralty and a Copper Gong in Causeway Bay? We might call these "homotopes", i.e., references which are neither equivalent in sound (transliteration) nor in meaning (translation) but which are equivalent by virtue of their designating the same place, but using different associations. A bilingual might be forgiven if he is confused with Queensway being identified in Chinese as 金 鐘 道; if 金 鐘 is the Chinese equivalent of Admiralty, then why shouldn't 金 鐘 道 not be "Admiralty Road" rather than Queensway? Perhaps the strangest homotope is the one for Lantau Island. The name looks like a transliteration, but it isn't. The

---

[3] There is an interesting coincidence here, since the transliteration of the Cantonese pronunciation of the Chinese word for "mountain gap" 峽 is identical to the spelling of the English word "gap" — meaning the same thing. We might call these interlingual equivalents "phononyms" — where the pronunciation of a word in one language is exactly the same as in another language, both of which have the same meaning.

Chinese name for the island is 大嶼山島, which, literally translated, would mean "Big small-island mountain island". Although this is literally what is printed on the signs, local Cantonese just say 大嶼山, avoiding orally the redundancy of "Big Island Mountain Island" in the written form. But the English version, "Lantau" Island, bears no relation to the current Chinese nominalism; it's a transliteration of an earlier, but now discarded name 爛頭, which means "Rotten Head", perhaps referring to the fact that, according to local lore, the island was formerly only sparsely forested and decrepit in appearance.[4]

If we consider the anomalies of place-names in Hong Kong, we have to be alert to when something is transl*ated* from Chinese to English, when it is transl*iterated* from Chinese to English, when it is transl*ated* from English to Chinese, and when it is transl*iterated* from English to Chinese. Consider the poor tourist on the MTR who cannot read Chinese: he needs to negotiate between Chai Wan 柴灣 ("Brushwood Bay") , Wan Chai 灣仔 ("Little Bay"), and Tsuen Wan 荃灣 ("Fishtrap Bay"). Chinese passengers of the MTR will be able to read the signs in Chinese, but those who can only negotiate English might be forgiven if they are hopelessly confused in a muddle of "Chai's" and "Wan's". Might these names not be more serviceable for those who are illiterate in Chinese if they were rendered in translation? Surely, "Brushwood Bay", "Little Bay", and "Fishtrap Bay" would be easier to remember and easier to differentiate one from the other. And wouldn't "Garrison Gate" be more attractive than Tuen Mun 屯門 ? After all, translations of place-names that were originally Chinese abound: there is "Diamond Hill" for 鑽石山, Fortress Hill for 炮台山, and North Point for 北角. And, while we're at it, why not "Bullhead Corner" for 牛頭角 Ngau Tau Kok (or should that be "Bullhead Horns"?), and "Multicolored Rainbow" for 彩虹 (Choi Hung), and "Prospect Pond" for 觀塘 (Kwun Tong), and "Fire and Charcoal" for 火炭 (Fo Tan), and "Sandy Field" for 沙田 (Sha Tin).

Transliterations have a way of obscuring and even obliterating some of the most colorful etymologies of the place-names in Hong Kong. Ho Man Tin 何文田, for example, is not very obvious even in the original, although legend has it that the area was first settled by three families with the surname Ho 何, Man 文, and Tin 田 (Liang, p. 60). Hong Hum 紅磡 is easy enough to translate: "Red dockyard", but its significance is not immediately obvious. However, if we resort to legend, we will find something at least plausible: it appears that workers building a shipyard at the water's edge were startled to see red water gushing up out of the seabed. Not until a geomancer was called in to quell the waters did work on the dockyard resume (Liang, p. 62).

Of course, not all failures to translate are to be regretted: Yau Ma Tei 油麻地 is probably better left in the transliteration, since it means "place of oily hemp", and present-day polluted Hong Kong 香港 itself (Cantonese: Heung Gong) might not wish to be reminded that its name

---

[4]   I am indebted to Chan Wing Choi, Honorary Secretary of the Institute for Linguistics (Hong Kong branch) for this detail.

originally meant "Fragrant Harbor" in Chinese.[5]

In our survey of Hong Kong place names, there appears to be no obvious pattern in why some names, originally Chinese, are translated, and others transliterated. There are, to be sure, many names originally in English that are transliterated in Chinese. However, there appear to be many fewer instances of names originally in English that have been translated into Chinese. The most obvious are those connected with English royalty, such as 皇 后 大 道 for Queen's Road, 公 主 道 for Princess (Margaret) Road, and 太 子 道 for Prince (Edward) Road. Then, there is 界 限 街 for Boundary Street; 軍 器 廠 街 Arsenal Street; 中 峽 道 Middle Gap Road; 摩 囉 廟 街 Mosque Street;[6] 舊 山 頂 道 Old Peak Road; 差 館 上 街 Upper Station Road; and 聖 十 字 徑 Holy Cross Path.

What speculations might we venture with this sketch of the place-names in Hong Kong? First, the lack of uniformity might reflect the sporadic expansion of the British settlement, first established in Hong Kong Island and the southern tip of the Kowloon Peninsula, later spreading northward towards the New Territories in Kowloon, and southward on Hong Kong Island. Second, the names that seem oblivious of the existence of the other, as if referring to two unrelated places ("homotopes"), may reflect concurrent "hegemonies" where English and Chinese cultures co-existed. Third, we notice that there are many street names transliterated from English which are in fact named for historical figures, as in Des Voeux Road, Pottinger Road, D'Aguilar Street, Hennessey Road, Harcourt Road, Chater Road, Connaught Road. By contrast, there are almost no street names of Chinese origin that derive from the names of Chinese luminaries. Indeed, this contrast can be extrapolated as a major difference between the West of post-Renaissance Europe and the United States, on the one hand, and Asia on the other. In the U. S. especially, places are named after people: Washington, Jefferson, Franklin, Madison, Monroe, Lincoln, et al — are all commemorated by cities (Washington, D. C.; innumerable Jeffersonvilles; Madison, Wisconsin; Franklin, Indiana; Monroe, Michigan — not to mention many counties and street names that are named after individuals). In the United States, even a relative non-entity like Lt. Zebulon Montgomery Pike can be enshrined with a place name — in Pike's Peak. Yet, despite their renown and their importance, you will search the length and breadth of Asia and not find a single town or city named after Confucius, Buddha,

---

[5]   As for the source of the "Fragrant" in "Fragrant Harbor," there are at least four variously dubious derivations: one involves a woman pirate named "Fragrant damsel" who occupied the island, and for whom the island was named (although scholars find this dubious) ; a second relates to a temple situated where Causeway Bay is now, in front of which there was a censer that produced a fragrance that the winds wafted out for miles: in time the mountain behind the temple was called "Red Fragrance Censer Mountain" 紅 香 爐 港, later shortened to "Fragrant Harbor" 香 港; a third recalls some fragrant waters; and a fourth alludes to fragrant trees (see Jao Chiu Tsai 饒 玖 才, pp. 105-110).

[6]   Actually, 摩 囉, is not a transliteration, but a Cantonese term designating Indians: the term clearly does not differentiate between Muslims and Hindus, Indians and Arabs.

Laozi, or Mao Zidong: no "Confuciustown" 孔子城, no "Buddhaville" 如來村 no "Laozi Capital" 老子京 and no "Chairman Mao Village" 毛主席村莊.[7]

If one were to learn about Hong Kong from its place names alone, one would find out almost nothing about the terrain from most of the English names, and almost nothing about the civic leaders from any of the Chinese names. Of course, this propensity reflects more than the traditionalist Chinese (indeed, Asian) practice of naming places and people after the terrain, and the modernist Western tendency of using places to commemorate people. During the colonial period, it was inevitable that the names of the colonials and not of the natives would be monumentalized. Although there was, before the 1997 return of Hong Kong to the motherland, a flurry of interest in removing all vestiges of colonial hegemony, there does not appear to be much enthusiasm for such wholesale nativization of place names now. Some areas, in fact, resolutely retain their English flavor. The area around Kowloon Tong, with its Suffolk Road 沙福道, Dorset Crescent 多實街, Somerset 森麻實道, Norfolk Road 羅福道, Devon Road 德雲道, Kent Road 根德道, Stafford Road 施他佛道, Essex Crescent 雅息士 — all run along that most triumphant of English place names, Waterloo 窩打老道.

What are we to make of these different transpositional strategies, and how does our analysis affect our understanding of the relationship between translation and post-colonialism? First, we notice what is missing: there is no draconian erasure of local names in favor of names redolent of empire (as one finds in Friel's *Translations*). We find a variety of adamic practices: accommodations of meaning (translation), nominalistic fidelity to sound (transliteration), and calcifications of native language idiom and custom (homotope). Perhaps it's my pedantic way of dispelling the myth, promulgated by theorists bent on abstractions or by rhetoricians eager to make a point, that cultures cannot be monolithized into entities that can be conjured up, abrogated, or appropriated. (Indeed, the only post-colonial abrogation I have noticed since the "handover" of Hong Kong to the People's Republic of China is the removal of the word "Royal" from "The Royal Hong Kong Jockey Club" — hardly a revolutionary adjustment of attitude; "The Royal Hong Kong Yacht Club", in fact, refuses to give up its "Royal".)

A study of Hong Kong place-names in the context of postcolonial theory is an awkward affair. Either the reality evinced in the historical record seems not to fit the theory, or postcolonial theory appears to be irrelevant. The Hong Kong instance neither confirms nor disconfirms the theory. One of the most recent de-colonized territories, yet it would be difficult to characterize Hong Kong as either "colonial" or "postcolonial".

---

[7]   There is, as far as I know, one glaring exception, and that is "Ho Chi Minh City" — which is a recent coinage. There *are* in Hong Kong occasional streets — like Ho Tung Road 何東道 — named after local celebrities or people who owned the land, there are no "honorific" street names recalling nationally and internationally renowned Chinese (or non-Chinese) eminenti.

Perhaps it would be more accurate to say that Hong Kong is both, and it is neither.

In one respect, however, Hong Kong is indubitably post-colonial and postmodern. In the best postmodern tradition, Hong Kong is resolutely not centrist, or to put it more accurately, it is multicentrist. "Central" is the English "translation" for 中 環 a district which might be more accurately rendered as "Central Hub". But "Central" is also identified in Chinese by 中 區 meaning, literally, "Central district". And the building known as Central Plaza is not situated in Central, but east in Wan Chai, and now we have another building called "The Centre" on Queen's Road Central , which is, indeed, in the western sector of the district called Central. The Chinese name of this building is 中 環 中 心 which, rendered literally, would be "Central Hub Center" or, if we adopt the convention of "Central" for 中 環, would yield, "Central Centre". Hong Kong, therefore, has not only different locations marked by the notion of center; it also has different nominalizations as well. Whatever the etymologies of these variant terms, it is clear that the word "center" doesn't mean in Hong Kong quite what it means elsewhere. The "center" in Hong Kong appears in different places. Curiously, the versions of "center" in Hong Kong are neither transliterations, nor translations, nor even homotopes. Perhaps in this, as in so many other respects, Hong Kong was postmodern way ahead of its time.

Works Cited

Alam, Qaizer Zoha. 1992. "Humour and Translation." *IJT: International Journal of Translation*. 4:1-2 (Jan-Dec.), 81-93.

Ashcroft, Bill, Gareth Griffiths, and Helen Tiffin. 1989. *The Empire Writes Back: Theory and Practice in Post-Colonial Literatures*. London: Routledge.

Bassnett, Susan and Harish Trivedi, eds. 1999. *Post-Colonial Translation*. London: Routledge

Baudelaire, Charles. 1947-53. *Correspondance générale*, ed. Jacques Crépet, 6 vols. Paris: L. Conard

Benjamin, Walter. 1968. *Illuminations: Essays and Reflections*. New York: Harcourt, Brace and Jovanovich.

Benson, John Benson and Giles Constable, eds. 1991. *Renaissance and Renewal in the Twelfth Century*. Toronto: University of Toronto Press. (First published: Harvard University Press, 1982).

Berlin, Isaiah. 1981. *Concepts and Categories: Philosophical Essays*. New York: Penguin Books.

Boodberg, Peter. 1979. *Selected Works of Peter Boodberg*, ed. Alvin P. Cohen. Berkeley: University of California Press.

Boorman, Howard and Richard Howard. 1968-1970. *Biographical Dictionary of Republican China*. 3 vols. New York: Columbia University Press).

Bowers, Fredson. 1956. Hamlet's 'Sullied' or 'Solid' Flesh: A Bibliographical Case-History. *Shakespeare Survey* 9. 44-48.

Bowers, Fredson. 1959. *Textual and Literary Criticism*. Cambridge: Cambridge University Press.

Cheng, Chen-to. 1975. "The Translator Who Knew No English: Lin Shu." *Renditions* 5. 26-31.

Certeau, Michel de. *Culture in the Plural*. 1997. Translated & with an Afterword by Tom Conley. Minneapolis: University of Minnesota Press.

Ch'en, Kenneth. 1964. *Buddhism in China: A Historical Survey*. Princeton: Princeton University Press.

Ch'ien Chung-shu [Qian Zhongshu]. 1975. "Lin Ch'in-an Revisited." *Renditions* 5. 8-25.

Cheyfitz, Eric. 1991. *The Poetics of Imperialism*. New York: Oxford University Press.

Child, Jack. 1996. "Spanish-English Translation: Crossing the Cultural Bridge." *ATA Chronicle*, January, p. 22-23.

Compton, Robert William. 1971. *A Study of the Translations of Lin Shu, 1852-1924*. Ph.D dissertation, Stanford University.

Coward, Harold. 1988. *Sacred Word and Sacred Text. Scripture in World Religions*. Maryknoll, New York: Orbis.

Dabney, J. P. 1837. *The New Testament of Our Lord and Saviour Jesus Christ*, by William Tyndale, the Martyr. Andover: Gould & Newman.

Dahood, Mitchell, S. J. 1965. *Psalms 1-50*, The Anchor Bible. Garden City: Doubleday and Company.

Davenport, Guy. 1996. *The Hunter Gracchus*. Washington, D. C.: Counterpoint.

Dimic, Milan. 1975. "Translation and Interpretation in Bicultural and Multicultural Societies." In *Translation and Interpretation: The Multi-Cultural Context*, 13-34. Vancouver: CAUTG.

Eagleton, Terry, Fredric Jameson, and Edward Said. 1991. *Nationalism, Colonialism, and Literature*. Minneapolis: University of Minnesota Press.

Eliot, T. S. 1934. *Elizabethan Essays*. London: Faber and Faber.

Eoyang, Eugene. 2002. "Western Agon / Eastern Ritual: Confrontations and Co-optations in World Views," in: *Thresholds of Western Culture: Identity, Postcoloniality, Transnationalism*. London: Continuum International Publishing (forthcoming).

_____. 1997 "Hong Kong and the Human Trinity: Language, Education, and Culture." *Asian Thought and Society*, vol. XXII, No. 66 (September-December): pp. 242-248.

_____. 1993. *The Transparent Eye: Translation, Chinese Literature, and Comparative Poetics*. Honolulu: University of Hawaii Press.

_____. 1983. "Translation as Excommunication: Notes Toward an Intra-worldly Poetics." Paper presented at First Sino-American Symposium on Comparative Literature. In: Eoyang, Eugene (Ed). *The Transparent Eye: Translation, Chinese Literature, and Comparative Poetics*. Honolulu: University of Hawaii Press. pp. 111-168.

_____. 1988. "Maladjusted Messenger: Rezeptionsasthetik in Translation," *Chinese Literature: Essays. Articles. Reviews* (CLEAR) 10 (1988), pp. 61-66.

_____. 1985. "Changing the Canon: The Challenge of Non-Western Literatures," Unpublished paper. American Comparative Literature Association conference, Ann Arbor, March 1985.

Fanon, Frantz. 1990 (1961). *The Wretched of the Earth (Les Damnés de la Terre)*. Harmondsworth: Penguin Books.

Faur, José. 1986. *Golden Doves with Silver Dots: Semiotics and Textuality in the Rabbinic Tradition*. Bloomington: Indiana University Press.

Foley, John Miles. 1986. *Oral Tradition in Literature: Interpretation in Context*. Columbia: University of Missouri Press.

Foster, John Burt, Jr. and Wayne J. Froman, eds. *Threholds of Western Culture: Identity, Postcoloniality, Transnationalism*. New York: Continuum, 2002.

Friel, Brian. 1981. *Translations*. London: Faber and Faber.

Gadamer, Hans-Georg. 1975. Truth and Method. New York: Crossroads.

Greenslade, S. L., ed. 1963. *The Cambridge History of the Bible: The West from the Reformation to the Present Day.* Volume 3. Cambridge: Cambridge University Press.

Habicht, W. 1993. "The Romanticism of the Schegel-Tieck Shakespeare and the History of Nineteenth-Century German Shakespeare Translation" in *European Shakespeares: Translating Shakespeare in the Romantic Age*, edited by Dirk Delabastita and Lieven D'Hulst, pp. 45-53. Amsterdam: John Benjamins.

Hamill, James F. 1990. *Ethno-logic: The Anthropology of Human Reasoning.* Urbana, Ill.: The University of Illinois Press.

Hardy, G. H. 1967. *A Mathematician's Apology.* Cambridge: Cambridge University Press.

Haskins, Charles Homer. 1957. *The Renaissance of the 12th Century.* New York: Meridian Books.

Henderson, John B. 1991. *Scripture. Canon. and Commentary: A Comparison of Confucian and Western Exegesis.* Princeton: Princeton University Press.

Herman, Mark. 1996. "Humor and Translation." *ATA Chronicle.* April 1995, p. 26; June 1995, p. 35; Sept. 1995, p. 41; Jan., p. 33.

Highet, Gilbert. 1957, 1967. *The Classical Tradition: Greek and Roman Influences on Western Literature.* London : Oxford University Press.

Hobbes, Thomas. 1960. *Leviathan*, ed. Michael Oakeshott. Oxford: Basil Blackwell.

Hoffman, Daniel. 1990. *Poe Poe Poe Poe Poe Poe Poe.* Garden City, N. Y.: Doubleday, 1972; New York: Paragon House.

House, Juliane. 1977. *A Model for Translation Quality Assessment.* Tübingen: Gunter Narr.

Hsia, C. T. 1961. *A History of Modern Chinese Fiction, 1917-1957.* New Haven: Yale University Press.

Hughes, Richard. 1985 (1929). *A High Wind in Jamaica.* London: Panther Books.

Jameson, Fredric. 1986. "Third World Literature in the Era of Multi-national Capitalism." *Social Text* 15, 65-88.

Jao Chiu Tsai 饒 玖 才. *Hsiang-kang ti-ming tan-suo* 香 港 地 名 探 索. Hong Kong: Cosmos Books Ltd, 1998.

Johnson, Mark. 1987. *The Body in the Mind: The Bodily Basis of Meaning, Imagination and Reason.* Chicago: The University of Chicago Press.

Kelber, Werner H. 1983. *The Oral and Written Gospel: The Hermeneutics of Speaking and Writing, in the Synoptic Tradition. Mark. Paul. and Q.* Philadelphia: Fortress Press.

Kelly, Louis. 1979. *The True Interpreter: A History of Translation Theory and Practice in the West.* New York: St. Martin's Press.

KJV. *The Holy Bible:Authorized King James Version.* New York: Oxford University Press, 1931.

Lambert, M. "La Traduction il y a 4000 ans." *Babel* 10 (1964): 17-20.

Laurian, Anne-Marie. "Possible/Impossible translation of jokes." *Humor* 5-1/2 (1992), 111-127.

Lawler, James. "Daemons of the Intellect: The Symbolists and Poe." *Critical Inquiry* 14 (Autumn 1987), 95-110.

Lederer, Richard. *Anguished English*. New York : Dell, 1989.

Legge, James. 1960 [first published in 1871]. *The Chinese Classics*. Vol. IV: *The She King*. Hong Kong: Hong Kong University Press.

Levi, Peter, ed. 1985. *The English Bible from Wycliff to William Barnes: 1534-1859*. West Sussex: Churchman Publishing Limited.

Liang Tao [梁 濤]. *Origins of Kowloon Street Names* [九 龍 街 道 命 名 考 源] Urban Council Journals [市 政 局 刊 物], 1993.

Liu, James J. Y. 1975 "Polarity of Aims and Methods: Naturalization or Barbarization?" *Yearbook of Comparative and General Literature* 24, 60-68.

Lopez, Donald, Jr., editor. 1988. *Buddhist Hermeneutics*. Honolulu: University of Hawaii Press.

Mallarmé, Stephane. 1945. *Oeuvres complètes*, ed. Henri Mondor and G. Jean-Aubrey. Paris: Éditions Gallimard.

Matthiessen, F. O. 1931, 1951. Translation: An Elizabethan Art. Cambridge, MA: Harvard University Press.

Maurer, Herrymon. 1985. *Lao Tzu / Tao Teh Ching: The Way of the Ways*. New York: Schocken Books.

McCarroll, Tolbert. 1982. *The Tao: The Sacred Way*. New York: Crossroad.

Miyoshi, Masao. 1974. *Accomplices of Silence: The Modern Japanese Novel*. Berkeley: University of California Press.

Morris, Colin. 1972. *The Discovery of the Individual, 1050-1200*. London: S.P.C.K. for the Church Historical Society.

Morris, Ivan. 1964. *The World of the Shining Prince*. Harmondsworth: Penguin Books.

Mueller-Vollmer, Kurt, ed. 1985. *The Hermeneutics Reader*. New York: Continuum.

Neusner, Jacob. 1983. *Midrash in Context: Exegesis in Formative Judaism*. Philadelphia: Fortress Press.

Niranjana, Tejaswini. 1992. *Siting Translation: History, Post-Structuralism, and the Colonial Context*. Berkeley: University of California Press.

Parker, William Riley. 1968. *Milton: A Biography*. Oxford: The Clarendon Press.

Pohling, H. 1971. "Zur Geschichte der Übersetzung." *Studien zur Übersetzungswissenschaft, Beiheft zur Zeitschrift Fremdsprachen* 314. Leipzig.

Pound, Ezra. 1955. *The Classic Anthology Defined by Confucius*. London: Faber and Faber.

Pound, Ezra. 1935. *Make it New*. New Haven: Yale University Press.

Qian Zhongshu [Ch'ien Chung-shu]. "Lin Ch'in-nan Revisited,"
    Renditions. Autumn 1975, pp. 8-21.
Read, Anthony & David Fisher. 1994. *Berlin: The Biography of a City.*
    London: Pimlico.
Reid, Alastair. "Basilisks' Eggs". *The New Yorker*, November 8, 1976,
    pp. 175-208.
Robert, Roda P. 1992. The Concept of Function of Translation and Its
    Application to Literary Texts. *Target: International Journal of
    Translation Studies* 4: 1-16.
Ruthven, K. K. 1979. *Critical Assumptions.* Cambridge: Cambridge
    University Press. Sager, Juan Carlos. 1983. "Quality and
    Standards — the Evaluation of Translations." In: Picken, Cathona
    (Ed). The Translator's Handbook. London: Aslib. 121-128.
Schillebeeckx, Edward. Jesus: An Experiment in Christology. New York:
    Seabury Press, 1979.
Sondrup, Steven and J. Scott Miller, eds. *The I of the Beholder: A
    Prolegomenon to the Intercultural Study of Self.* Provo, Utah:
    ICLA Intercultural Studies Committee, 2002
Sternberg, Meir. 1981 Polylingualism and Translation as Mimesis."
    Poetics Today 24: 221-239.
Stock, Brian. *The Implications of Literacy: Written Language and Models
    of Interpretation in the Eleventh and Twelfth Centuries.*
    Princeton: Princeton University Press, 1983.
Tamaoka, Katsuo and Toshiaki Takahashi. "Understanding Humour from
    Another Culture: Comprehension of Parental Brain Twisters by
    Japanese University Students Learning English as a Second
    Language." *Psychologia* 37 (1994), 150-157.
Thomson, James A. K. *The Art of the Logos.* London: George Allen &
    Unwin, 1935.
TLS: *Essays and Reviews from The Times Literary Supplement, 1965.*
    1966. London: Oxford University Press.
Venuti, Lawrence. *The Scandals of Translation: Towards an Ethics of
    Difference.* London: Routledge, 1998.
Waley, Arthur. *The Book of Songs: The Ancient Chinese Classic of
    Poetry.* New York: Grove Press, 1960 [first published in 1937].
    _____. "Notes on Translation," *Atlantic Monthly*, November 1958.
    _____. *The Real Tripitaka.* London: George Allen and Unwin,
    1952.
    _____. 1919. *The Poet Li Po A.D. 701-762.* London: East and
    West Ltd.
    _____. *The Tale of Genji: A Novel in Six Parts by Lady Murasaki.*
    London: George Allen and Unwin, 1935.
Wenzel, Peter. 1988. "German Shakespeare Translation: The State of the
    Art." In: *Images of Shakespeare: Proceedings of the Third
    Congress of the International Shakespeare Association, 1986,*
    edited by Werner Habicht, D. J. Palmer, and Roger Pringle, pp.
    314-323. Newark: University of Delaware Press.

Williams, William Carlos. 1995. "An Essay on Leaves of Grass." In:
    Hindus, Milton (Ed). *Leaves of Grass One Hundred Years After*.
    Stanford: Stanford University Press.

Appendices

Wade-Giles / Pinyin Correspondence

(Adapted from the Library of Congress Pinyin Conversion Project)

a	a	chou	zhou	hou	hou
ai	ai	ch`ou	chou	hsi	xi
an	an	chu	zhu	hsia	xia
ang	ang	ch`u	chu	hsiang	xiang
ao	ao	chü	ju	hsiao	xiao
cha	zha	ch`ü	qu	hsieh	xie
ch`a	cha	chua	zhua	hsien	xian
chai	zhai	chuai	zhuai	hsin	xin
ch`ai	chai	ch`uai	chuai	hsing	xing
chan	zhan	chuan	zhuan	hsiu	xiu
ch`an	chan	ch`uan	chuan	hsiung	xiong
chang	zhang	chüan	juan	hsü	xu
ch`ang	chang	chüan	quan	hsüan	xuan
chao	zhao	chuang	zhuang	hsüeh	xue
ch`ao	chao	ch`uang	chuang	hsün	xun
che	zhe	chüeh	jue	hu	hu
ch`e	che	ch`üeh	que	hua	hua
chen	zhen	chui	zhui	huai	huai
ch`en	chen	ch`ui	chui	huan	huan
cheng	zheng	chun	zhun	huang	huang
ch`eng	cheng	ch`un	chun	hui	hui
chi	ji	chün	jun	hun	hun
ch`i	qi	ch`ün	qun	hung	hong
chia	jia	chung	zhong	huo	huo
ch`ia	qia	ch`ung	chong	i	yi
chiang	jiang	en	en	jan	ran
ch`iang	qiang	erh	er	jang	rang
chiao	jiao	fa	fa	jao	rao
ch`iao	qiao	fan	fan	je	re
chieh	jie	fang	fang	jen	ren
ch`ieh	qie	fei	fei	jeng	reng
chien	jian	fen	fen	jih	ri
ch`ien	qian	feng	feng	jo	ruo
chih	zhi	fo	fo	jou	rou
ch`ih	chi	fou	fou	ju	ru
chin	jin	fu	fu	juan	ruan
ch`in	qin	ha	ha	jui	rui
ching	jing	hai	hai	jun	run
ch`ing	qing	han	han	jung	rong
chiu	jiu	hang	hang	ka	ga
ch`iu	qiu	hao	hao	k`a	ka
chiung	jiong	hei	hei	kai	gai
ch`iung	qiong	hen	hen	k`ai	kai
cho	zhuo	heng	heng	kan	gan
ch`o	chuo	ho	he	k`an	kan

181

Wade-Giles / Pinyin Correspondence

(Adapted from the Library of Congress Pinyin Conversion Project)

kang	gang	liu	liu	nou	nou
k`ang	kang	lo	luo	nu	nu
kao	gao	lou	lou	nü	nü
k`ao	kao	lu	lu	nuan	nuan
ken	gen	lü	lü	nüeh	nue
k`en	ken	luan	luan	nung	nong
keng	geng	lüan	luan	o	e
k`eng	keng	lüeh	lue	ou	ou
ko	ge	lun	lun	pa	ba
k`o	ke	lung	long	p`a	pa
kou	gou	ma	ma	pai	bai
k`ou	kou	mai	mai	p`ai	pai
ku	gu	man	man	pan	ban
k`u	ku	mang	mang	p`an	pan
kua	gua	mao	mao	pang	bang
k`ua	kua	mei	mei	p`ang	pang
kuai	guai	men	men	pao	bao
k`uai	kuai	meng	meng	p`ao	pao
kuan	guan	mi	mi	pei	bei
k`uan	kuan	miao	miao	p`ei	pei
kuang	guang	mieh	mie	pen	ben
k`uang	kuang	mien	mian	p`en	pen
kuei	gui	min	min	peng	beng
k`uei	kui	ming	ming	p`eng	peng
kun	gun	miu	miu	pi	bi
k`un	kun	mo	mo	p`i	pi
kung	gong	mou	mou	piao	biao
k`ung	kong	mu	mu	p`iao	piao
kuo	guo	na	na	pieh	bie
k`uo	kuo	nai	nai	p`ieh	pie
la	la	nan	nan	pien	bian
lai	lai	nang	nang	p`ien	pian
lan	lan	nao	nao	pin	bin
lang	lang	nei	nei	p`in	pin
lao	lao	nen	nen	ping	bing
le	le	neng	neng	p`ing	ping
lei	lei	ni	ni	po	bo
leng	leng	niang	niang	p`o	po
li	li	niao	niao	p`ou	pou
liang	liang	nieh	nie	pu	bu
liao	liao	nien	nian	p`u	pu
lieh	lie	nin	nin	sa	sa
lien	lian	ning	ning	sai	sai
lin	lin	niu	niu	san	san
ling	ling	no	nuo	sang	sang

Wade-Giles / Pinyin Correspondence
(Adapted from the Library of Congress Pinyin Conversion Project)

sao	sao	t`i	ti	tsu	zu
se	se	tiao	diao	ts`u	cu
sen	sen	t`iao	tiao	tsuan	zuan
seng	seng	tieh	die	ts`uan	cuan
sha	sha	t`ieh	tie	tsui	zui
shai	shai	tien	dian	ts`ui	cui
shan	shan	t`ien	tian	tsun zun	
shang	shang	ting	ding	ts`un cun	
shao	shao	t`ing	ting	tsung	zong
she	she	tiu	diu	ts`ung	cong
shen	shen	to	duo	tzu	zi
sheng	sheng	t`o	tuo	tz`u	ci
shih	shi	tou	dou	wa	wa
shou	shou	t`ou	tou	wai	wai
shu	shu	tu	du	wan	wan
shua	shua	t`u	tu	wang	wang
shuai	shuai	tuan	duan	wei	wei
shuan	shuan	t`uan	tuan	wen	wen
shuang	shuang	tui	dui	weng	weng
shui	shui	t`ui	tui	wo	wo
shun	shun	tun	dun	wu	wu
shuo	shuo	t`un	tun	ya	ya
so	suo	tung	dong	yai	yai
sou	sou	t`ung	tong	yang	yang
ssu	si	tsa	za	yao	yao
su	su	ts`a	ca	yeh	ye
suan	suan	tsai	zai	yen	yan
sui	sui	ts`ai	cai	yin	yin
sun	sun	tsan	zan	ying	ying
sung	song	ts`an	can	yo	yo
ta	da	tsang	zang	yu	you
t`a	ta	ts`ang	cang	yü	yu
tai	dai	tsao	zao	yüan	yuan
t`ai	tai	ts`ao	cao	yüeh	yue
tan	dan	tse	ze	yün	yun
t`an	tan	ts`e	ce	yung	yong
tang	dang	tsei	zei		
t`ang	tang	tsen	zen		
tao	dao	ts`en	cen		
t`ao	tao	tseng	zeng		
te	de	ts`eng	ceng		
t`e	te	tso	zuo		
teng	deng	ts`o	cuo		
t`eng	teng	tsou	zou		
ti	di	ts`ou	cou		

Stephen Mitchell's *Tao Te Ching*

Mitchell's "Translations"	Antecedents
The Tao is great. The universe is great. Earth is great Man is great. These are the four great powers. Man follows the earth. Earth follows the universe. The universe follows the Tao. The Tao follows only itself. (#25)	Tao is great. Heaven is great. Earth is great. Man is great. The universe has four greats. And man is one of them. Man follows earth; Earth follows heaven; Heaven follows Tao; Tao follows itself. (#25, Herrymon Maurer)
There is a time for being ahead, a time for being behind. . . . a time for being vigorous. . . Return is the movement of the Tao . (#29)	Hence, there is a time to go ahead and a time to stay behind. . . . There is a time to be vigorous. Returning is the direction of the Tao. (#29, Tolbert McCarroll)
The Tao never does anything, Yet through it all things are done. (#37)	Tao never does anything, And everything gets done. (#37, Maurer)
Yielding is the way of the Tao. All things are born of being. Being is born of non-being. (#40)	Yielding is the way of the Tao. The ten thousand things are born of Being and Being is born of Nonbeing. (#40, McCarroll)
When a superior man hears of the Tao, he immediately begins to embody it. When an average man hears of the Tao, he half believes it, half doubts it. When a foolish man hears of the Tao, he laughs out loud. If he didn't laugh, it wouldn't be the Tao. (#41)	When a superior man hears about Tao, He goes after it diligently. When an average man hears about Tao, He both gets it and loses it. When an inferior man hears about Tao, He laughs loudly at it. If he did not laugh, It would not be Tao. (#41, Maurer)

Stephen Mitchell's *Tao Te Ching*

Mitchell's "Translations"	Antecedents
The Tao gives birth to One. One gives birth to Two. Two gives birth to Three. Three gives birth to all things. (#42)	The Tao gives birth to the One. The One gives birth to two. Two gives birth to three. And three gives birth to the ten thousand things. (#42, McCarroll)
Without looking out your window, you can see the essence of the Tao (#47)	Without looking out of the window You can see heaven's way. (#47, Maurer)

In the pursuit of knowledge,
every day something is added.
In the practice of the Tao,
every day something is dropped.
Less and less do you need to force
  things,
until finally you arrive at non-
  action.
When nothing is done,
nothing is left undone.
(#48)
	In the pursuit of learning,
	every day something is added.
	In the pursuit of the Tao,
	everyday something is dropped.
	Less and less is done
	until you come to action with
	  striving.
	When you follow this practice,
	nothing remains undone.
	(#48, McCarroll)

For governing a country well there is nothing better than moderation. (#59)	For governing others and serving heaven there is nothing better than moderation. (#59, McCarroll)
Governing a large country is like frying a small fish. (#60)	Governing a big country is like cooking a small fish. (#60, McCarroll)
My teachings are easy to understand and easy to put into practice. (#70)	My words are easy to understand and easy to put into practice. (#70, McCarroll)

It takes from what is too much
and gives to what isn't enough.
(#77)
	It is the way of heaven to take
	  where there is too much in
	  order to give where
	there is not enough.
	(#77, McCarroll)

Index